D0775148

Extreme Continental

Giles Whittell grew up in Kenya, Nigeria and Algeria and read history at Cambridge. After the revolutions in Eastern Europe in 1989 he rode a bicycle from Berlin to Bulgaria and described the trip in *Lambada Country* (1992). He has also written a guide to Central Asia and is Los Angeles correspondent for *The Times*.

GILES WHITTELL

Extreme Continental

BLOWING HOT AND COLD
THROUGH CENTRAL ASIA

Everything it never occurred
to you to ask about
Central Asia, & nothing
about sex (see p. 114).

Happy reading,

Giles.

INDIGO

First published in Great Britain 1995
by Victor Gollancz

This Indigo edition published 1996
Indigo is an imprint of the Cassell Group
Wellington House, 125 Strand, London WC2R 0BB

© Giles Whittell 1995

The right of Giles Whittell to be identified as author of
this work has been asserted by him in accordance with
the Copyright, Designs and Patents Act, 1988.

Extracts from *Through Russian Central Asia* by
Stephen Graham reproduced by permission of
Macmillan Publishing Co., Inc.

A catalogue record for this book is
available from the British Library.

ISBN 0 575 40006 2

Printed and bound in Great Britain by
Guernsey Press Co. Ltd,
Guernsey, Channel Isles

96 97 98 99   10 9 8 7 6 5 4 3 2 1

Contents

❦

Acknowledgements

Besides Mikhail Gorbachev, without whom most of the region explored in this book would probably still be closed to the world, I would like to thank Stephen Graham, Jane Kokan, Peter Hopkirk, Stephen Glynn and Varia Shavrova for helping me get started. In Moscow Oliver Phillips was the very opposite of diminutive in his support, while Kolya Astafiev and Tania Shalygina of Soviet Travels, Dima Litvinov of Greenpeace and Marcus Warren all offered excellent advice.

Dozens shamed me with their generosity in Central Asia, among them Professor R. Nepesova, Yusup Kamalov of the Union for the Defence of the Aral and the Amu Darya, Nikolai Shchetnikov, Valery Denisov and Vica Timonova in Bishkek, Valentin Dyerevyanka in Kara-Kol and Sasha Silienka in Tashkent. Chris Bowers was a great host (and banker). Hugh Pope and Richard Lightbody likewise came to my rescue at a moment of acute illiquidity.

My thanks to Georgia Garrett and Bill Hamilton for their encouragement in London early on, to Richard Owen at *The Times* for his forbearance during my first six months in Los Angeles, and especially to Liz Knights and Viv Redman at Gollancz for their heroic patience and enlightened criticism.

Finally, I would like to thank my parents for painting my bedroom while I was away, among many other things; Crispin for putting up with me at the end of the landing; and Joanna for everything, ever since the first *colossal* at *Le Tremplin*.

To Mr and Mrs W

Prologue

❧❧❧❧

I did exactly as Comrade Vuchetich intended, and it seemed to work. From the bus stop I crossed the road and started up the first monumental flight of steps. Granite soldiers with veins standing out on their forearms cleared the way with their bayonets. From the top of the steps an avenue of poplars sloped upwards to the next battalion. These men, apparently defending a pond, were cast in solid bronze. Beyond them troops crowded in on all sides, some charging, some kneeling to shoot, some wounded, some carrying the wounded. Then the way ahead was blocked by a low cliff and for a moment Mr Vuchetich had me flummoxed.

I had turned to look back towards the river when the sound of violins wafted over from an illuminated cavern to the right of the cliff. The music led me up a curved stone ramp into an enormous underground drum in the middle of which a sculpted hand burst from a dark slab of marble holding a flaming torch. The single, curving wall of the drum was faced with dark red marble and etched in gold with the names of seventy thousand of the one million Russian soldiers who died here, at Stalingrad.

People's sculptor E. V. Vuchetich designed this memorial in 1963 and supervised its construction over the next four years. I managed to think it strange that those lives which had been counted so cheap at the time had been remembered so expensively. But otherwise I was in thrall to the sculptor as I continued up his ramp with the orchestra swirling round me and a lump in my throat, and at last came out above the low cliff.

To the right, at the top of a hill, blotting out the sun, stood the woman known as Mother Russia in whose name Stalingrad was fought. The Intourist leaflet said she was 52 metres high and weighed 8000 tonnes. Her toes were the size of giant turtles and beneath a flowing cotton dress she had the body of an

Olympic javelin thrower. Glancing northwards as if to check that Russia was following, she brandished a twenty-metre sword towards the East.

Hoping for a view, I set off up the hill in the direction of her feet. It was a fresh May morning. Hardly anyone was about. A steady wind flattened the grass and numbed my ears. I reached the bottom of the statue, clambered on to its massive square base and sat on one of its vast toes looking out across the river.

The land on the far bank was utterly flat and neither farmed nor forested. It was steppe. After a few dozen horizons it would be desert, and with each degree of latitude towards the equator the heat would intensify until in the Kara-Kum desert down by the Afghan border you could fry a chicken on a hub cap in the sun (or so I had read). Eventually, in all directions, mountains would appear above the haze. I fantasized about being up there already in the Tien Shan, the Mountains of Heaven, in some cool green valley never seen before by western eyes.

An old couple came slowly up the zig-zag path towards the statue. I reckoned from their graven looks and the medals on the husband's jacket that they came here often. To mourners, Mother Russia is presumably meant to say, 'They died for me, and not in vain. Bring your infinite grief to my infinite concrete bosom and I will give you infinite solace.'

But I was just passing through. To me she said, 'Forget Communism. They put me here to commemorate a battle for Russia. We won it, and as one of many consequences we hung on to Central Asia.'

The couple paused for a few minutes at the foot of the statue, to pay their respects and admire the view, then turned to walk back down the hill. I slithered off the toe and went round to the other side of the base to be in the sun.

'Of course, at the time we didn't think of it as hanging on,' the statue said over her shoulder. 'It was grander than that. Asia was our birthright.'

The wind gusted and died down.

'We knew our strength then, after the war. No one argued about where Russia stopped and Asia started. Russia was Asia and Asia was Russia, west of the Volga and east of the Volga, beyond the steppe, right up to the mountains . . .'

She was becoming querulous.

'Asia is our destiny, don't you see? Why else did they put me here, waving a sword as if I were about to charge down the hill and terrorize everything this side of India?'

I felt for her, in a way. I took a picture of her 250-tonne scarf and walked back to the bus stop, imagining eight thousand tonnes of woman wading the Volga in two giant strides and causing the earth to shake and the Aral Sea to empty like a puddle as she pounded eastwards to Samarkand, Bukhara and Tashkent. How humiliating to do that, and then be recalled by an empire collapsing from within.

To Baku

~~~~~

Volgograd was a hushed sort of place, following the west bank of the river for fifty miles like a line of solemn Party stalwarts turned out to see the Leader in his motorcade.

The Battle of Stalingrad utterly destroyed the city, and in addition to the Soviet dead it killed 200,000 Germans. The new Stalingrad was decorated with its own Order of Lenin and with flowerbeds between its carriageways. Its population, topped up by forced resettlement, is one million, but you wouldn't know it. They seemed a subdued million. They didn't natter on buses in the way of Muscovites. They queued in virtual silence for salami and no one busked for their devalued kopecks.

Maybe those not awed by their history were awed by their river. It is hard to stray far from this great flat groove that drains in total silence an area the size of Western Europe. The Volga looks wider than the city, sliding relentlessly southwards under a smooth silver skin. It used to be transparent to a depth of four metres but nowadays murk sets in at forty centimetres and the sturgeon tend to serve up toxins with their caviar.

At least the river is moving. For most of its 2292 miles the Volga is dammed and lake-like, but Volgograd is downstream of the lowest barrage on an elbow where the water turns towards the East and begins its only free run, to Astrakhan and the Caspian Sea. Even here its width puts it in a league beyond the kind of European rivulet that can be straddled by a single city. On one bank the land is green or urban grey, and undulating. On the other it is brown and flat and virtually deserted. There is not a single bridge. This is a frontier, whatever Mother Russia said.

My plan was to cross into former Soviet Central Asia and take a two thousand mile eastward swing through it to the Altai mountains, which Russia calls her Switzerland, at the junction of Kazakhstan, Siberia, Mongolia and China. The journey would skirt the northern frontiers of Iran and Afghanistan and the western end of China. I would have a companion of sorts; a Scot who took the same route in 1914, approaching from the Caucasus and Baku. With his journal in my pack I wanted to carry out some amateur research, and maybe even find what he had once called 'very paradise'.

For now I was alone and conscious of it. I felt cut loose in a soundproof bubble. No one here knew me. No one I knew knew I was here. No one I knew had ever been here before. No one I met spoke my language and I spoke theirs very badly. To be honest, I was not convinced I was in Volgograd at all.

It felt as if I had a bet on with my mum: 'Look, I'm off now. I'll phone in a couple of weeks – but I bet you'll never guess where from.' She would probably have guessed Ulan Bator, or Mogadishu, or Punto Arenas. Then to be clever she would have said Basildon or Chingford. Not Volgograd. There can be few cities of a million souls giving off such faint vibrations to the outside world as Volgograd.

It was no less likeable for that. The air was clean and cool. The streets were wide and swept. The hotel was grey outside but grand within. Its restaurant was a large round hall with alcoves behind gilded columns, and my room (eight dollars) was so vast I could have shared it with the Bolshoi.

The river station was vaster still and almost empty; a long glass-clad oblong of a building with an unrevolving revolving restaurant on top. An entire hillside of grey stone steps led down to it from the Avenue of Heroes. By painful transliteration I made out the words Kazan, Rostov-na-Donu and Astrakhan on the arrival and departure boards.

I approached a ticket window.

'Please, is it possible steamer to Astrakhan?'

The woman behind the window smiled. The soundproof bubble burst. She didn't mind me torturing her beautiful language. And yes, it was possible. Tomorrow. One-thirty. Lyoox?

'Lyoox?'

Beautiful, comfortable, one gentleman only, de luxe.

That sounded good to me. I bought the ticket and returned to the hotel for a dinner of sturgeon and cognac, served with bewildering panache by a *babushka* in a corset and lace-up boots. Most of the tables in the restaurant had been rearranged for a group of twenty-six Germans come to visit Mother Russia. They said prayers before and after their meal and woke me next morning with their hymns.

It was a warm morning. I sent home some postcards of Mother Russia and bought some rock cakes and a jar of instant coffee at the bazaar. Back at the river station, from nothing, someone had conjured pandemonium.

Three important-looking steamers were tied up at the quayside, all white and elegant, all playing amplified music from loudspeakers on their upper decks. Lean men in flares and flip-flops trotted up and down gangplanks loading beer and unloading empties. Two live sturgeon were carried on in sacks, showing only their splayed silver tails. Passengers on holiday cruises, from upstream and down, had half an hour of shore leave in which to buy cigarettes and tomatoes from trestle tables set up in the shade of the terminal's glass walls, or to ignore Volgograd and sunbathe. Most were going for the tomatoes.

My boat was the *Capitan Rachkov*. My cabin looked like Hercule Poirot's first-class compartment on the Orient Express. It smelt of clean linen and was reached by a dark veneered companionway with a polished brass handrail. I was in heaven, even before we cast off to a final tootle of brass band and found ourselves suddenly in silence in the middle of the Volga.

Going with the current the *Rachkov* only had to idle, leaving hardly a wake. Volgograd and Europe slipped backwards on the starboard side. Mother Russia disappeared behind factories and apartment buildings which eventually gave way to meadows and low trees and tiny tributaries. The east bank was still technically Russia and would be all the way to Astrakhan. But the river had turned east of south, from six o'clock to four, and with every thrum of the engine Central Asia came a few feet closer on the port bow.

Because of the dams above Volgograd the river was too shallow for heavy shipping except along a lane kept open by dredgers pumping sludge ashore, day and night, along pipes floated on pontoons which the current pulled into long pendulous curves.

Lunch was served. The first-class dining room was astern above the sun deck, with a panoramic wall of windows and lace curtains obscuring them. There was also a piano. Once the tweedy couple whose table I shared realized I was foreign I was left to eat my sawdust-flavoured discus of chicken in uncomfortable silence.

I had learned some Russian, but clearly not enough, with a Muscovite in Knightsbridge. Some of the wonderful rasps and rolls I recognized, but native speakers in full flow tend to camouflage their every word with inflections, perfections, devilish root vowel changes and downright unfair colloquialisms. For a queasy hour or two it felt as if the soundproof bubble was reforming. Back in my cabin, trying to ignore it, I thought about the next six months. Nothing about them – not one meal or bed or poste restante – was fixed. This was usually an exhilarating thought, but occasionally, like now, it gave me butterflies.

I ate a rock cake. My porthole faced east. Gazed at idly, the riverbank in that direction seemed lifeless, but a closer look revealed a steady inshore traffic of outboard-motored skiffs scurrying between fishing huts and secret inlets. The sun was low. The afternoon was fading. Enough of this. I headed aft to mingle.

Now the communication thing began to work. A lithe Russian woman in a flesh-coloured bikini asked me to take her picture on the sun deck. We established that she was on holiday from Kazan, the ancient Tartar capital on the upper Volga. And she was married. Her husband sauntered over from a deckchair. He was young, muscular and tanning well.

'Ha!' he said, when told the photographer was an *Anglichanin*, and without a pause he steered us to their stateroom. He stepped into their adjoining bathroom to pull some trousers over his swimming trunks, and emerged with two bottles of champagne, one of vodka and a bunch of radishes.

'Ha!'

He was Sasha, and his wife was Lena. He was businessman and she was Rechflot *offitsant*. (Rechflot was the Soviet river transport company.)

'Ha!'

'Hmm! Very good. Excellent steamer.'

'*Nyet*. Ridiculous Soviet steamer. Fine American steamer Mississippi – yes, that excellent. This, unfortunately, rubbish.'

I protested but he cut me short with a square-ended finger.

'Now. You. First *Anglichanin*. First foreigner. Therefore: hundred grammes.'

Russians toast by weight. We toasted our meeting. We toasted business (two lingerie shops in Kazan). We toasted my mother, my grandmother, Margaret Thatcher, Brezhnev, Stalin, Reagan, Bush and, after much persuasion by the *Anglichanin*, Gorbachev, to whom, I suggested, Sasha owed his shops. The vodka had not lasted much beyond family. Now the sweet, over-bubbly Soviet *shampanski* was climbing up the inside of my nose. As night fell over the river, Sasha and his laughing wife and their excellent ridiculous Soviet stateroom began, like a fairground waltzer in a dream, to spin.

We docked at nine in the morning. Astrakhan's port was busy with steamers, hydrofoils and bulk grain carriers, but none of them was going down the Caspian to Turkmenistan. I took a taxi to the railway station hoping instead for a train to Baku and a shorter crossing to Turkmenistan from there. But there were no trains to Baku any more. Azerbaijan was independent now, and at war with Armenia. The only option was to go to Makhachkala and take pot luck from there.

The station was teeming. Men (on the whole) queued ten and twenty deep from a dozen ticket windows. To judge by the vinegary air they were sweating freely into their thick jackets and zip-up acrylic jerseys. Women and children sat in circles on the floor, grazing on mutton bones and hardboiled eggs unrolled from cloth bundles. Stunted palm trees stood limply in each corner of the hall, dwarfed by their pots.

A formation of gold-toothed gypsies closed in on me, hands out, the babies they carried pleading with their eyes. I gave one of them a note and then had to stride away like a celebrity pursued by paparazzi. I came to rest at a giant map of the Soviet railway network; a hopelessly gangly protozoon magnified a billion times. It showed Makhachkala halfway to Baku on the west side of the Caspian. The east side is where Central Asia starts. This was turning out to be a complicated way of getting there.

I queued for two hours for a ticket, then left Astrakhan heading into a desert I hadn't known existed.

My map called this the Black Land. It was actually khaki, white and blue. The khaki was sand, the white was salt and the blue was from occasional shallow mirrors of standing water left by spring rains.

I was sharing a compartment with three thickly stubbled Azeris. It smelt as if we had only a few lungfuls of rotting air between us. We sat, two facing two, exchanging mumbled courtesies and fidgeting in our grimy clothes. When I pulled down a top bunk and lay on it banter began to flow below. It turned raucous, briefly, when the door opened and a bundle of xerox'd porn was thrown in, apparently on a no-obligation trial basis. A glimpse or two of photocopied pudenda was enough for the oldest of the three. Assailed by remorse, he went huffily to sleep. The other two fell silent, reading.

This train was dozy compared with the purposeful Moscow–Volgograd express. In sixteen hours it covered three hundred miles, all along quintessential branchline. There is nothing arterial about Astrakhan–Makhachkala.

Still, there was a restaurant car. As we turned gradually southwards, following the shore of the Caspian, but separated from it by dunes and salt pans, a heavy-set woman with a black stripe of make-up between her eyebrows brought me bortsch and bread. The sky turned pink. Occasionally a stork would flap across it.

The cook came and sat opposite. He looked at my map and said I must be a spy. Those on nearby tables – all men; an assortment of dour, sunburnt Russians and swashbuckling Tartars – had turned to listen. Horrible things happen to spies. No, I said, I was not a spy, and the cook roared with laughter.

We repaired to his compartment and downed a hundred grammes. Makhachkala, it turned out, was the capital of Dagestan (a tribal federation that had repulsed Russia's armies for twenty solid years in the middle of the nineteenth century under the inspirational Imam Shamyl). Now the Dagestanis wanted independence and Makhachkala was dangerous. Watch out for mafiosi, said the cook, there and in Baku. He was a Dagestani himself, chubby and loquacious, but he switched from high humour to deep sighs and earnestness in a way I already thought of as Russian. It was time for a sigh. He offered a short discourse on money. Exhibit one: a wad of rubles from his back pocket. Most important characteristic: worthless. Moral: Never trust a Democrat.

'*Kagda Brezhnev byl, vce kharoshyi byl. Vce dyoshevo byl.*'

When Brezhnev was around, everything was fine. Everything was cheap. *Kagda Brezhnev byl* . . .

It was to become a depressingly familiar refrain.

He stared mournfully out of the grubby window. Then Brezhnev and rubles vanished from his face and he said, delightedly, that in fourteen years on the Dagestan line he hadn't seen a single foreigner till now. It seemed possible. In Soviet times this was not an 'open' line. Anyway, I chose to believe him, and felt instantly promoted from bum to pioneer.

The following day was nervy. I didn't stray from the station at Makhachkala for fear of missing any Baku train that might show up. By the time one did, on the last leg of a two-day slog from Moscow, I had fallen in with a crew of self-appointed minders who squatted in a line over a crack in the platform, armpits on knees, cracking their knuckles, eating strawberries and spinning green strawberry tops on to the tracks. They said hey, don't bother with a ticket, and we jumped on the back of the train as it pulled out.

Only one of this crew was Russian and his name was Boris. His face was red and his breath fetid from vodka in the restaurant car the night before. He would taunt the others ('What's your real name, Abdul, your Russian name?'), then laugh as if to forgive himself, and kiss them. He tried kissing me once but I managed to be distracted by a wasp. For some reason he was tolerated. Abdul even laughed with him once or twice. The two of them swaggered down the crowded third-class wagon commandeering benches. Sleepy families made room in silence. Embarrassed, I sat opposite an old greybeard in a skull-cap and tried to look inordinately grateful. The old man stared straight at me. Eventually he said, 'You are Estonian. True?'

I practically whispered my reply, but he picked it up and absorbed it like a co-conspirator. Then, with his eyebrows, he seemed to issue a series of instructions to his companions. They sat me on a sun-warmed window seat and put in front of me an unleavened loaf, a lump of salami and a glass of steaming tea.

The guard arrived within a few minutes, followed by an expressionless militiaman with a stubby gun slung over his shoulder. I was anxious, mainly about having no visa for Baku. Before the guard could ask for my papers the old man addressed him solemnly and at length. They ended by shaking hands. The guard leaned over to shake mine, wished me a safe journey, and then herded Boris, Abdul and company out of the wagon to be fined and thrown off the train at the next station.

The old man borrowed my Russian pocket dictionary and explained by pointing at the relevant words that until Baku I should behave like an Estonian diplomat.

There was a crack in the window and I put my nose to it. (The rest of the wagon stank of urine.) Outside, the northern Caucasus sloped down in a series of grand green ramps towards the railway and the sea. We were approaching the mountains from an angle and the highest were the furthest off, dark and lush beneath a collar of cloud. The closer slopes were patterned with sunflower fields and rows of vines. Villages of one-storey houses with red-tiled roofs and deep verandas slid past every now and then. They could have been in the Auvergne. We stopped at every station – places with quarrelsome-sounding names like Kaspiysk and Izberbash – but not at the Azeri border. Independence did not seem to extend yet to frontier police, and I took this as a hopeful sign.

The coast and the Caucasus converge on Baku. As the mountains drew alongside I peeled a generous taxi fare off the wad of fifty-ruble notes under my shirt, hoping to avoid dithering on arrival. But the city was slow in coming. There followed a long, hot trundle across the peninsula that shelters it from the prevailing northerlies. This is black gold country. Under the Apsheron Peninsula and the sub-marine plateau around it lie what were the Soviet Union's richest oil reserves outside Siberia. The first evidence was a line of flares out to sea and some idle well-heads near the railway, but by the time we passed Baku's northern outskirts there seemed to be a pump in a careless pool of crude in every garden. Everything was black or brown.

'*Azerbaijanski bagatstva*,' said Old Greybeard with a proud nod, standing ready for the station mêlée.

Azeri wealth. You betcha. I soon found out that for Central Asia this simply meant endemic petrol shortage.

We had arrived. One moment the platform was empty. The next it had vanished under the feet, bags, bundles and boxes of sixteen wagons' worth of human beings. Where windows opened or were broken, VCRs and bicycles and sacks of onions plopped out as if from faulty howitzers, to be caught by posturing young males who had jumped off as the train rolled in. Dark, bobbing, yelling heads clustered round the doors. I squeezed out and swam with the tide.

Baku was hot. It smelt of oil, burnt and unburnt, which made a change from bodies. If there is an art of looking as if you know where you are going when you don't I had not mastered it. I hesitated in the station hall and two slick youths in lurid jackets homed in at once 'for a chat, over here, where it's quiet'. I escaped in a big black taxi with my rucksack squashing my face.

'The port.'

'Which port?'

'I don't know. The big one. Krasnovodsk.'

We screeched a bit getting there. The driver seemed to want to show what his baby could do. He said there was a war on and plenty bad people around, though to be honest my first impressions of Baku, framed by a shoulder strap, were of quiet, shady streets, desultory roadworks and a spectacular blue bay.

The Apsheron Peninsula curled round to the north, a pale sliver that eventually merged with the horizon. To the south a television mast had pride of place on top of a long protective headland. In between, the fourth city of the former Soviet Union overlooked the Caspian from its natural grandstand.

The ferry terminal stuck out into the bay from the kind of tarmac desert dictators build for march pasts. There would be a boat to Krasnovodsk the following day, but a man with epaulettes flicked my inadequate visa and said 'aeroplane'.

Across the tarmac, the Palace of Government reared up half a dozen storeys facing out to sea. It was heavy, hostile, built in reddish stone and sprouting neo-Gothic spikes at every corner. It was flanked by a pair of colossal hotels. The one nearest the ferry terminal would not accommodate a foreigner without a visa but the other hardly blinked. CNN and ITN and all the free world's lesser info-scavengers had been here and left stickers. The receptionists used BBC World Service biros.

Wishing I was a body-armoured pro on expenses, I paid forty dollars for a room on the eighteenth floor and took refuge in a long, hot shower.

Mr Graham

~~~~~

It was May 1992. The Soviet Union had been dead five months.
The five republics of former Soviet Central Asia were emerging
from seven decades of enforced isolation with as little knowledge of the outside world as that world had of them.

Their confinement had begun when the Bolsheviks claimed
power in Tashkent in November 1917. Three years before
that, in the last spring before the First World War, with the
Tsar still safe on his imperial throne and Communism nothing
but a dangerous fad, a lone and lanky European had steamed
into Baku on a train from Moscow. His only luggage was a
modest knapsack. Thirty years old, tall and fair, he would have
cut a striking figure on the station platform, and if the look
on someone's face can be imagined from his turn of phrase it
would have been a savvy look, a confident gaze over the heads
of his fellow travellers towards the sea. If street urchins had
laughed at him he would probably have answered with a beatific
smile.

His most commercial talent was a fluent, unselfconscious
prose, but he was also an ardent walker with rare stamina and
not much need of creature comforts. 'Tramping' was his word
for walking, and he considered it 'a gentle art'.

'Know how to tramp', he wrote much later, 'and you know
how to live.'

Among the items in his knapsack were a sheet sewn into a
sleeping bag, a coffee pot, a bar of soap, a comb, a broad-
brimmed hat, a mosquito net, a mug, a knife, a notebook,
several handkerchiefs, a book of poetry and an insulated glove
with which to pour his coffee.

He spoke fluent Russian and knew Baku from an earlier walk
across the Caucasus. He stayed no longer than it took to get a
ticket on a boat to Krasnovodsk, from where, he announced in

a despatch to *The Times*, 'I go into the depths of the Russian East . . .

> . . . to Tashkent, the limit of the railway, and then take the road, with my pack on my back, through the deserts of Sirdaria and the Land of the Seven Rivers towards the limits of Chinese Tartary and Pamir, then along the Chinese frontier, north to the Altai mountains and the steppes of southern Siberia . . .

He wrote that he might be stopped and turned back hundreds of miles from the nearest railway station, in which case, he warned, 'silence may engulf my correspondence for a time'. But he was not turned back. His only difficulties were in finding fuel for camp fires and water for his coffee. He surmounted both by adopting local nomadic practice and burning dung and drinking horses' milk.

His name was Stephen Graham. I had stumbled on his book *Through Russian Central Asia* in a locked, glass-fronted bookcase off the Portobello Road the previous autumn. Published and reprinted in 1916, it had 235 thick parchment pages and thirty-seven photographs with captions like 'Lepers in a frontier town', and 'Fine-looking Sarts in Old Tashkent'. At the back there was a pull-out map, hand-drawn in pen and ink, 'Shewing [sic] Traveller's Route'.

I bought it for thirty-six pounds and read it in one go, drooling over its mountainscapes, gawping at its cameos and shadowing its author across a big new map of the Soviet Union which I had bought at the same shop and laid out on my bed. By the end I was already subtracting air fares from my bank balance and working out how much would be left, per day, for board and lodging. *Through Russian Central Asia* was not an armchair travel book. It was a get-a-life-and-do-it-yourself travel book.

The next day I looked up Stephen Graham in a heavy green volume of the British Library catalogue. He had an entire page of titles but the one that danced off the paper with infectious and unfashionable enthusiasm was *Part of the Wonderful Scene*, his autobiography.

His father had edited *Country Life* for quarter of a century, but Graham junior did not start out as a journalist and never went to university. His first job was as a clerk in Somerset House, which he left in 1908, inspired by a sermon.

'No one has achieved much in life', boomed Canon Scott Holland from the pulpit in St Martin-in-the-Fields one Sunday, 'who has not at one time or other staked everything upon an act of faith.'

Stephen Graham staked everything upon a trip to Moscow, where he learned Russian and struggled to break into journalism. For six months he lived on pork fat and black bread, sending articles to the *London Daily News* and getting nothing published. Eventually the paper took a piece on ikons. He cashed his pay cheque at the Moscow branch of the Credit Lyonnais and went on a binge of bortsch and cabbage pies. Gradually his strike rate with Fleet Street's editors improved and he saved enough to start his exploration of the Russian Empire. In 1910 he headed south to walk across the Caucasus. For weeks he tramped through alpine scenery 'where the poet might well say "I love not man the less, but Nature more".'

Back in London, he wrote a book about his walk. Lord Northcliffe read it. Northcliffe owned *The Times*. He was a god who performed for Graham the miracle that starving writers dream of:

Very early on November 11th, 1913, there was a double knock at my front door and I went down to receive a telegram. It had been telephoned to St James's Street post office at 4.18 a.m. and was from Lord Northcliffe: COULD YOU CALL AT CARMELITE HOUSE AT TWELVE FIFTEEN? That was the great chief's self-introduction. I had not heard from him before.

I looked out a clean tie and a map of Russian Central Asia and presented myself. We met standing, no waiting. Northcliffe was wearing a trim navy suit with a red tie . . . His first words after shaking hands were: 'My papers are at your disposal. Go where you like and write what you like. I'll look after the financial side.'

(I read that again. *Go where you like and write what you like. I'll look after the financial side*. This was pure fantasy. I photocopied

it, then went outside to a payphone to ask Aeroflot about visa
requirements and flights.)

So Stephen Graham went to Central Asia on expenses. He
was moderately interested in those he met, but did not dissect
them; he did not pretend to be both novelist and anthropologist
as well as travel writer. He preferred swift sketches: a Tashkent
money-changer was 'a fat, ill-shaven, collarless old man'. A Russian peasant in the Altai was 'a comical fellow, somewhat over
six foot high, with a giant's shoulders, an ogre's stomach, but
the walk and manners of a child'.

He generalized freely and none-too-reliably on 'Mohammedans': 'They are robbers by instinct, and non-progressive not
only in life, but in ideas . . . All is play to them. They are playful
in their attire, in their business, in their fighting, in their talking
. . . They are not serious enough to get rich in our Western
way.' On the other hand, 'They are picturesque, and have given
to a considerable portion of the earth's face a characteristic
quaintness and beauty. They cannot be dismissed.'

His most serious enquiry was into the nature and extent of
Russian settlement – which he regarded as unquestionably civil-
izing – along the northern foothills of the Tien Shan. He wrote
earnestly of poods and versts and grants of land and agricultural
techniques. For the benefit of would-be emigrants from western
Europe he listed railway fares and distances from Black Sea ports
to major Central Asian towns. He set out in detail tax incentives
offered by the Russian government, and military service stipu-
lations.

He was a Russophile at a time of widespread Russophobia.
He was a professional in that what he earned he earned by
writing. But above all he was a tramper; an indefatigable strider-
out of a fine morning, a lover of wide-open, unspoilt places and
fresh air, an unashamed Romantic. In Russian Turkestan, as the
Tsar's Central Asian colonies were then known to the outside
world, he found his sort of nature in abundance and the words
flowed from it into his notebook:

As I lay on the heath and looked upward the Asiatic mountains drew their cloaks round them, hardened their faces, and
slept as they stood away in the background . . . All night

long the breeze rippled and flapped in my sleeping-sack and crooned in the neck of my water-bottle. Far up in the hills lights twinkled in the Kirghiz tents, and in the illumination of moonlight I faintly discerned black masses of cattle beside which boys watched all night, playing their wooden pipes and singing their native songs to one another.

Those Kirghiz tents were yurts; round frames of wooden slats with shallow conical roofs, clad in felt and furnished with embroidered rugs and cushions. The Kirghiz migrated from Manchuria and Mongolia to the Central Asian highlands in the sixteenth century, bringing with them the *Manas*, an epic oral history of their race which once begun could not be interrupted and might take days to finish. They raised vast flocks of sheep, goats, cattle, yak and horses – anything that gave milk and meat and travelled well, when necessary, to fresh pastures. They were said to be the finest horsemen in Asia and they hunted with eagles trained to pluck out the eyes of their prey.

North-east of the Tien Shan, in the Altai, the solitary tramper found a milder sort of mountain where Cossacks and a few Russians lived in log cabins and bred maral deer for the pain-killing properties of their horns. There were places here, he wrote, 'that are so placid and beautiful that you exclaim: "Good heavens, this is a very paradise!"'

He found lodging with a maral farmer and idled away a fortnight swimming in mountain streams and making jam from redcurrants that 'hung like bunting on some of the bushes, and were so thick that you could pick a potful in a quarter of an hour'.

Russian Central Asia, he concluded, was 'likely to remain for a thousand years one of the most peaceful places upon earth'.

Stephen Graham says he was the first person to have a byline in *The Times*. He was certainly one of the last non-Russian visitors to Central Asia before war and revolution changed it utterly. When Archduke Franz Ferdinand was killed in Sarajevo Graham was picking redcurrants in the Altai mountains. When news reached the Altai that Russia was mobilizing on the Austrian border, he hurried west to try his hand at war reporting.

The land he left behind was soon lapped by Europe's bloodbath.

In 1916 the Tsar's Governor General in Tashkent announced the conscription of Central Asian Muslims to serve on the Eastern Front. Relations between colonists and colonized were already tense. After conquest and expropriation, conscription for a war between Christians in an unknown Christian world was not to be endured. A rebellion started on the road from Tashkent to Samarkand and spread quickly to Fergana and the Kirghiz highlands. It was crushed without mercy. Some rebels fled to China. Those who were caught were shot. Whole Kirghiz villages around Lake Issyk-Kul were torched.

By the time the Bolsheviks took Moscow in October 1917 most Central Asians were ready to cheer wildly at the downfall of the Tsar. They might even have turned *en masse* to Lenin, who in those first feverish months of revolution promised self-determination for the former colonies. But Tashkent's Bolsheviks were cut off from Moscow. In January 1918 their hand was forced by a 23-year-old commissar called Ossipov who wearied suddenly of Communism and shot eight fellow commissars. Ossipov got prematurely drunk to celebrate, whereupon his coup collapsed. The secret police rounded up four thousand suspected collaborators, who were convicted by a tribunal of worker-judges and shot.

The Red Army was as brutal. In February it snuffed out a fledgling independence movement in Kokand, the chief city between Tashkent, one hundred miles away to the north-west, and the great fertile bowl of the Fergana Valley. Kokand's mud walls were flattened by artillery and most of its inhabitants were slaughtered.

The suicidal business of resisting Bolshevism then fell to a guerrilla brotherhood known as the *Basmachi*, whose foot-soldiers were brigands and whose commanders were Sufi mystics; Muslim holy men known to the likes of Stephen Graham as whirling dervishes. Their dream was an independent Turkestan united under Allah. Their greatest leader was a turncoat, Enver Pasha. He had fled Turkey after leading it to defeat in the First World War. He then undertook to pacify Central Asia for Lenin, but defected to the counter-revolutionaries within a day of arriving in Bukhara. He took control of present-day Tajikistan, took arms from the King of Afghanistan and for eight months hacked bravely at the underbelly of the godless bear. But in July 1922 the Red Army cornered him and killed him in the Pamirs.

Enver's death marked the end of hopes of Central Asian independence and the beginning of a new role for the region: that of laboratory.

The Soviet government performed three bold and fateful experiments in Central Asia. The first was an assimilation project on one of the world's most complex ethnic mixtures, outlawing its religion and replacing its history, languages, literatures and other cultural traditions with new ones that were invented or alien or both. The second was an experiment with the land, turning a string of fragile oases into modern industrial cities serving a plantation belt designed to make a twentieth-century superpower self-sufficient, with export surpluses, in a uniquely thirsty cash crop. The third was an adventure in top-secret nuclear physics, sealing off an area of savannah the size of Texas for the detonation of up to fifteen atom bombs a year for forty years *and hoping nobody would notice.*

The assimilation project began in earnest in 1924, when the Soviet authorities carved up the emirate of Bukhara and the khanates of Khiva and Kokand into 'republics' on the pretext of recognizing ethnic differences. In fact those differences were much too blurred to correspond to lines on maps. The Kazakh, Kirghiz, Uzbek and Turkmen peoples are all descended from the waves of Turkish nomads who came south from the steppe during the ten centuries up to roughly 1400. They have their own languages but they are all Turkic languages; the Turkic peoples of Central Asia understand each other. The Soviet policy was not so much to create long-desired homelands as to divide and rule.

At first, in the early 1920s, hand-picked Central Asians were admitted to the ruling class, but most fell prey to Stalin's morbid fear of pan-Turkist conspiracies and were denounced in the show-trials of the 1930s or just liquidated. They were replaced by Russians.

Russian replaced the local languages except in uneavesdropped private conversations. The Cyrillic alphabet replaced the Arabic. Between the revolution and the Second World War at least 25,000 mosques were closed. Squads of atheist evangelists fanned out into the hills and melon fields, and a University of Atheism appeared in the city of Dushanbe. In 1918, pursued across the Pamirs by soldiers and census-takers, another wave of Kirghiz nomads had left for China. According to an escaping Austrian prisoner-of-war who travelled with them these were 'the last of all genuinely free peoples of earth'.

Urban Central Asians were squeezed into Russian suits, hats, libraries and opera houses. Their ballads were forgotten and their lutes, tambours, silken robes and skull caps mostly banished to museums.

Meanwhile the slaying of the Central Asian ecosystem had begun with the launch in 1928 of Stalin's first Five Year Plan for the modernization of the Soviet Union. The Plan gave the southern Central Asian republics – Tajikistan, Uzbekistan, Turkmenistan – a single and vital role in the economy of the Union as a whole: to grow cotton.

Cotton's dreadful thirstiness stems from having to be washed as well as watered. If it is grown using chemical fertilizers and pesticides it must be washed frequently. If the land is arid water must be brought in via artificial irrigation channels. If the channels are unlined and open to the sun much of this water is lost in seepage and evaporation. If the total water supply is fixed and yet cotton output is required to increase year-on-year at whatever cost, something else must suffer. Something did. In 1959 the Aral Sea began to shrink.

The Aral was once the largest body of water between the Caspian and the Pacific, fed by two great rivers, the Syr Darya and the Amu Darya. One drains the Tien Shan westwards, the other drains the Pamirs northwards and both had an almost mythic allure for Alexander the Great, who had read of them as the Jaxartes and the Oxus in the writings of Herodotus. Nowadays they provide all the water used to irrigate and wash Central Asia's cotton. They also fill scores of canals and about a hundred reservoirs to give some thirty million former Soviet Central Asians running water, fish and beaches. The planners and engineers involved knew what they were doing. One wrote in 1961: 'It is inevitable that the Aral Sea will disappear.' Inevitable, and reckoned to be worth it; a reasonable trade-off for the ten-fold leap in cotton output that had already been achieved since the revolution.

It is worth being clear about this. The Soviet government accepted that its policies might entail the disappearance *of an entire sea*. It was not a stunt humankind had contemplated before.

In three decades the Aral Sea's surface shrank by half and its volume by two-thirds. In 1986 a plan that had been germinating for decades to divert much of the flow of the Ob and Irtysh rivers to the Aral along a canal that would have been one of the biggest civil engineering projects of all time – the so-called Siberian Rivers project – was finally abandoned by the Politburo in what was seen by most Central Asians as a major victory for Russian nationalism. In 1991 not a drop of water reached the Aral from the Amu Darya and scientists said the whole sea would be gone by 2020. Its main port was already sixty miles from the shore, and foreign photo-journalists struck gold with images of rusting trawlers stuck on sand dunes. Seldom had the wreckage of the Soviet Union been so snappable.

Those who predicted the disappearance of the sea also said its bed would form a stable crust. In fact it has stayed as shifting sand which the steppe's unimpeded winds dump in vengeful storms on the fields and ex-fishing communities of the ex-littoral.

As the Aral dried up a lake called Sary-Kamysh south-west of it swelled with water poisoned from washing pesticides off cotton. This was intended. But for every drop that made it to Sary-Kamysh (and similar sumps across the cotton belt), several more seeped down instead to the water table, poisoning that and causing it to rise. This brought endemic liver and stomach disease to those cotton-growing areas which use wells for drinking water, and poisoned the topsoil on which the cotton was meant to grow.

The early Five Year Plans also required for Central Asia as for the rest of the Union the collectivization of agriculture in general; the pooling of resources and livestock and the reorganization of the land itself into collective and state farms. It went against the grain. Kirghiz and Kazakh livestock-rearers killed their animals rather than hand them over. Thus died, between 1929 and 1934, four million horses, six-and-a-half million head of cattle and thirty-one million sheep and goats. Those accused of obstructing collectivization were generally executed or sentenced to a slower death by forced labour on irrigation projects or hydro-electric dams (sixteen were built on the Syr Darya alone), or on the TurkSib railway or the new mines and mining towns of northern Kazakhstan. Eight hundred thousand Kazakh nomads and peasant farmers are estimated to have died like this – which at least began to clear the decks for experiment number three.

Soviet Russia emerged from the Second World War on the winning side but deeply worried at having lost the first leg of the nuclear arms race to America. She determined on catching up in peacetime and in secret. The first Soviet atom bomb was built and detonated two thousand miles east of Moscow on the Kazakh steppe in 1949. More than four hundred nuclear devices were tested above and below ground since then at a site near Semipalatinsk whose existence was not officially acknowledged until 1989. The town of Kurchatov, from which it was run, had never until then appeared on any map. But nuclear testing is a noisy business and sooner or later someone was bound to notice. For decades, terrified locals pretended not to, but eventually, under cover of *glasnost*, a Kazakh poet called Olzhas Suleimanov observed that the people of eastern Kazakhstan had never been consulted about this percussive use of their ancestral homeland. He published data on its high levels of cancer and genetic mutation, demanded a test ban and in 1991 obtained it.

By this time the longest-running experiment, the one carried out on humans, threatened mayhem. It was a scene of cracked petri dishes, synthesized cultures spreading into one another, Bunsen burners left alight and lab doors banging in the wind as scientists fled in panic. Perhaps it was inevitable. This experiment had always been the most ambitious, and Brezhnev, in his terminal torpor, seemed to have given up on it. After the zealous proselytizing of the twenties and the brutal social engineering of the Stalin years, lanquid Leonid turned the mother of all blind eyes on the fiasco that was Soviet Central Asia.

Russification had failed. Most Central Asians learned the language, but in the end few used it except to study and to talk to Russians.

Sovietization had failed. At a given time, no more than five per cent of Central Asians were ever members of the Communist Party. Power resided with bureaucrats and gangsters who were golden-handcuffed to each other by blackmail and congenital corruption. In the Uzbekistan of Brezhnev's era crime was elevated to a form of government. For twenty years, Uzbek Party General Secretary Sharaf Rashidov rounded-up the Uzbek cotton crop by about a million tonnes a year and extracted payment from Moscow not for what was bought but for what he said was grown. The proceeds funded an extraordinary pyramid of bribery, with a base of cotton pickers and Rashidov's inner circle playing at feudal barons at the top.

The drive to stamp out Islam had failed. Stalin himself admitted it by reopening Central Asia's major mosques (and two madrasas to provide them with a clergy) as a sop to would-be Muslim mutineers in World War Two. This was 'official' Islam; censored and apolitical but acknowledged. Meanwhile the true faith burned quietly behind closed doors, fanned by the mystics who had led the *Basmachi*. In the last years of the Soviet Union the doors opened and the fire spread and the mullahs of Fergana and Tajikistan called for Islamic rule.

By 1991 it seemed certain that Soviet Central Asia would follow Moldavia and the Caucasus to hell. Two hundred people had died the previous summer in street fights over land rights between Kirghiz and Uzbek farmers in the Kirghiz town of Osh. Tajikistan was toppling into civil war between ex-Communists and the Islamic opposition. Western foreign ministers saw fundamentalists in every newly independent closet. At any rate, they knew that Soviet Central Asia was poor and hungry even by the desperate standards of the rest of the collapsing Soviet bloc. A Harvard specialist wrote cheerfully that 'the Armenian-Azerbaijanian conflict is nothing more than a small ripple on the surface; the real storm will come in Central Asia.' Ethnic Russians, fearing the storm, were streaming back to the motherland in their tens of thousands.

Poor old Turkestan. I suppose, since I was going there, it should have been in a UN jeep as an adviser on transitions to democracy, or a hydrologist hot from the Sahel, or a dermatologist with grizzly tales from Chernobyl. At the very least I should have had a hamper of urgently needed vitamin supplements. In fact my most specialized piece of equipment was a pocket geiger counter borrowed in Moscow from a former army electronics engineer, and my reason for going was nothing if not self-indulgent.

I wanted to find a part of Central Asia that was untouched by Soviet experiments; a piece of Stephen Graham's 'very paradise'. I would do in the aftermath of the Soviet era what he had done on its eve, following his route from the Caspian through the deserts of Turkmenistan and Uzbekistan and along the northern edge of the mountains of Kirghizstan and Kazakhstan to the Altai, making notes on what had changed in the interim and what, by any chance, had not – a single valley (if that was all there was) without a road or electricity, without a bust of Lenin or collective farm, where people (if there were any) still lived in log cabins or in yurts, raising maral deer and sheep and yak and horses, burning dung, drinking mare's milk, hunting with eagles.

The idea was irresistible. Here, suddenly open for more or less the first time in the century, was an area two-thirds the size of Australia containing two deserts, the entire western steppe and three of the world's major mountain systems, one of them, the Tien Shan, a thousand miles long. Surely even a totalitarian nuclear superpower could not wreck it all.

Kara-Kum

For Azerbaijan the end of the Soviet Union had been marked by a savage war with Armenia, its western neighbour, but from the haven of downtown Baku it was hard to envisage what the foreign press was writing home about. The only pointers to the fighting were two Red Cross Landcruisers in the hotel car park. Otherwise war seemed to entail billiards on the boardwalk and a continuation of the ancient Azeri traditions of tea-drinking and carpet-making.

There must have been at least a hundred billiard tables under the trees in the park between the waterfront and the Avenue of the Oilworkers. All were in use, all exclusively by males. Most of them were young, with the hopeful beginnings of moustaches. There was much laughter but virtually no potting talent. One player stood out. He wore an immaculate dark green three-piece suit, patent leather shoes, a Homburg hat and a heavy gold watch. The clips of three gold pens decorated his left breast. He smoked a pipe and held his cue vertically by the thick end, waiting his turn. He was slim, handsome and looked about seventy. His turn came. It was a tricky shot right down the side of the table, close to the cushion. He took it without hesitating and seemed to miss-hit the cue-ball. It climbed on to the rim of the table, rolled along the wood to the middle pocket, dropped back on to the baize (but not into the pocket), continued along the cushion, hit the red ball and pushed it into the corner pocket. He winked at me and turned away.

Baku's waterfront is used to outstanding individuals. Gary Kasparov learned his chess here. Further along towards the ferry terminal a giant chess board was marked out on paving stones beneath a trellised vine. Another thin man, this one with an anguished look, was standing among his knee-high pieces looking for a way out of trouble. His opponent was nowhere to be seen, but on a chair of wood slats beside the board stood a teapot and two glasses.

It took twenty-four hours and three visits to the ferry terminal to get a ticket to Krasnovodsk. On those visits I learned that in the Soviet Union and its successor states to call yourself *picatyl* – writer – was to pull rank. Not here the sympathy and smiles afforded those who call themselves writers in the West. In Baku writer still meant Writer. Mere functionaries opened doors for Writers. If a Writer was to be disgraced or rehabilitated, the Politburo or whatever had replaced it would decide.

So the word *picatyl* kept policemen at bay and eventually got me a cabin. Meanwhile I wandered along the waterfront and back, with forays up the streets descending to it.

I had read that the Caspian can be wild; a frothing capsizer whipped by a wind called the Khazri. But just now it was calm and strangely full. You don't expect a sea to come within a foot of flooding the promenade. Perhaps it was somehow getting all the Aral's water.

The park beside the promenade was hot and empty until early evening. Then at five o'clock a miniature train that had been sulking in a playground opposite the Palace of Government screeched into life. For grown-ups there was unsweetened green tea at a rouble a pot and if you were hungry a snack of bread and salami served at tables on a part-time bandstand.

Those who sought something better from independence than bread and salami were busy being businesspeople. A block up from the waterfront on Shaumian Street it seemed that every door not leading to a ministry led to a *komysion*; a private shop. Stretch-fit women's wear was the hot seller, festooning the shelves of once-sober Soviet bookshops, can-canning across barbershop mirrors and dangling over pavements from protruding wooden rails. Underneath it were tracksuits, leather jackets, perfume, lipstick, ersatz chocolate, cigarettes and water-heating elements, all hefted across one or other of Turkey's newly opened borders, all generating an inordinate amount of yearning.

No one seemed to take any notice of the carpet-weavers. They worked and sang and chattered through a line of open windows opposite the sixteenth-century palace of the Shirvan Shahs, south of Shaumian Street in the old town. They sat on benches in front of carpets taking shape on vertical steel frames, tying from memory four thousand knots per square decimetre in patterns which take up as many bytes of human brain as a Mozart symphony. They snipped and thwacked down each knot on the one below with what looked like a cross between a cheese knife and a scimitar, all so fast their fingers were blurred, all attracting hardly a glance from outside. I stopped and stared and was rewarded with sudden silence – except for the thwacking of the knots, which probably wouldn't have stopped for an earthquake. I attempted a Prince Charles grin ('What you're doing seems to me to be absolutely tremendous') and the chatter resumed, though the singing did not until I'd left the window and headed back to the hotel for an evening of *War and Peace* and hard currency coffee.

I had been told to collect my ferry ticket at 11 p.m. I did so, enraging a pair of muscular Kazakhs who seemed to think they had been queue-barged by an Estonian.

'*Picatyl*,' I said. That shut them up.

A bus took us to the other end of the bay where we shivered on a quayside till four in the morning while the crew ate and slept. The flat eastern horizon was already glowing as I fought stroppily up the gangway of the good ship *Kirghizia*. I paid a steward extra to have a cabin to myself. I locked myself in, exterminated a large community of mosquitoes with a pump-action spray from the British Airways travel shop in Regent Street, and fell almost instantly asleep in its narcoleptic haze.

Stephen Graham had left Baku in comparative serenity:

> The night is very dark and starless, and so the eight-mile semicircle of lights is wonderful to behold; the handsome lanterns of the pier, the lights of the esplanade, of the three variety theatres, of the cinemas and shops, the thousands of sparks of homes on the mountain-side. This is the real beginning of my journey, and it is very thrilling.

When I woke up, Jean-Claude Van Damme was playing in the video salon. Mr Van Damme, a kick-boxer by training and a minor Hollywood star by virtue of his physique and his unusual (for Hollywood) Brussels accent, seemed to be an idol in Central

Asia. The Kazakh musclemen and about forty other males were crammed into dark airlessness watching him break out of a *légion étrangère* prison barracks in the Sahara, swim the Atlantic, kick-box a bloody name for himself in the New York underworld, rescue a long-lost sister from prostitution and eventually win a million-dollar jackpot against the North American kick-boxing champion in an underground car park in Las Vegas.

As soon as the film ended blinds covering the portholes went up. The sea was calm and the sky very bright. The salon turned out to be a bar. Most of the audience filed out, but the Kazakhs stayed, looking at me.

'Good film,' I said.

'Interesting,' one of them agreed. He was fondling a string of prayer beads.

'*Da. Intyeresnaya*,' said the other. 'We also will go to America.'

I glanced over their shoulders at the bar, hoping for sustenance. Three brown bottles on a glass shelf were all that could be seen.

'And, um, in America, you will . . . ?'

'Work,' said one.

'Business,' said the other.

'We are businessmen.'

Not smiley businessmen.

'Why do you come from Estonia to Turkmenistan?' asked the one with the prayer beads.

'I don't come from Estonia. I come from England.'

'England?'

'Serious?'

'Serious.'

They looked at each other and smiled for the first time.

'No you don't.'

'Yes I do.'

'You have document?'

I showed them my passport, a pre-EC black one with the splendiferous green and gold frontispiece. It absorbed their attention more completely than had Jean-Claude Van Damme. At last the one with the prayer beads looked up from an American visa and said, 'England is America, yes?'

I asked them what line of business they were in and they said general business – buying, selling, import, export. They bought clothes and cosmetics in Istanbul and sold them from their flats in Chimkent in southern Kazakhstan where they had many hot women friends to whom they would introduce me if I ever visited. They also did retreads of old tyres.

'You want to export tyres to America?' I asked.

'Maybe.'

'No.'

They conferred.

'No. America has enough old tyres. We go to work.'

I mentioned immigration quotas and green cards. They were interested but not bothered.

'*Inshallah*, we go,' said the one with the prayer beads. 'We are kick-boxers too. We can, if necessary, kick-box to America.'

Passengers were gathering on the foredeck, from where Turkmenistan was visible as a thin khaki strip between the blues of the sea and the sky. There were no gulls. The air was still and hot. We entered a channel between sandbanks and passed a low beacon on the end of the northern claw of the bay of Krasnovodsk.

The town looked like a Greek fishing village; single-storied white houses and a few low trees descending in tiers to the water. Giant silver oil tanks glinted opposite them on the south side of the bay. Cliffs rose behind, hiding the desert.

We passed a wreck and docked next to the *Kirghizia*'s sister ship, the *Azerbaijan*. There was no rush on deck, no hubbub on shore. I shuffled with the quiet crowd down the gangway on to Central Asian concrete, and took the last space in a taxi into town.

Krasnovodsk gets no moisture from the sea. It may be a port, but it is also the easternmost oasis of the Black Sands desert, the Kara-Kum. No one lived here until a Russian garrison arrived in 1869, and it arrived for strategic reasons only. Krasnovodsk was to be the start of the Trans-Caspian railway, which in due course brought the largest and most warlike tribe of Turkmens, the Tekke, to their knees and the British and Russian empires to the brink of war.

Stephen Graham thought the Krasnovodsk of 1914 'one of the hottest, most desert and miserable places in the world'. Since then a piped extension of the 1100-kilometre Kara-Kum Canal from the Amu Darya has eased the pressure on its wells and allowed a modest crop of apricots. When you clean your teeth in Krasnovodsk you do it with snowmelt from the Pamirs. But it was still a hot and potentially miserable place, a staging post for oil and people, twelve hours by boat from Baku and twelve by train from Ashkhabad, the Turkmen capital. It felt far from life, which is why I was glad to be eavesdropped in the inter-city telephone office by Sergei Rostovtsev.

Night had fallen. The streets were lit but empty, except outside the telephone office. People were booking calls to Ashkhabad and Moscow, and shouting urgently into the Bakelite handsets when their numbers came up. I was ringing a high-ranking academic in Ashkhabad – my next stop – called Rosa, whose number I had been given by a journalist in London. I had introduced myself to her by fax from Moscow. She picked up after only one ring and said in English that all was beautiful; she was expecting me. I hung up and headed for the hotel round the corner.

A man stepped out of the shadows.

'Good evening.'

I jumped.

'Perhaps you would like a conversation?'

I was surprised not to have seen him there, because he was bleached. His face, hair and hands were as white as copy paper. He apologized in punchy English for having listened to me on the phone, and again suggested a conversation – awkwardly, as if trying to sell something.

His father had come to Krasnovodsk in the Great Patriotic War (he called it that without irony) as commandant of a camp for Japanese prisoners of war. With the job went a spacious flat in a solid nineteenth-century townhouse on the town's main square, where he had been born and still lived. We went there.

In a sense Sergei was a leftover, washed up on the Turkmen coast by the last flood tide of Russian empire-building. He had studied English at university in the Ukraine but had returned, leaving a girlfriend behind, to teach at the Krasnovodsk Pedagogical Institute. Krasnovodsk would always be home. Sergei would shortly be proposing to his girlfriend ('a young man should not live alone'). If she accepted she would have to come and live with him here.

We sat in the flat, in the room overlooking the square. The only furniture was his bed, two chairs and a desk. Bookshelves hid one wall, Turkmen rugs the others. He smoked filterless cigarettes, flicking their burning ends with an apparently fire-proof finger to get the ash into a glass. He made tea, and when the tea was finished we drank vodka.

The conversation started as an oral exam:

'What is your profession?'

'What are your hobbies?'

'Who are your favourite authors and composers?'

His own favourite author was Dumas. 'All educated Russians have read *The Three Musketeers*,' he said, putting me to shame. 'It is the criterion of education.'

After a while the tobacco and vodka emboldened him to touch on more modern themes. The Baltic states had fought for inde-pendence and so deserved it, he said. The Central Asian ones had neither fought for it nor wanted it. A sure sign of this passivity was the fact that no standard-bearer had come for-ward for an independent Central Asia – no Lech Walesa, no Lansbergis.

Look at the Turkmen President, Sergei said. Saparmurad Niyazov. Raised in a state orphanage, a Party man almost liter-ally from the day of his birth, and now unchallenged despite the wholesale oustings of Communists from Kiev to Vladivostok.

'The career of Niyazov is similar to the career of John Major,' Sergei said.

I nearly choked. 'You've heard of John Major?'

'I follow your developments.'

Ahem. I was no particular fan of Mr Major's, but something seemed a little skewed here. Democracy? Elections? The rigours of facing a free press? Come now, Sergei. Such things make a difference.

'Niyazov and your Major are both Party animals which follow the leader and then, at the last jump, they have luck.'

I caved in. Sergei had clearly given this more thought than I had.

In the morning, before beetling off to work in a dark suit that made his head look like a lightbulb, he pointed me in the direction of Krasnovodsk's museums.

It was 9 a.m. and baking. On the street corner a squat yellow tank on two wheels and a wooden leg dispensed sweetened water by the glass. A posse of Turkmen women sauntered down Rilova Street ahead of me, dressed from neck to ankle in dazzling machine-woven silk. They walked and looked like supermodels, each step planted directly in the path of the preceding one, or even an inch or two across it. Statistically they were likely to be Olmuts, the dominant tribe of eastern Turkmenistan, but in Krasnovodsk you never know. A long propaganda mural at the end of the street, with faces in every hue of brown and beige, declared that sixty-eight nationalities lived in peace and socialist brotherhood in this town of only 60,000.

The Museum of Local and Natural History occupied the old Russian fort. It contained a black yurt (*kara oi*), desert sibling of the more famous white yurts of the Tien Shan. There was a painting of a Turkmen ambassador in golden slippers seeking Russian protection for his people at an audience with Peter the Great in St Petersburg in 1714. (Nothing was ever exhibited by a Soviet curator for mere passing interest. The myth of having been invited, albeit in Tsarist times, was central to Soviet Russia's justification of its presence in Central Asia.) And there was a lammergeier, stuffed, mounted, three metres from wingtip to wingtip, casting its shadow over a glass-fronted display of lesser desert fauna. The bearded vulture lives off skeletons picked bare by other scavengers. Like bomb-aimers, they drop the bones from great heights on to rocks, then glide down to tear a meal of marrow off the splinters. Only fifteen pairs survived in the western Kara-Kum, according to the caption, presumably because trucks' bones are heavier than camels', and less nourishing.

A short walk away near the sea, the Museum of the 26 Baku Commissars was being de-commissioned. Until 1919 the Baku Commissars were just another twenty-six Bolshevik zealots but then they were abducted from Baku by counter-revolutionaries and gunned down in a sandy hollow in the Kara-Kum, not far from Krasnovodsk. There was a whiff of British imperialist involvement, and the Commissars went straight to Communist heaven. A monument went up in the sandy hollow and others appeared in Baku and in the towns where the Commissars were born. Theirs were the heroic jaws that had saved the revolution as it fought for life in a world of wolves. Theirs was the ultimate sacrifice adopted by Soviet propagandists to inspire the faithful and sway the doubting until the even greater sacrifices of the Great Patriotic War spawned their own cult. Now their bronze faces had gone from the Baku monument, leaving only pale circles on a curving white wall. A big bronze head was still there, bowed over cupped hands which had held an eternal flame, but the flame was out and the square was up for a new name.

The museum at Krasnovodsk was a bungalow where the Commissars were held before being taken into the desert and shot. A large canvas, so detailed it could have been a photograph, showed two British officers in immaculate green tunics giving orders to the firing squad. Since the canvas was painted a British historian had established beyond reasonable doubt that no Britons were present at the execution. In the spirit of *glasnost* his writings now had pride of place in the display beneath the painting.

But the Commissars themselves were being de-idolized more slowly here than in Baku. The museum's director recited a two-minute hagiography for each of them. She was unstoppable. I took in almost nothing, made no notes, asked no questions. Still she spoke. For an hour the terrible museum ache spread up from my heels.

Escape was sweet. I met Sergei for an odd lunch of noodles and hot chocolate in a canteen by the bazaar, then bought a ticket for the next day's train to Ashkhabad.

The train left at dawn. I spent the night in Sergei's study, where he put me to sleep with an agonizing translation of an article in *Turkmenskaya Pravda* about Princess Diana attempting suicide. He took great care over conjunctions and prepositions and got most of them wrong; pronouns too. Diana was always 'he'.

As I crept out at four in the morning trying not to wake him,

Sergei sat up suddenly in bed, slight and wiry in only a loose white pair of pants.

'I want to say more on the historical background of Krasno-vodsk,' he said.

He might have been sleep-talking. Following on from nothing in particular, he said that the first president of independent Latvia was arrested by Stalin's men in Stavropol in 1939 and exiled to Krasnovodsk.

'He was my father's friend. In 1942 he died, but no one knows his grave.'

'Thank you, Sergei. Goodnight.'

'Goodnight.'

And he went straight back to sleep. I should have wished him luck getting his girlfriend out here to share his solitude.

The train clanked round the bay and into the desert, which from here stretched five hundred miles east to the Amu Darya, two hundred north to Kazakhstan and two hundred south to Iran.

The black sands of the Kara-Kum looked more sand-coloured than black. As far as land is concerned, they are what Turkmeni-stan has to make do with. A lifeline consisting of a road, a railway line and some telephone wire lines on posts used by camels for backscratching is pegged out across the desert. It links Krasnovodsk to the capital, to the oases of Tedzhen and Mary and to the river port of Chardzhou. The Kopet Dagh mountains rise to the south along its middle section but are out of bounds. They are in Iran and the border is closed.

At Nebit Dagh, three hours inland, all the guards got off the train and squatted in the sun for fifteen minutes. I had a break-fast of one and three-quarter deep-fried dough-splats called *chiburreki* from which the oil ran down my fingers. The last quarter I dropped into the jaws of a panting mongrel.

From here on the only civilized response to the heat was surrender. I lay on my bunk and concentrated on breathing. The man on the bunk opposite fanned himself to sleep with a hand towel. The fanning did not stop even once he was asleep. It got faster and faster until the breeze woke him up.

We clanked on. Every hour or so I stood over the coupling with the wagon in front and let the hot wind billow up my trousers to dry off the sweat. Those who lived along the railway seemed immune to the heat. At Bacharden an old man emerged from a yurt pitched beside the station building and stood watching the train from under a tall black sheepskin *tilpek* head-dress, like a busby. He had a full beard, and wore a thick suit under a heavy overcoat. I wondered idly what he'd wear on a winter trip to Moscow.

In the relative cool of the evening we passed through Geok-Tepe, where in 1881 General Mikhail Skobelev besieged and stormed the last great stronghold of the Tekke. For nearly five centuries the Tekke had had the run of the central Kara-Kum. Their women wove exquisite carpets on flat wooden frames laid flat on the floors in their tents. Their men raised the sheep for the wool for the carpets but also earned themselves a bad name in Europe and the Levant for plundering passing caravans. Any Russians whom they captured tended to be taken north to the wicked city of Khiva and sold as slaves. They were, and are, a tall handsome tribe, with straight European noses and deep European eyes. Skobelev crushed their buccaneering spirit. After a month-long seige, he blasted a mortal breach in Geok-Tepe's defences, extracted a formal surrender from the tribal elders and awarded his men a three-day binge of looting, rape and slaughter. Twenty thousand Tekke died. Their living heirs, with the notable exception of Professor Rosa, seemed a placid bunch.

We pulled into Ashkhabad at dusk.

'WELCOME TO THE CAPITAL OF THE TURKMEN SSR', said a notice in large red letters over the entrance to the station concourse. The concourse was not busy even when our train had emptied into it. No one offered a taxi. No one proffered a stump for money. No one tried to sell me bubble gum.

An electric trolleybus pulled up outside, absorbed a tidy queue and pulled away. For an eerie moment Ashkhabad seemed to be a city without noise.

I walked two blocks south up Lenin Prospect and two west on Freedom Prospect to the Hotel Ashkhabad. Smart types, men and women with briefcases, were standing at high tables at the bar slurping coffee and molten ice-cream. I phoned Rosa to say I'd arrived.

Rosa had been described to me as a viper but she turned out to be more of a boa. The journalist who had given me her number had been in Ashkhabad to do a story for the *Index On Censorship* about Turkmenistan's tiny, outlawed opposition. Rosa was not the opposition. If anything she was the regime. I had faxed her from Moscow offering to support her application for a British visa in return for accommodation while in Ashkhabad. She accepted. I knew she would. For any poor beggar trying to get into the bastion of comfiness and opportunity we used to call the West (which was a cruel joke even then; a tenth of the world's population masquerading as a hemisphere), visa support is gold dust. Without it the applicant needs hard currency in quantities the average Turkmen wage-earner would take decades to accumulate. That said, Rosa was not the average Turkmen wage-earner.

In her hive she was queen bee, while in the real world she was a manic social climber. With her family and subordinates she was bossiness made flesh, while on those she thought might be of use she lavished endless attention and bucketfuls of oily charm. She was embarrassingly kind and generous to me. Once or twice I found her poignant. In the end she was insufferable.

I was waiting outside the hotel when she swept up in the back of her son's Lada, sitting next to her husband. They got out and approached in a phalanx, Rosa leading. Her face was round, her skin pale, her hair black, her eyes fierce, her girth substantial, her mein imperial. When the truth hit her, that her ticket to the London glitz was the teenage-looking scruff with the rucksack, her concrete smile cracked for an instant and was re-cast with a hiss of disappointment.

'I am Rosa, Professor of Comparative Linguistics at the Turkmen Academy of Sciences, and President of the Ashkhabad-Alberquerque New Mexico Twinning Committee. This is my husband, Batir. This is my son, Batir. He is married with one child. You are hungry, exhausted and excited for a bath? We go.'

We went, fast, through empty sodium-orange streets. The husband and son looked like boxers and did not speak. Rosa said she had prepared a light supper and a programme of excursions for the next three days. Her son would be my chauffeur. Her son spoke excellent English.

Her son grunted. He swung us violently into a parking space behind a squat block of flats. (All of Ashkhabad is squat. The city was flattened by an earthquake in 1948 and rebuilt, with a few recent exceptions in special earthquake-proof concrete, to a maximum height of four storeys.)

Supper was served in a sitting room festooned with claret-coloured rugs. As the coffee table disappeared beneath an invasion of hors-d'œuvres I tried to say it all looked more than I could manage.

'Don't teach me about food and drink,' snapped Rosa. She had changed into a loose purple robe made with enough fabric for a small tent.

'I like to feel the evening on my body.'

I nodded, hoping to convey uncontroversially how nice that must be for her. Her husband walked in wearing pyjamas, carrying a pillow from the bedroom. He lay down on his side on a rug on the floor, propped himself up on an elbow with the pillow under his armpit and ate a radish.

'My husband is a lawyer,' Rosa said. 'He works with the president.'

Batir senior ate another radish then sat up cross-legged to face me like an old bull. Using his wife as interpreter he conveyed his astonishment that I should be undertaking this journey without fluent Russian and knowledge of at least one Turkic language. When my programme of excursions in Ashkhabad was completed he, or one of his colleagues, would fly with me to Mary and arrange onward transport to Chardzhou and Bukhara. I would stay with highly placed associates of his along the length of my route. Every conceivable assistance would be afforded me with no question of a charge being made. That way I would come to no harm. My heart sank.

Rosa poured ice-cold vodka and we toasted Anglo-Turkmen relations, which had recently been inaugurated with a gift from President Niyazov to Prime Minister Major of an Akhal-Tekinsky racehorse (now in quarantine). Then Rosa lifted the top off a small terracotta jar to reveal a glistening blob of caviar.

'I was a visiting professor at Dayton Community College,

Dayton, Ohio. I presented to my American friends a kilo-gramme of Turkmen caviar and they were dumb. They could not speak. It was the most splendid gift of their lives.'

There wasn't much you could say to that. The caviar in front of me had the texture of dried-out raspberry jam and tasted mainly of salt. I said it was exquisite.

'What?'

'Perfect.'

'I know. Eat it. Eat it all.'

The Islamic festival of Kurban Bairam began the following morn-ing and Rosa was excited about it. Kurban Bairam commemor-ates Abraham's preparedness to sacrifice his son to the god of the Old Testament, but celebrating it had been forbidden in Turkmenistan for the preceding seventy years. Traditionally, a lamb is sacrificed by the head of the household and consumed over three days by his extended family. Rosa had in mind, instead, a visit to a collective farm with her colleagues from the Academy of Sciences.

She wore velvet. (The Batirs were ignoring the feast. Father had flown to Moscow for the day, apparently on presidential business. Son, far from chauffeuring, was broking melons at the commodity exchange.) We rendezvoused in front of the earth-quake-proof Palladian façade of the Academy of Sciences with four assistant professors, all women, all full of deferential greetings, all dressed in full-length gowns that were nearly as splendid as Rosa's but not quite. Then we drove north in con-voy out of the city.

The highest peaks of the Kopet Dagh rose close behind Ash-khabad. We left them behind, heading straight for the desert, but the desert did not come. We crossed the Kara-Kum Canal, a concrete trough of red water as wide as a respectable river, and continued for half an hour through vineyards. I congratu-lated Rosa on her people's conquest of the Kara-Kum and she agreed that it had been a stupendous Soviet achievement.

We ate *plov* (pilau) beneath portraits of Gorbachev and Lenin in a collective farm committee room. Then, at her own sugges-tion, Rosa posed for my camera on the veranda of a beach hut beside an artificial lake constructed by, and apparently for, the collective farm's manager. The water came from another larger reservoir near Geok-Tepe, but originally, I remarked, from the Pamirs.

'Yes, from the Pamir. It is wonderful,' said Rosa. 'The great Kara-Kum Canal means that we may, per capita, expend six hundred litres of water a day. That is even more than in your European capitals.'

You could practically see the water evaporating into uselessness. The beach hut did not seem to have been used by anyone in years. Its front stilts were sinking into the lake bed, causing the whole thing to tilt crazily towards the water. Rosa held on tight to the railing round the veranda. Later she posed on a swingboat at a Socialist Pioneer Youth Camp run by the farm. At regular intervals she would tell us all how much she was enjoying herself. The assistant professors smiled and nodded and were snapped at if they tried talking among themselves.

Back at the flat in the afternoon Rosa declared herself 'excavated' and went into a trance in front of the video of *My Fair Lady* (a gift from her friends at Dayton Community College, Dayton, Ohio). The embassy ball roused her.

'Have you ever been to a ball like that?'

'No.'

'I have, many times. I was invited to the opening of the American Embassy here.'

I was privileged that evening to see Rosa in her ball-gown. We attended a wedding in the Sports Club Grill next to Ashkhabad Dynamo's football ground, where a non-league match between Krasnovodsk Agricultural Workers and Ashkhabad B was in progress under lights. Batir senior, back from Moscow, spoke gravely with an inner circle of friends and an outer one of hangers-on.

'He is very popular and knows many people in the republic,' Rosa confided in my ear. 'It is true, we are well known.' She estimated there were two hundred guests present. 'It is little. When my son was married we had five hundred guests, not here but in a banquet hall.'

Her outfit was a diaphanous sixty-five dollar pink two-piecer from Sears in Dayton, Ohio, with matching pink stilettos. It made of her a fifty-year-old dominatrix in pubescent party gear, which as a concept was not without its own depraved allure. As a reality it was resistable. She made a fuss of me within earshot of the high table and was later called to the microphone between dances to introduce her foreign guest. She pulled me with her. After her speech the band launched into a slow tune which she recognized.

'"Feeling"! My favourite! This is for us!'

We danced.

In my embarrassment I went too fast and Rosa's big soft arm turned into a leaden metronome. She crooned the words of the song in my ear, interrupting herself to say what a fine singer she had been before a thousand hours of lectures broke her voice.

'But as you see,' she said, 'I am still a dancer.'

The bride and groom looked miserable throughout, glued to their seats, desperately young, desperately formal, ignored by their guests – except when women whose dancing had been admired with rubles turned to stuff them into a jar at the bride's elbow.

Unable to find Ashkhabad uplifting I blamed it on the asphyxiating Rosa. Breaking loose from her turned out to be straightforward, however. On day three I typed a letter to the British Embassy in Moscow promising a bed and sustenance for visa applicant Rosa N— for the duration of her stay in London. She read it, filed it, kissed me and assented at once to my request to skip the excursion planned for that morning to the exhibition of Economic Achievements of the Turkmen Soviet Socialist Republic. (Rosa did not like to acknowledge the end of the Soviet Union.)

Having escaped, I went to the exhibition anyway. It was a long, hot walk away past dusty square plots created by the city's grid of avenues and never filled. It was closed; the pavilion that Turkmenistan's economic achievements had occupied was being converted for trade fairs. But inside it you could still see the world's biggest Turkmen rug, folded four times, hung from a giant steel rail and filling a glass curtain wall the size of a basketball court. The rug was eighty metres long and ten metres wide and took four women three years to weave. This was quick work, achieved by simplifying the octagonal gol motif which is the hallmark of all Tekke rugs and limiting the number of shades of red to the point where the end product was dull – and all the duller for being so big. It was a definitive piece of Soviet gigantism.

The Soviets played other games with Turkmen carpets. In the Art Museum there were carpet portraits of Lenin and Stalin, and the plinth of Ashkhabad's principal Lenin statue was clad in ceramic versions of a selection of Turkmen tribal rugs. The great leader in his mausoleum two thousand miles away would surely have been touched by this gesture of affection for his person, which had never once set foot in Central Asia.

Ashkhabad was full of undefaced monuments and grandiose reinforced concrete ministries and institutes in shades of pink and grey. It had wide, clean streets, generous shade and start-lingly few people. It seemed to be a city of 400,000 stay-at-homes. A city going through the motions. A shamelessly Soviet city that would have asked to be rebuilt from scratch if there hadn't been an earthquake. What other sort of city could have begat Rosa?

'I want to buy a carpet,' I said crossly to a taxi driver on my last morning there. He drove north into the desert almost as far as the collective grape farm, but further west, and bumped off the road to park with hundreds of others on a cracked earth football pitch. He pointed across the road and said 'bazaar'.

Inside a walled enclosure were perhaps two hundred real Turkmen rugs, the finest in the world, known to collectors as Bukharas because Bukhara was their entrepôt, but woven in the Kara-Kum with the wool of Kara-Kul sheep grazed on the foot-hills of the Kopet Dagh, or with silk from Fergana, or with a mixture of both. They hung from rails and were laid flat only for prospective buyers. Some were antique, some new; some big enough for a feast and twelve crossed pairs of legs, some meant as door flaps for *kara oi* or prayer mats or saddle bags (still to be sewn up). All glowed red, the older ones from the root of *rubia tinctorum* boiled in vats of camel urine. All were beyond my means, so I stared at them, and their tidy, mesmerizing gols stared back.

Along one wall of the enclosure toothless elders sat among heaps of *tilpek* hats, arguing loudly and shaking their fists at my camera. Along another, women did a brisker but more placid trade in silk. Outside, an amphibious army jeep on sale for $2500 in rubles was being ignored by most in favour of pens of chickens, cows and fat-tailed sheep, plus a pair of tethered camels.

Trust Ashkhabad to put all this outside its city limits. In 1914 Stephen Graham found as much life in forty-five minutes on the station platform.

> It was crowded with all the peoples of Central Asia – Persians, Russians, Afghans, Tekinski, Bokharese, Khivites, Turkomans – and every one had in his hand, or on his dress, or in his turban, roses . . . Persian hawkers, with capacious baskets of pink and white roses, moved hither and thither; immense and magnificent Turkomans lounged against pillars or walked about, their bare feet stuck into the mere toe-places they call slippers . . . In the third-class waiting-room was a line of picturesque giants waiting for their tickets, and kept in order meanwhile by a cross little Russian gendarme. Behind the long barrier, facing the waiting train, stood the familiar band of women with chickens and eggs, with steaming samovars and bottles of hot milk.

Graham passed through a month or so before me, in the brief desert spring. Hence the roses. I had envied him until I found the bazaar, which seemed to even things up. It did more besides. It made me start to whistle and hum again. There had been very little whistling *chez* Rosa.

I had said goodbye to her that morning. She had put on a white suit edged in red, and high white shoes with red leather bows on the backs of the heels. In a roundabout way she had offered to change money at a very favourable rate (for her) as a very generous favour to me. I declined but tried to give her some dollars, having asked originally to be a paying guest. She bridled.

'You have offended . . . You have insulted me. Let us stop. Forget all. This conversation did not happen.'

Then she melted and became very tactile. She tried to give me a bottle of vodka, not to drink, she said, but to wash my face with on long journeys. I'm afraid I laughed ungratefully. Her next offering was a grenade-sized bunch of fresh garlic, which I also declined.

She didn't take the money I had offered, but she did commandeer my parents' house and most of their energies for two weeks later in the year in London, at which time, mercifully, I was in Kazakhstan.

The last thing I did before leaving Ashkhabad was bump into a tall, dark-haired British reporter covering Central Asia from his base in Istanbul. He looked like Superman and wore desert boots and a complicated black leather money belt. He carried an electronic personal organizer in the breast pocket of his dark green button-down shirt and had a knuckle-crunching handshake.

Central Asia wasn't happening yet, he said. Tajikistan was simmering, but where was the bloodbath, the full-blown civil war that foreign desks the world over assumed would flare up as soon as the Afghan Mujaheddin had smuggled enough guns across the border to their Tajik brothers? Superman wasn't filing much. Just loading up with contacts so he could hit the ground running when it all boiled over. He was on a four-week swing, a republic a week. Azerbaijan, Turkmenistan, Tajikistan, Uzbekistan. Kirghizstan and Kazakhstan could wait. Who did I file for? A book? Nice one. Envied me the freedom.

We lunched in the Hotel Ashkhabad, then I left town in a bus, heading east, chuffed to be envied.

Halfway to Tedzhen the road brushed the Iranian border. Leaning out of the bus you could practically touch the barbed wire, which formed a fence ten feet high with horizontal struts and more barbed wire on top. Behind it there was a swathe of desert cleared of scrub and mined. This fence stretches from the Caspian to the Pacific; over the Pamirs, along the Tien Shan, through the Altai, skirting Siberia and finally telling Manchuria when to stop.

The road and the border veered off southwards to become

the northern corner of Iran. Delineating the Soviet Union was a big job. Defending it, of course, was an even bigger one. About twenty khaki battle tanks had been enlisted to the task at an army base on the outskirts of Tedzhen. They had since been decapitated and were drawn up beside the road in one long line, their gun turrets sitting uselessly beside them on the desert floor.

Tedzhen itself was a natural oasis unnaturally enlarged by the Kara-Kum canal, and apart from its name was bafflingly anonymous. The low white houses along the dusty street that led off the main road to the station had no windows in their outside walls. What shops there were seemed to manage without signs. If Tedzhen had a history it had left no trace. And then there were the tribespeople who strode about in billowing blue robes with white turbans wound round their heads from the chin up, leaving only eye slits. At the bus station dozens of them were gathered in the shade of a willow tree looking like domesticated highwaymen and waiting for transport to the old Silk Route oasis of Sarakhs, eighty miles south-east on the Iranian border.

I had planned to go straight on to Mary, Turkmenistan's industrial capital and the second largest city, but Sarakhs seemed the more exotic prospect.

The first half-hour of the bus-ride was through thicket: dense, green and naturally watered. We were in a shallow basin that had just collected the spring rains from a hundred miles of mountains. A camel crashed out of the bushes and ran distractedly alongside us. It seemed to be having an attack of claustrophobia.

Inside the bus, most heads were swathed in white. I asked one of them why. A hand unwound about three feet of cloth, revealing the face of a hot young man.

'*Akhal-Tekinsky*,' he said, and wound himself up again. A subgroup of the Tekke tribe, then. Apart from that, conversation in the bus was limited. I sat on the shady side by an open window and did not feel the heat until getting out at Sarakhs, when it mugged me.

There was a tiny hotel opposite the bus stop, a guesthouse with white-framed windows each side of a large front door.

Cylindrical stoves bulged out of the walls of the hall from floor to ceiling. 'For winter,' said the manager. 'Minus twenty.' I phoned a number on a list given me by Rosa's husband, who, to my relief, had dropped the idea of providing me with an escort. Within minutes an army jeep pulled up outside. Within a few more I was in an air-conditioned sanctuary gazing at a mural of mountains, lakes, and birds of paradise. Bagench, a youthful, cross-eyed procuror (something legal), was giving instructions to his wife and bidding me lie down. Bagench was a protégé of Batir senior's, and the mural covered one wall of his sitting room. It was pukesomely vivid, yet still mouthwatering.

'Batir is a great man,' Bagench said.

I nodded. He lay down beneath the mural and tucked a pillow under his arm – in the manner of who else but Batir senior – and gestured for me to do likewise. He had got the afternoon off work and had invited two friends round to meet the English associate of Batir of Ashkhabad. Mrs Bagench carried in an enormous meal of boiled chicken joints and *plov*, followed by watermelon, tea and soft-centred strawberry sweets instead of sugar. After each trip she would leave the room – but then spy on us, I think, because she managed to anticipate our every whim. After lunch I took two Anadin for the heat and we drove off in the jeep to the mausoleum of the Sufi mystic Abul Fazl, built by Muhammad Bini Atciz Az Seracksin around 1023. It had been badly damaged by the Mongols and recently restored.

A fearsome one-legged holy man keeping watch over the mausoleum from under an awning forbade photography, so the jeep roared back to the mayor's office to obtain permission for the associate of Batir of Ashkhabad to take a photograph. Meanwhile I climbed, panting, on to a huge unexcavated oblong mound. Until the youngest son of Genghis Khan destroyed it in 1221 this mound had been Sarakhs. Al-Fadl ben Sahl, Grand Vizier to the Caliph of Baghdad, was killed here in his bath in 819.

The border split Sarakhs in two and its Iranian half was a mere shout away, with pistachio trees where the desert curled up towards the east end of the Kopet Dagh. The jeep returned, permission having been obtained, and I took a picture of the cuboid mausoleum and its modest dome, then we all went swimming in a nearby reservoir.

The water was tepid. We dried off in minutes without towels and squatted in the patchy shade of a thorn bush, avoiding soldier ants. The Brezhnev conversation came round again; the same conversation I'd had with the cook on the train to Makhachkala. One of the friends rated him the greatest Soviet leader, but Bagench seemed to favour Andropov and Stalin.

'Stalin?' I asked, to be sure I had understood.

'Stalin. Of course.'

'But didn't he kill millions of people?'

'There were millions of bad people at that time.'

Sarakhs was not that interested in gulags. It was an innocent place and late that night, with the blazing heat of the afternoon a mere mirage in the memory, it was even magical. While the men slurped mutton broth indoors beneath the birds of paradise, Bagench's wife, mother, grandmother and daughter sat out on the wide veranda with the crickets, talking quietly and chuckling at the moon.

In the morning Bagench fixed me a lift to Mary in an army petrol tanker driven by a brooding German with the Russian name of Sasha. Twenty per cent of Sarakhs' population was German. Their ancestors settled on the Volga in the eighteenth century and drifted towards Asia in the nineteenth, or were sent by Stalin in the twentieth (he expelled those ethnic Germans still living in the Russian heartland when Hitler invaded in 1941).

The truck was an eight-cylinder Kamaz turbo diesel. Fast, deafening and indestructible, Kamaz are the pride of the Soviet truck-building industry. Sasha drove it like the devil, aiming for desert rats and lizards when they crossed the dirt road, never slowing down for potholes, stopping once in four hours and then only to top up the radiator from an irrigation channel.

He wanted out – a one-way trip to Germany and the German citizenship to which he was entitled by birth. He wanted a real job, a real house, a real life, and never to return. He said his piece then stuck to smoking, not bothered if in the course of lighting up he swerved us off the road. He seemed to have a death wish.

We delivered the petrol to a helicopter base outside Mary. Twenty Hind gunships, the kind used against the Mujaheddin in Afghanistan, sat on soft tarmac under their drooping rotors.

Mary felt Godforsaken. But in fact, under the desert a short distance north of this dirty, ugly, flyblown fan-assisted oven of an oasis, God had hidden 600 billion cubic metres of natural gas. It was found in 1968 and the prospectors called their bore-hole Shatlik (Joy). This is the key to Turkmenistan's future prosperity, and Sasha said it was being linked by pipeline to Iran. We went to Shatlik for him to be paid and for a silent canteen lunch of grey ravioli eaten under a yellowing mural, in three panels, of Soviet engineers reclaiming the desert so that two big-breasted Turkmen women might take their evening walk along a verdant riverbank.

Outside the canteen trucks came and went, belching fumes and leaking diesel. Workers traipsed to and from shifts over a wasteland of dust and bald concrete. It was hard to imagine the 600 billion cubic metres of gas underneath us; a gigantic fart, as old as the world, being bled by a valve called Joy.

Sasha left me at a hotel in the centre of Mary and returned to Sarakhs. I got a room with an air-conditioner and cooled down. Then, realizing too late that cooling down just gives the heat a headstart on you, I set off on foot, losing energy and fluid with each step, to look for ruins.

There should have been tremendous ruins because Mary has a tremendous past. Until 1937 it was Merv, 'Pearl of the East', and northern gateway to Afghanistan. (London's Russophobes were stricken with Mervousness when a Lieutenant Alikhanov claimed it for the Tsar in 1884; British troops were even mobilized on the Afghan border the following year.) As eastern capital of the Turkish Seljuk empire in the eleventh and twelfth centuries Merv was leader of the Muslim world and the greatest city on the Silk Route, ever. It was the victim of the Mongols' most horrific single act of butchery (at least half a million died) and of their most comprehensive orgy of destruction. Hardly a building was left standing and the Persian branch of the Silk Route, which Merv controlled, never really recovered. Still, there were meant to be ruins.

I was looking in the wrong place. Merv had depended for its

water on the River Murgab. So did Mary, but the Murgab had changed course since the Mongol invasion. Now it ran through a concrete channel past the ferris wheel in Mary's Lenin Park. Old Merv was fifteen miles away and desiccated. In the end I went there in a taxi with Tania of Intourist.

Tania had studied English in Ashkhabad.

Under Rosa?

Who else.

'Rosa treated me well, but she was very strict with the others. Sometimes like a man.'

I went a little further and likened Rosa to Rosa Klebb, the granite-faced KGB colonel who nearly does for James Bond with a poisoned spike in her shoe at the end of *From Russia With Love*. Tania was not familiar with James Bond but seemed to enjoy the comparison, anyway.

As we swept over the Kara-Kum Canal she clicked into auto-babble and explained how the canal provided each Turkmenian citizen with up to six hundred litres of water a day. I seemed to remember hearing this somewhere before. The climate of the Murgab oasis had been found to be highly beneficial to sufferers of kidney ailments, she said. They came from across the former Soviet Union to clinics to lose ten litres of water a day in sweat and replace it by eating the famous local melons. I said I'd read that the Murgab oasis was historically disease-ridden and now had a poisoned water table from excessive cotton cultivation. She clicked off and looked out the window.

'It's true. We live like animals.'

Tania wanted desperately to travel to England. She had learned English to be a citizen of the world, not an Intourist guide in Merv. But you had to be invited to get a visa, and her letters abroad were still being intercepted by the authorities. I knew all about visa support, and cursed myself for having lavished it on the wrong person.

The bit about intercepted letters took a while to sink in. When it did, I had a small anxiety attack. I had let off steam about Rosa, in brutal language, in a letter home. I told Tania.

'She will read it. Of course. She has excellent connections with the authorities.'

Oh God. We laughed.

We were at Merv.

It looked as if Cecil B. DeMille had recently finished an epic on Genghis Khan and the Seljuks. The set had been all but struck. A few of the biggest mock-ups still stood as skeletons on the baked brown plain, waiting for an especially big crane to come and take them down safely. They were miles apart, making no sense.

On the subject of Merv there are only theories. The best is that the River Murgab continually shifted its course, before the Mongols came as well as after, and that Merv moved with it. This would explain the remains – mostly mere traces – of five separate sets of city walls, scarcely overlapping, each from a different age. We stood on a hummock and Tania pointed at other hummocks, reciting their names. Erk Kala, Giaur Kala, Sultan Kala, Abdullah Khan Kala, Bairam Ali Khan Kala.

Sultan Kala was the one that counted. The sultan in question was Sultan Sanjar, last Seljuk Viceroy of Merv, patron of scholars, ruler of half the world. His mausoleum was still standing. So were three strange fluted walls of a palace where he hosted parties at which all the guests were men and all the women slaves.

Old Merv was definitely old, but so beaten up and blown away that my imagination gave up on it. I couldn't see the Sultan or his concubines, couldn't fear the Mongols' fires on the lowering horizon, wasn't seized with a desire to dig for amulets. The heat, the desolation and an unpleasant vision of Rosa as an octopus with dormant tentacles in every corner of Turkmenistan, made me anxious to push on. The next day I crossed the desert to Chardzhou.

The territory between Mary and the Amu Darya is virgin; no gas under it, no cotton over it, only sand held in unspectacular waves by slow-growing saxaul bushes and their deep, divining roots. I crossed it in a taxi, with tea and raisins included in the fare of twenty dollars. It was extravagant, but it made a change from buses and trains and earned the driver two months' wages in a day.

The hotel at Chardzhou was full. Reluctantly I looked up another name on Rosa's husband's list. The name was Nikolai.

Nikolai had a Hitler moustache and was watching a documentary on Hitler when I arrived. At first he seemed agitated by the prospect of having to deal with an uninvited foreign guest, and he kept patting his short grey hair while regaining his composure. He made one or two aggressive jokes that I didn't understand and then barked at his wife for food. Whenever he caught sight of Hitler on the television he would point and say 'our beloved Adolf', and laugh. Chicken legs and tomatoes came, and vodka. He quizzed me incredulously for half an hour, relaxing slowly with the help of the alcohol. Then he made a phone call and announced a grand tour of Chardzhou.

I didn't know it at the time, but Chardzhou is the pits. It consists of rows of sad naked apartment blocks rising square off the desert like a bar chart.

Within a few minutes of Nikolai's call an athletic man walked in wearing a black shirt. This was the driver, a Tartar of few words. It turned out that Nikolai was a very big cheese; manager of the Chardzhou cotton combine, which collected cotton grown along the first few hundred miles of the Kara-Kum Canal, and cleaned it, combed it, spun it and shipped it. In Chardzhou, cheeses didn't come much bigger than Nikolai. His apartment was the usual three-and-a-half rooms but his car was a gleaming white Nissan Laurel and it came with a driver.

First we called on Abul Fazl, a bulging Azeri with whom Nikolai had done national service in the Caspian fleet. He climbed in. The next stop was for Timur, Nikolai's deputy manager, who seemed envied for his house. He sat us in the shade at the edge of his courtyard and clapped his hands for *plov*, apricots and more vodka. Timur didn't drink himself and didn't join us on the tour, which proceeded to a butcher's shop.

We strode in as a gang and Nikolai shouted for the butcher. I did not catch his name, being already drunk. A back room was hurriedly prepared and the butcher joined us there for yet more vodka, this time with bread and onion. He was fat. He unbuttoned his white tunic, which was browned with blood, and stuck a fat little finger in his navel. He seemed happy like that. We downed another bottle. Nikolai received a parcel of meat and we moved on, to a dacha on the west bank of the Oxus.

Like Alexander the Great some 2321 years earlier, I had been anxious to see this river. Alexander's anxiety had been how to get his army across it once Bessus, a Persian regicide, had burned the only bridge. My anxiety was that the river might be empty. The Macedonians had floated over on leather bundles filled with twigs. I stumbled down a short path from Nikolai's allotment and was relieved to see a swathe of silty water half a mile wide.

We swam. Nikolai had a lean face but a slack stomach with a deep slit from an appendectomy scar.

I remembered hearing it was dangerous to swim when inebriated, especially in strong currents, so I concentrated very hard on keeping my head above water, and survived. Nikolai and Abul Fazl survived too. They had done this before, usually with *dyevuchki*. Girls. Drying off in the dacha Nikolai made much of some soft porn on the walls and said his wife never came here. It was a grubby little sex hovel with a narrow unmade bed and orange curtains. He seemed to be offering to get me a woman when Abul Fazl pulled me outside and poured a bucket of cold water over my head. To wash the river off, he said. The Tartar driver laughed. I gasped and wondered fleetingly if these people were dangerous.

We drank more vodka then drove back into town along dirt roads. It was getting dark and Nikolai recognized someone walking in the twilight. Another deputy manager. All of Chardzhou seemed to deputy-manage the cotton combine. This man piled in and was brought up-to-date on the hilarious saga of Nikolai's unexpected guest. He invited us to dinner.

This was served on an enormous dais under the stars and lasted about two hours. I do not remember what we ate, but by the end I was grotesquely bloated and desperately drunk. We dropped Abul Fazl at home, then went to an apartment building that I thought was Nikolai's, though it was actually Lisa's.

Nikolai told the driver to return at six in the morning. Lisa met us at the top of three flights of stairs and ushered us into her sparsely furnished flat. She was perhaps thirty-five, with thick black hair and a voluminous body sheathed in something black and velvety. Nikolai had a quiet word with her. She looked over his shoulder at me and asked him, 'Does he understand?'

Nikolai answered for me and we went through a bedroom on to a balcony where Lisa brought us tea. As we drank it the bed was made up with clean sheets and I caught sight of another woman, younger and slimmer than Lisa.

'Everything OK?' asked Nikolai.

'Everything OK,' I croaked.

'You will sleep well,' said Nikolai.

'Yes. Then I will take the train to Khiva. In the morning I will take the train to Khiva.'

Nikolai got up and came unsteadily towards me. He had been mumbling something I hadn't understood. He stood over me and raised his fist and held it there for a bit. Then he hit the side of my face. I was very surprised.

He hit me again, harder. Lisa rushed out and stood between us, pleading with him. I pulled away, picked up my shoes and camera at the door and ran out of the flat. I ran down the stairs and along a path between apartment buildings to a dimly lit road. On the far side I found some shadows and sat down to put my shoes on, facing the way I'd come. Nikolai didn't follow. I felt my jaw, which ached, and remembered with a sick feeling that my rucksack, my notebook and $2000 in cash were in Nikolai's flat. I didn't know his surname or address and his grand tour of Chardzhou had taken the edge off my homing instinct.

It turned out that Nikolai enjoyed hitting people when drunk, and meant nothing by it. After waiting a while for him to simmer down and for my marinaded nerves to unfray I crept back to Lisa's flat. She was looking out for me at the bottom of the stairs. The younger woman whom I had glimpsed from the balcony led me to a back bedroom next to the kitchen and said 'Sleep, everything OK,' at which point Nikolai hammered on the front door.

He did not get in, and eventually found his way home. I had a bad night, with a bruised face, a shrinking brain, a distended stomach, a churning bowel and a crack squadron of mosquitoes conspiring to interrupt sleep.

The driver turned up as arranged at six in the morning. When he heard what had happened he doubled up laughing.

Nikolai had showered and changed into a suit by the time we picked him up at a pre-arranged street corner.

'Everything OK?' he said, smelling of shampoo and grinning like a schoolboy. *Vsyo narmalne?* The phrase was beginning to grate.

It was a Sunday. We went and sat outside a school being used as a polling station for a mayoral election in which the incumbent was the only candidate. He was the other person in Chardzhou with a chauffeur-driven car, and one of only two people for whom Nikolai stood up. (Hard-boiled Russian technocrat offers solemn greeting to stolid Turkmen figurehead whom he afterwards derides, to stifled mirth, as a turnip.) The other passer-by honoured with a public sign of respect from Nikolai was a white-haired Greek, veteran of the Great Patriotic War in which he had lost his left hand to a grenade and after which, as a Communist who hated the cold, he had exiled himself to Turkmenistan. (Two lonely Europeans clasp each other briefly with three hands and a stump, and much seems to pass between them even though nothing is said.)

There was a train to Khiva at midday, and I wanted to catch it as the first stage of a side-trip to the Aral Sea. With half an hour to go Nikolai swung into action. Timur of the enviable courtyard and the apricots was despatched to the station to procure a ticket. I was catapulted in the Nissan Laurel to Nikolai's apartment, where his wife and daughter, wearing expressions which said, 'We know he has brought shame on our family; be merciful and do not breathe a word of it to Batir of Ashkhabad', were standing by with a steaming bath, clean towels, a hot meal and an entire set of brand new clothes. These included a white T-shirt of finest Turkmen cotton and a pair of Chinese training shoes. But I liked the coarse grey woollen Y-fronts best. They were beyond horrible. On the right loins they would have passed for Calvin Klein.

Nikolai was waiting at the station when we slewed to a halt outside it at 12.02 p.m. Central Asian trains never go faster than 40 m.p.h. and their odysseys are measured in days, not hours or minutes. But, barring acts of God, they leave each station dead on time. Nikolai had cashed in all his favours with the station master to hold the Khiva train until we got there.

He trotted with me to the platform and pressed a first-class ticket and a two hundred ruble note into my hand.

'Please say nothing about last night,' he said quickly. 'You are always welcome in Chardzhou.' He squeezed a tear of contrition from one eye. I thanked him from my heart and pledged undying comradeship. Then, mercifully, the train pulled out.

The Aral Sea

~~~~~~

For all its shrinkage, the Aral Sea was still very large and obvious on my map, yet it proved hard to get to. There were no roads over the former sea bed to the former port of Muynak on what had been the southernmost shore, and the whole area was closed to foreigners anyway. The closure was said to be because of chemical weapons testing on Barsar-Kelmez, the Aral's second largest island, but you got the feeling it was also because the Uzbeks were ashamed of the sadly shrivelled pond in their back garden.

They were also puzzled. Why visit Muynak?

'There is nothing to see,' a KGB underling told me helpfully at one of many interviews. He had a point. *The* point. *There is nothing to see*. Not boring, anonymous nothing, but the traumatic, lingering absence of a great, blue, liquid, living thing that had disappeared. It would be like hearing silence at Piccadilly Circus.

From Chardzhou the train trundled north-west for two hundred miles, shadowing the wide trench between the Kara-Kum and Kizyl-Kum deserts which contains the Amu Darya. These were straightforward miles. The river could not mistake its course and sweated along unmolested. But the moment it hesitated, cotton pounced. At Gaz Achak, the first of hundreds of distributaries which form the Amu Darya's delta had been canalized and given branches of its own. Likewise downstream, all the way to Muynak, side-channels that had once been seasonal and apt to change course on a whim were now permanent and fixed. The result is impressive on satellite pictures: 100,000 square kilometres of green in an ocean of aridity, 60 per cent of it producing cotton.

The green smudge has been this big before. Left to its own devices the Amu Darya used to wander over the desert like a restless tail as the wind moved its banks and its red silt fell out of suspension into bars and ridges. They say it once flowed into a giant swamp. It has fed the Aral Sea, by one route or another, for a mere four thousand years, watering en route the oases of Khorezm.

For a few sweet decades between the tenth and thirteenth centuries Khorezm was a player in world politics. Its kings, the Khorezmshahs of Gurganch, prospered by their position on the northern Silk Route to southern Russia and waxed when Merv and Baghdad waned. But Gurganch was always at the mercy of the Amu Darya, or anyone who meddled with it.

The Mongols meddled with it. In 1220 they broke a wooden dam a mile upstream of the city in revenge for the killing of a Mongol envoy two years before by Mohammed II, the last and most bumptious Khorezmshah.

Gurganch was washed away and the Khorezmian oasis spawned only one more independent city before the Russians came. This was Khiva, impregnable and dastardly.

Khiva spent most of the eighteenth and nineteenth centuries amassing wealth and notoriety in equal measure by selling slaves, most of whom were brought in from the Kara-Kum by Turkmen raiders. It was a compact citadel set back twenty miles from the west bank of the river. Its inner wall, thirty feet high, incorporated forty massive rounded bastions. It was ruled by hereditary Khans who threw prisoners from their minarets for fun and thought themselves, according to a Captain James Abbott who visited in 1840, the equals of the kings and queens of England. If Khiva irked Victorian Britain, it infuriated Tsarist Russia, and was desperately remote.

By 1992 that remoteness had eroded somewhat. There were two trains a day from Moscow, flights from Tashkent to Urgench (twenty miles away and as ugly as its name), and buses to everywhere at every hour of the day and night. Foreigners turned few heads in Khiva. At first I took this as a personal affront but I soon decided that affecting ennui towards tourists was an Uzbek national pastime. Uzbeks also seemed, on balance, shorter, noisier, less elegant and fonder of tradition than their Turkmen neighbours. Near Khiva's old town even young men wore straight-sided skullcaps known as *tubetekkei* and a type of dark quilted coat, fastened with a sash, that I recognized from Stephen Graham's photographs.

The twelfth-century citadel was intact to its last sun-baked brick, though heavily restored and inside out; human life spread up to its walls from outside instead of in. This had been arranged for tourists, of whom I thought I was the only one until a shuffling sound came up the spiral stairs of the Islam Khodja minaret.

I was joined in the lookout lantern at the top of Khiva's tallest tower by Gary and Jean from Queensland, Australia. Jean drove minibuses in Cairns. She had won a trip to Moscow and St Petersburg and had traded it in for the Silk Route. Gary was a telecom engineer by profession but a botanist by calling. As he looked out over the empty old town and the cotton fields beyond, he said that ecologically Central Asia was shafted because neither Russians nor Muslims gave a knick-knack for ecology. Russians were so used to scary vast untrampled territories that they found a bit of human spoilation actually reassuring. Muslims left big things like the fate of the planet to fate. Gary sighed.

'But have you seen Tash Kowli?' he asked.

I hadn't, but I went there next and found that it was, as Gary put it, something else.

Tash Khauli was a palace built for Allakuli Khan in 1838, and on the painted ceilings of its harem nothing had been left to fate. Or else fate has a peerless eye for colour and symmetry and detail – the abstract detail to which Islamic artists are restricted though it dazzles none more than the unsuspecting infidel. Turquoise hexagons slotted into brilliant orange stars, cobalt cloverleaves danced over fields of rape and bunches of purple flowers seemed to fall towards the floor only to be lassooed at the last moment by swirly pink tentacles.

These roofs, intended for the eyes of concubines and eunuchs only, were as psychedelic as the Kara-Kum was bleak. But they were also cheerful, dammit. I had not seen anything as cheerful since the equally un-Soviet market outside Ashkhabad.

The delta of the Amu Darya is long. Khiva was still two hundred miles from Muynak. I continued north-west, through cotton fields in which the bushes grew out of a sterile salty crust, to Tashauz, the main town of northern Turkmenistan. Here a surreal silver Lenin pointed skywards from an empty plot opposite the hotel, against a background of unfinished concrete building frames.

It made a brave ensemble. Lenin seemed to be defying passers-by to decorate his eternally waistcoated tummy with spray paint. 'Get Me Out of Here' might have been appropriate, or 'Mad Vlad' (a brief caption for the pedestal). It was not clear why he was pointing at the sky. Maybe he was hailing an aero-taxi back to good old, grim old Moscow, where proletariats and their grudges did not have to be magicked out of the desert.

In the lobby of the regional offices of the former Soviet Ministry of Land Reclamation and Water Resources in Tashauz there was a collection of posters of the ministry's greatest works: the Samarkand headworks on the Zerafshan River in Uzbekistan, irrigating 80,000 hectares for cotton; the Nurek dam on the Vakhsh River in Tajikistan, one of the highest in the world, irrigating 400,000 hectares for cotton; the Kara-Kum Canal in Turkmenistan, taking 400 cubic metres of water from the Amu Darya every second to irrigate 500,000 hectares for cotton; and the Golodnaya steppe of southern Kazakhstan, converted with the help of 650 kilometres of 'lined distributors', 5700 kilometres of 'flumes' and 15,600 kilometres of 'subsurface horizontal drainage' into fifty brand new state farms, forty-three of them to produce, exclusively, cotton.

Most ministry employees had gone home but a stoutish young man on duty invited me into his office, whereupon the telephone rang. He grunted into it for five minutes, writing figures in columns in an old ledger. It was a form of telemetry. He was making sure Tashauz and its surrounding cotton fields were getting their dues in water. He hung up and asked how it was in the hotel. I said it was fine. I had spent the afternoon there, air-conditioned, reading *War and Peace* and finding war on the whole more exciting than peace, while the entire hotel staff had gathered in the foyer to watch an omnibus edition of *Los Ricos Tambien Lloran* (*The Rich Also Cry*), a 1970s soap opera about lachrymose rich Mexicans to which the former Soviet Union was addicted. Foreign journalists in Moscow had been suggesting that as inflation, unemployment and the mafia ran wild, only *Los Ricos Tambien Lloran* was holding former Soviet society together. (The soap was aid. All five hundred episodes had been presented to the CIS by Mexico's President Salinas.) Thrice weekly 290 million mostly desperate people from 130 ethnic groups in 16 republics sank into a peaceful torpor of televisual thumb-sucking. They were not just reassured to be reminded that the rich also cry. They worshipped the characters and aspired with all their souls to live in palatial Mex-American condominia and wear kipper ties and purple twin-sets.

'But what about the water?' asked the man with the ledger. 'Can you drink it?'

The water seemed fine too, I said.

'It is eighty per cent bad, and we drink it all the time,' he said. He seemed depressed. He flexed a stiff knee and winced. Arthritis, apparently. 'Everyone in Tashauz is ill in some way from the water and I have to measure it out.'

Tashauz wasn't even on the front line, but Nukus was. The war of attrition between ideology and nature (grand metaphors are sadly apt) had been fought to the death up at Muynak. But in Nukus, capital of the autonomous region of Karakalpakstan, a polite little guerrilla war was still in progress.

I arrived in a sandstorm and got a room on the top floor of the ostentatious ten-storey Hotel Tashkent. My passport was withheld for inspection by the authorities, who arrived within the hour. At first I thought they were a couple being shown to the wrong room. The man was baby-faced and Mongol-featured. The woman was older. They were from Avir.

'Avir?'

'Ovir.'

'O.V.I.R.'

'*Otdel Viz i Registratsii.*'

'Kagebe.'

'Kagebe?'

'Ka-ge-be.'

The woman wrote it on a piece of paper. KGB.

They came in and sat down.

Wasn't the KGB defunct? I asked.

'Not in Uzbekistan,' said the woman.

'You do not have Nukus on your visa,' said Baby-face.

'I have only the main cities of my itinerary on my visa,' I said.
'If I had every city on my visa it would be many pages long.'

'But Nukus is a major city. It is capital of Karakalpakstan.'

'I am sorry.'

They seemed to like apologies.

'We too are sorry. You cannot stay in Nukus.'

'But I want to visit Muynak.'

'Impossible. Muynak is a closed city.'

'Why?'

'It is closed.'

I pleaded that I'd travelled five thousand kilometres to see
the Aral Sea.

'Impossible,' said Baby-face, but then he offered a chink of
hope. 'Perhaps if you have an invitation you may obtain permission from the Foreign Ministry of Uzbekistan in Tashkent.'

Tashkent was seven hundred miles away so, for the time
being, I chose to misunderstand the nice people from OVIR,
and hung around in Nukus. This was for two reasons: I hoped
to meet a man called Yusup Kamalov, chief spokesman for the
Union for the Defence of the Aral and the Amu Darya, but he
was stuck in Tashkent trying to get a flight back from a meeting
with sympathetic Americans.

There was also a chance of going back upriver by boat, but it
depended on repairs being carried out on a mothballed tug at
a river port called Takhiatash. The spring rains had been exceptional and for the first time in decades the lower Amu Darya
was navigable.

Baby-face and Older Woman returned the following evening
with a confession to be signed and a fifty ruble fine to levy. I
promised to be on the next day's bus to Bukhara and we parted
amicably.

The bus went without me. I checked out of the hotel and
stayed at Mr Kamalov's house for a couple of days at the invitation of his son, while Mr Kamalov remained stuck in Tashkent.

It was a big house by Soviet standards, with a walled garden
and a garage. Half of the bathroom was a muddy crater overlaid

with a coarse mesh of pipes. Instead of flushing the lavatory you had to scoop lime into it from a bucket.

I went out only twice, in taxis, to see how the boat repairs were going. They were going slowly. The rest of the time Yusup's fourteen-year-old son played host like one born to it. His name was Idris and his talents, which included speaking English, were diverse. He performed 'Let It Be' at a large upright piano in his bedroom, first with the original lyrics then with his own ones in Karakalpak. He clobbered me at 'Cotton Harvest', a version of Pacman he had devised on a computer borrowed from the Academy of Sciences, where his father had a daytime job as a wind power researcher. He waited on me at a small table in the large front room and sat on a sofa-bed discussing Boney M and business software while I ate. When his mother was out teaching he cooked. He sketched my portrait, and it came out like Jean-Claude Van Damme.

He said his father had taken many journalists to Muynak and was not afraid of OVIR or of prison. He also explained that his father was an inventor as well as an environmentalist. Most of the inventions seemed to depend on wind. There was a stack of home-made windsurfers outside under an extended eave, and a home-made hang glider. (What Idris could not show me because they were not ready were his father's wings.)

Yusup Kamalov sounded at least mildly unhinged. I expected someone restless and gaunt, eaten up by his own energies. There was someone like this, but it wasn't Yusup. It was 'Uncle Tolik', a nervous, underweight Russian with grey hair and a moustache, who drove a wheezing Niva jeep and paid Idris a commission to sell Turkish pantyhose to the girls at school. Uncle Tolik did not seem to be anyone's uncle but he dropped in constantly in a threadbare tracksuit for tea. He also ran a subscription video channel at the Hotel Tashkent, from a room on the top floor. I think it was Uncle Tolik who eventually grassed on me.

Yusup was a different sort of dude. When he finally made it home it was as if an unwanted guest had got up and left. Everyone grinned. Idris and his younger sister and the dog (there was a dog) dashed for the door when they heard the chuckling outside. Yusup herded them all back in with big arms and bunches of bags. This was not a natural windsurfing physique walking in the house. It was more of a baked potato.

Yusup wore a T-shirt and a pair of Levis obtained during an international wind power conference in California. He distributed gifts from the sympathetic Americans, including a scroll of the American Declaration of Independence for Idris.

The homecoming fest lasted until Idris and his sister were sent to bed. Eventually, under a bare bulb in a den full of papers at the end of the house, Yusup talked in broken English about the Aral Sea and other apparently related themes.

What had been lost? He wondered if I knew. It was not just a sea full of fish, but a jungle full of man-eating tigers that had also been a seasonal staging post for billions of migrating Siberian birds. The Aral and the Amu Darya delta had been somewhere in which *homo sapiens* had to know his place.

Was it worth getting back? (Yusup's question again. I had assumed it would be an article of faith for him that you don't drain a sea and get away with it, and that before anyone did anything else the sea should therefore be refilled. But Yusup was far more practical.)

No. If the sea was re-filled it would not be for its own sake. Not with two million people now needing decent water in Karakalpakstan and Khorezm.

'For the population here what means the sea if there is no water for drinking?' Yusup asked.

What he was after was a little justice.

'I want the Aral to be the first case in the world where nature and man are granted equal rights. Like man with man, so man with nature. It is the only way.' He squeezed and shaped the air with his hands as he spoke, cranking up the expressiveness of his limited English.

Like man with man. That was another thing. He spread on the floor two large-scale pilotage charts given him by a *Washington Post* correspondent who had visited the previous year. Together the charts formed a giant picture of the Aral basin: deserts, Pamirs, Tien Shan and all. Yusup paced round it, chortling.

'Made in the USA by the CIA from American spying satellites. It is the best map of my country in the world. Now.' He took in the mountains with a sweep of a windsurfer sail batten and predicted a war over water, fought between the highlands which had it and the lowlands which needed it.

'Why should Karakalpak people have bad water while Tajik people have good water? Is it because we are second-class citizens? Why do we have to beg for water?'

Silence for a moment.

I asked about the Union for the Defence of the Aral and the Amu Darya. Membership was down from three hundred to one hundred because people were concentrating on surviving. Environmentalism was a luxury. It was also prejudicial at the best of times to one's reputation with the KGB – and everybody else.

'In Nukus they say green man is crazy man. If I start to talk about nature they say you must talk only about money, business, car, video.'

Yusup did not stop at nature. He talked about flying like a bird. Idris had mentioned his father's wings and I had thought it was a joke. It was not a joke. Yusup got down two dog-eared folders tied with ribbons, full of diagrams of insect wings and bird wings and human adaptations of them. Airflows and upthrusts were all worked out; Yusup knew his calculus. He was within a flap or two of floppy flight – and a serious cash prize which he believed had been offered by an Englishman to whoever pioneered it. He had met up with rivals once in Moscow. Many had since died experimenting, but Yusup was undeterred. If he was crazy he was happy being crazy. Anyway, his expenses-paid trip to the California wind power convention had earned him a unique status in Nukus. None of the money-business-car-video bunch had ever been to California.

He handed me a sheet of paper. On it was typed his plan for saving the Aral and the Amu Darya. It had been sent to the presidents of the five Central Asian republics, whom it invited to set up an Aral Bank to guarantee a minimum flow into the sea from the Amu Darya and Syr Darya rivers of, say, 30 cubic kilometres a year (30 billion cubic metres; three-fifths of the total annual flow of the two rivers combined). Surplus water would be sold by the Bank to commercial users and given to domestic ones. Those who chose to pollute it would pay for the privilege.

The Bank would own and lease all Aral Sea fishing rights, whose value would rise as the sea re-filled, encouraging the Bank to re-fill it at more than the statutory minimum rate. The Bank's revenues would be spent on lining and covering irrigation channels, and other water waste reduction schemes. With a 30 per cent cut in water wastage in the Aral basin and a steady inflow of 30 cubic kilometres a year the shrinkage of the Aral Sea could be reversed and a moderate recovery could be under way within ten years.

It was simple, feasible, the least that was worth demanding and the most that could be hoped for. None of the presidents had replied. Yusup did not imagine they would. He wasn't bothered. He wasn't obsessed. Not with the Aral Sea, anyway. With no private resources and no corporate resources in a country with no public resources or recognized channels for the expression of public opinion, there was only so much you could do.

Floppy flight was different. It was out there off the edge of some unsuspecting cliff, waiting to be accomplished, worthy of an obsession.

'I very want to fly like bird without noise of engine,' Yusup said. He laughed and re-tied the ribbons on the folders.

The boat repairs at Takhiatash had run aground. Something to do with a filter. There was, alas, no chance of chugging up the Amu Darya after all. Nor was there a realistic one of slipping past OVIR to Muynak without getting Yusup into trouble. He was happy to risk it but it didn't seem fair. It did seem worth taking OVIR at face value, however, and asking permission to visit Muynak from the Foreign Ministry in Tashkent.

The next morning Yusup went to the Academy of Sciences to type out an invitation and I went to the windswept long-distance bus station having arranged to meet him there before my bus left.

Baby-face was waiting for me. This was both a shock and a mystery. I tried ignoring him but was guided firmly into an interview room behind the ticket office.

'This is NOT BEAUTIFUL,' he said. 'You are the second

Englishman who has lied to me. What are you doing here? Three times to Takhiatash. Why? Where have you been staying?'

He was not so much aggressive as baffled, but he knew about my trips to Takhiatash and he knew I had been aiming for this bus. How?

I said I had stayed in Nukus to do an interview and obtain an invitation for my next visit.

'Where have you been staying? With whom was your interview?'

So this was it. Interrogation. Toe nails next. He could do what he liked but he wouldn't break me.

'With Kamalov,' he said, a disappointing hint of levity creeping into his manner. 'I know.'

Another confession followed, this time to be written as well as signed. Another fine. He said the confession could be written in English. It would be translated by a government interpreter.

'Write that you were staying with Kamalov.'

I wrote that I had been sleeping up a tree but crossed that out and put 'near the house of Mr Kamalov' when I realized I might be meeting Baby-face again.

He walked me to the bus. Yusup was waiting there with the invitation. For an exhilarating moment I thought he was going to pretend he didn't know me but instead he chuckled his crazy-man chuckle, handed me the invitation, slapped Baby-face on the back and climbed into a waiting jeep. Looking mildly embarrassed, Baby-face wished me a pleasant journey.

How did he know about Takhiatash? As the bus pounded southwards over the brown Kyzil-Kum I dreamed fitfully of Uncle Tolik's face in rearview mirrors. It had to be him.

Bukhara passed at midnight, Samarkand at six in the morning. (There would be another chance to see the blue domes of Gur Emir and Bibi Khanym that make Samarkand an international tourist destination.)

Nineteen hours and seven hundred miles after leaving Nukus I was in the Foreign Ministry's protocol department in the leafy heart of Tashkent, the Uzbek capital. An urbane ex-diplomat who spoke fluent English gave me temporary press accreditation, which made me feel extremely grand, and a visa stamp for Nukus.

'And, er, Muynak?'

'Muynak is closed. Permission is available only from Moscow.'

Moscow? I gave him what I hoped was a 'come off it' look.

'Or Nukus.'

'But in Nukus they refer everything to you.'

'We are sorry.'

So was I. Tashkent, like Samarkand and Bukhara, would have to wait. I had the Aral bit between my teeth and returned at once to Nukus by another overnight bus. Within minutes of checking back into the Hotel Tashkent reception had a message for me from OVIR: 'Do not try to go to Muynak.' I phoned Yusup. He sent to my room the only character in the whole charade with any truly sinister potential. His name was Habib. His eyes and hair were black and his brain was finely tuned to myriad conspiracies, real and imagined. He wore a double-breasted cream-coloured suit and spoke English (which he taught at the local university) with Holmesian precision. It was good to have him on my side.

'You may wish to interview me about the Aral Sea disaster or the struggle for autonomy in Karakalpakstan,' he said. 'Write down your questions.'

But before I could write down anything he volunteered his autobiography. He was a poet and a kick-boxer, raised by his grandmother in a village north-east of Nukus in the days when much of the delta had been water-meadow. She had pointed to an ox, he said, and told him to be strong. So he lifted weights to make the most of his slight frame. On military service in Potsdam he had broken most of his fingers in bare-knuckle fights.

'They respected only a strong man, not a witty man,' he said.

The phone rang. Habib answered. It was OVIR. The conversation was short and apparently sharp.

'They want to see you at nine tomorrow morning,' Habib said after hanging up. 'They wanted me to attend as interpreter but I said only if you pay me hard currency.' He let out a bark and paced the room.

'They are shadowing you. I said you have no links with military organizations. They wanted to know.'

I offered him twenty dollars to act as interpreter and help me get to Muynak.

'I will do my utmost,' he said. 'Now. I would like to urinate. Is that the right word?'

'You can say piss.'

He pissed, delighted with the addition to his vocabulary, and we set off on foot for Yusup's house.

Night had fallen; another ill-lit, not-quite-real Nukus night. A car containing Yusup and a passenger passed, stopped, picked us up and took us to the apartment of a Russian called Yevgeni.

Yevgeni was reddened by mead and apologized endlessly for his wife's absence and the consequent squalor of his tiny kitchen. He made his own mead from bees that he kept at his dacha, and he had Muynak contacts. He phoned one of them who happened to be in Nukus and would be returning the following day, but the contact didn't want to know. There were glum looks round the kitchen table. Conversation didn't flow. Yusup looked uneasy. Eventually he popped the question.

'Rustam?'

Yevgeni winced. Difficult, he said. Maybe not appropriate. Still, he made the call. Rustam arrived by car a few minutes later and we went out to meet him. Yevgeni addressed him quietly in the dark porch.

'This is our visitor from England. He wants to go to Muynak.'

'It's not my department.'

Rustam had a head like a bull. Yusup had said he was a KGB general. There was a long silence, which Rustam broke.

'Got any mead?'

You could have filled a wheelbarrow with the general relief. Yevgeni sacrificed a bottle of his finest vintage in a series of elegant toasts to Rustam's health, wealth and wisdom. Yusup flattered more subtly, with an awed reference to Rustam's *vliyaniye* – his influence.

Next morning the Deputy Prime Minister of Karakalpakstan instructed Mrs Kirilina, Baby-face's partner, to provide me with a permit to visit Muynak. A former Communist Party secretary would receive me there.

'Have a pleasant trip,' said Mrs Kirilina icily as she handed me the permit. I felt like snogging her.

It was a Friday. The Muynak bus was full of students making the 150-mile trip home for the weekend. Strips of cleared ground either side of the road were whitened by salt blown off the old sea bed, but beyond them the land was not visibly ravaged. There was more grass than cotton; long grass blown flat, and clumps of low trees, and every few seconds a telegraph pole. The students nattered or slept. Some of the men tipped their heads back and used the heels of their hands to funnel green tobacco powder under their tongues. Those who then continued talking did so without consonants. Most fell silent while the nicotine did its osmosis. Then they would lean forward and spit the spent green slurry into paper cones.

Habib had faded from the picture. I had a new minder, a colleague of his called Quat. Quat was short and dapper in a pale green suit whose jacket stopped above his hips. He had warned politely that the KGB was sure to interview him about this trip, and he would co-operate with them.

The bus stopped whenever anyone wanted to get off. In ones and twos people would wade into the grass at right angles to the road, to walk who knew how far. A mile? Ten?

The sky over Muynak was heavy with racing grey clouds. Lights were coming on in low houses along the road. People were scarce.

This was the place, then; the bereaved town. I had thought the question of the sea might be old hat, tiresome, absorbed and not much mentioned, but this was not so. The question of the sea was in your face. It was in everybody's faces. There was a trawler high and dry right next to the bus station, propped up with logs and tended like a war memorial.

Two children posed by the propeller and pulled sad faces. A policeman threatened to confiscate my film. A jeep pulled up and the driver told everyone to calm down. He introduced himself to Quat and took us to the house of his father, Tleuov, the former Party secretary.

A feast had been prepared: *plov* and chicken wings on garish china under bright lights in an otherwise sepulchral house. Men ate and women served, padding in with dishes prepared silently in semi-darkness. Only Tleuov initiated conversation. He was huge and heavy, with decades of solemnity behind him and slack cheeks at the corners of his mouth. Cross-legged on a cushion on the floor he formed a pyramid.

'Our train has gone,' he declared through the deferential Quat. 'The Aral Sea will never fill again.'

Thirty-four years of idle talk and Uzbek arrogance were to blame. Time spent on plans to divert Siberian rivers had been time wasted – wilfully, in his opinion. The solution had never been Siberian water or the Caspian or the upper Indus or wherever else red herrings had been sought. Eight-tenths of the water needed to re-fill the Aral lay in Uzbek reservoirs.

Tleuov never blamed cotton. Cotton was the cornerstone of Soviet Russia's great project to bring Central Asia from feudalism to Utopia in a single generation, and Tleuov had long since nailed his colours to the Russian mast. He spoke nostalgically of the 1940s and 1950s, when Muynak had been administered directly by Moscow as a place of exile – island exile. Not like the gulags, mind. Tleuov made the Muynak of old sound like a holiday camp.

No. The Aral had shrunk and the ecology and economy of Karakalpakstan had been wrecked to provide Uzbeks with boating ponds in the desert.

Quat chimed in that the Uzbek government had kept the Aral region closed since the end of the Soviet Union to prevent Karakalpaks mouthing off about Uzbekistan to foreigners.

'Tell America,' said Tleuov. 'Put it in your book.'

The trouble with Muynak's disaster, as I had been warned, is that you cannot see it. You cannot see the phosphates or the nitrates in the drinking water, nor the traces of Butifos, a defoliant outlawed everywhere else in the world by 1983. You cannot see the hepatitis or the thyroid and throat cancer affecting between them half the Karakalpak population. You cannot see the falling life expectancy or the rising infant mortality (seventy-two babies per thousand in 1992; four times the average for the former Soviet Union). And you cannot see the sea. In fact, but for an acre or two of dune and mud north of the town near the fuel depot, you might be forced to doubt that Muynak ever was a port.

It is true that some streets fade into sand that could have been a beach and some stop abruptly as if at a quayside. But only the dunes near the fuel depot settle the matter. In and on them lie the remains of Muynak's fishing fleet. Tleuov said there were 157 vessels once. One had been salvaged for the bus station. 144 had been carted off in pieces to the smelters of the northern steppe. Twelve were left, some still with their hulls, some stripped to their bones, all rusted almost black.

They were beautiful, especially the skeletons. Nothing shows the curves of a ship so well as its girders, each a cross-section, each (looking from the bow) pushing out the waist a little further than the one before. The exceptions were two flat-bottomed barges whose blunt front ends stuck twenty feet out from a mud bank. They looked like landing craft frozen in mid-invasion.

In 1957 the Aral was home to twenty-two species of fish. A quarter of a million tonnes of them were landed at Muynak that year. As the shore moved away successive ports followed it. The fifth and last, twenty miles to the north, was forced to close in 1986, by which time what remained of the sea was 39 per cent salt and devoid of life.

Because of the freak rains in Turkmenistan there were trickles of fresh water flowing through the trawlers' graveyard, and puddles under the barges' noses. Boys in shorts and bare feet were flipping little silver fish out of the puddles and keeping them alive by syringing water into their mouths. (It was better than eating them. The pesticide hexachlorophane, used on the cotton fields of Khorezm, contains a dioxin that attacks the human liver and nervous system and is present in concentrated form in fish from contaminated water.)

From the hulks Tleuov's son drove the rest of us back into town. Tleuov sat in the front passenger seat and hardly said a word. Silence was deemed the most fitting commentary.

We passed an abandoned cannery which had once produced twenty-three million cans of fish a year and had made Muynak a household name across the Soviet Union. For a while fish had been brought to the cannery for processing from the Baltic and the Caspian, just to save Muynak's jobs, but that arrangement had ended with the Soviet collapse.

To round off the tour we left town again, this time heading west along the spine of what had been Muynak Island. It had served time as the Muynak peninsula but was now just high ground in a desert. It rose to a cliff and here we stopped. A monument to Communism rose off the cliff: a silver spike, perhaps fifteen metres high, pointing northwards to a red star and the sky. Tleuov stood in front of it and his son and Quat seemed to understand that they should stand either side of him. I took their picture. Tleuov led me to the edge of the cliff and said that until 1938 the sea had come right up to its foot. Then Comrade Stalin's schemes for Central Asia had begun to have an effect, slowly at first. When the sea had retreated its first hundred metres a camp for Young Socialist Pioneers had been built down there on the beach. Now you could get to the sea only with a Kamaz truck or a helicopter. We looked out over the dunes and the saxaul. Except for a thin line of denser green following the fresh-water channel north-west from the fuel depot to the horizon, the view was like any view of the Kara-Kum between Mary and Chardzhou. A single set of footprints disappeared into the scrub. Tleuov thanked me for coming and intoned something to Quat.

'Whatever problems we may have here,' Quat translated, 'for us it is home, and paradise.'

Bukhara

❧❧❧

Paradise or no, Muynak was a long way off my route. I was glad to have made the detour and seen this strange and windy non-thing that was the lack of a sea, but I was also anxious to pick up Stephen Graham's thread again and follow it further east while there was still enough of the summer left for another side-trip, this time to the mountains.

I hurried south and did some sightseeing in Central Asia's holiest oasis. On my first evening there, while sitting scribbling in the lobby of the Intourist Hotel, I overheard a singular conversation and wrote it up more or less as it happened:

The sun has set over the ancient and noble city of Bukhara. In the old town there is scarcely a ripple on the surface of the pool at Lyab-i-Khauz. The synagogue down the dark alley leading off it is locked and silent. Likewise the Khudzhe Tabband mosque near Chor Minar, whose Imam works devotedly all day leading old men in prayer and teaching the Koran to younger ones; he is asleep in the house on the corner. And the thirteen monumental mosques and madrasas which made Bukhara's name – they too have closed for the night, none-too-exhausted by the day's trickle of tourists, nor daunted by the trickle to come in the morning. Bukhara is not Luxor, after all.

No harm will come to the old town tonight. The ghost of a Turkish subaltern, whose ancestors came from the Altai and whose kings are Karakhanids, keeps watch from the great stone lantern at the top of the Kalyan minaret, forty-seven metres above the jewellers' bazaar.

But outside the line of the old city wall there is a pocket of excitement in a small cone of electric light. Only one person appears to be involved. He is an American called McAlister. He has inserted a credit card into a telephone connected to a dish on the roof of the Intourist Hotel. This way he can talk without delay or intermediary to his employer five thousand miles away on the east coast of America. His employer is the *Boston Globe*.

'Hi. It's McAlister. I'm in Bo-kha-ra. Listen. This place is near Tajikistan and things are getting *hot* there. Yeah. We're leaving now, so tell Eltner. We'll be there in the morning. No. Ta-JEE-ki-stan. OK, and load me up with wire stuff in case Dushanbe has a hook-up. It's a city. Luvya. No. OK.'

Another American strides past McAlister towards reception.

'I'm getting a car,' he says.

'Get a *big* car,' says McAlister.

I had arrived in Bukhara early that morning, having returned to Nukus with Quat and wished Yusup well with pioneering floppy flight and saving the Aral Sea.

For most of the ten-hour bus ride over the barren and feature-less Kyzil-Kum I had slept and, without wishing to malign the desert that accounts for most of Uzbekistan's landmass, I don't think I missed much.

McAlister joined the other American at reception. I sidled up to ask if Dushanbe was safe.

'Well, they're shooting,' said the one getting the car.

'So not too safe . . .' said McAlister.

'. . . for vacations.'

I walked back to my own hotel, hyperventilating with envy. So Tajikistan was for heroes only; newsmen who home in like missiles on wherever is *hot*. Bukhara, by lily-livered contrast, was a place where passive tourists ogled passive buildings.

It was not ever thus. Eleven hundred years ago the *Boston Globe* would have been scrambling to open a bureau in Bukhara as it stunned the world by seceding from the Caliphate of Baghdad.

Since the death of the Prophet himself Baghdad's Abbasids and Ummayads had ruled the Muslim world unchallenged. Then, in AD 873, a band of Persian brothers from the noble house of Samani called the Caliph's bluff and declared them-selves kings of the lands beyond the Oxus.

Bukhara was to be their capital. The Caliphate was over-stretched and underpowered. Bukhara was too remote to fear a punitive invasion. The Samanids were home and dry. In a century they transformed Bukhara by bringing to it the industry of learning. Two hundred and fifty madrasas were built and students came from the ends of the known earth to fill them. Some sponged (there was a generous system of grants), but some worked. Avicenna wrote a medical encyclopaedia here, not superceded in the universities of western Europe until the nineteenth century.

Bukhara became Bukhara-i-Sharif; 'the Noble'. It was destroyed by Genghis Khan and it languished under Tamerlane (who was obsessed with Samarkand) but it rose again in the sixteenth century under the Uzbek Khans, who later called themselves Emirs.

There was much that was despicable about the Emirs of Bukhara. They traded in slaves. They kept hundreds of wives. According to a German doctor who passed through in disguise in 1820, they buggered little boys. They threw some unfortunates from the Kalyan Minaret and imprisoned others with scorpions and lice in a dungeon called the Zindan. Worst of all, they refused to sign and honour treaties with either of the two imperial giants of their era.

For most of the nineteenth century British India and Tsarist Russia wooed the Emirs with gifts and guns and promises thereof. The Emirs were on the whole vain and cruel but not stupid. They took what their rival suitors offered and played them off against each other. Eventually, in 1873, the Russian General Kaufmann abandoned conventional diplomacy in favour of the latest German artillery, with which he forced a treaty on the Emirate. But the royal family kept control of the city until after the Russian Revolution. In 1914 Stephen Graham could still call it 'the most wonderful city of Mohammedan Asia, a place that might have been produced for you by enchantment'. He continued:

Within toothed walls live 150,000 Mohammedans, entirely after their own hearts, without any appreciable interference from without, in narrow streets, in covered alleys, with endless shops, behind screening walls. The roads are narrow and cobbled, and wind in all directions, with manifold alleys and lanes, with squares where stand handsome mosques, with portals and stairways leading down to the cool and tree-shaded, but stagnant, little reservoirs that hold the city's water. Along the roadway various equipages come prancing – muddy proletkas, unhandy-looking, egg-shaped carts, with clumsy wooden wheels eight feet high, and projecting axles, gilt and crimson-covered carts made of cane and straw, the shape of a huge egg that has had both ends sliced off . . .

The bazaars are rich and rare, and in the shadow of the covered streets – there are fifty of them – the lustrous silks and carpets, and pots and slippers, in the shops each side of the way, have an extraordinary magnificence; the gorgeous vendors, sitting patiently, not asking you to buy, staring at the heaps of metallics, silver-bits and notes resting on the little tabourets in front of them, belong to an age which I thought was only to be found in books. What a wealthy city it is!

Seventy-eight years on the city walls were reduced to a few rounded fins of grey mud near the *kolkhoznaya* bazaar – the bazaar for collective farm surpluses. Most descendants of those 150,000 Mohammedans lived not in the old town but in suburban blocks and bungalows, and not 'entirely after their own hearts' but buffeted by endless new designs for living.

There had been Communism in all its guises, including the grotesque mutations wrought by Comrade Gorbachev. Now private commerce seemed to have been elevated to a prestigious way of life called Business, to which Democracy might or might not prove related. There was the option which President Karimov of Uzbekistan apparently endorsed of a return to the systemic sloth of Brezhnev's era. And there was religion. In Holy Bukhara Islam had never died even if at times its practice had been dangerous. Now it was resurgent and every Bukhariot was proudly *mussulmanski*. But even Islam was beset with options. Fundamentalist or moderate, was how outsiders saw it. Actually the question was whether *mussulmanskis* would be allowed to go on drinking vodka and watching Mexican soap operas. Whoever decided would outlaw them at his peril.

The 'little reservoirs' that had held Bukhara's water at the time of Stephen Graham's visit were now mostly filled in to deprive mosquitoes and bacteria of breeding grounds. Along the roadways Ladas came and went instead of egg-shaped carts. The covered markets in the old town still sold silks and carpets – but machine-made ones, for hard currency, to tourists.

'What a wealthy city it is!'

By 1914, thanks to the railway, Bukhara was selling rugs and silver to the world. But it was also seething. The mullahs abhorred the Emir for failing to ignite a holy war against the Russians. Secret societies of reformists abhorred the mullahs for standing in the way of a secular new Turkish empire that would stretch from Kirghizstan to Istanbul. The Emir seemed to sense the game would soon be up and retreated to a rambling summer palace called Sitorai-Mokhi-Khosa to enjoy himself. He spent lavishly on Chinese vases and European clocks and had a secret tunnel built under the garden from his palace to the harem, so that he could spy on the more succulent of his four hundred wives.

The Bolsheviks knew Bukhara was a hotbed of rival fanaticisms and handled it with care. They blew up its outer wall but rather than destroy the city itself they simply let it die.

Its cardio-vascular system was the network of covered street markets that Stephen Graham had found intact. In their clammy shade the city had lived. Like a termite hill in Africa it had reached an accommodation with the sun. The Bolsheviks took away the shade from all but three of the markets. While new factories and spinning mills sprang up in the suburbs the old town was quietly autoclaved by the sun. Between 1917 and 1926 its population halved. By 1992 it was, as the guidebooks proudly said, an open air museum.

Almost.

In a few places shade and water had survived together, and so had life. Lyab-i-Khauz was one of these. You reached it from the south along Sovietskaya Street, whose sides were blind brown walls. From the east and west the approach was via Lenin Street, beside a thin canal built by the Khan's Grand Vizier in the 1620s to fill a large, square pool: the *khauz* that gave Lyab-i-Khauz its name. He also built a madrasa and a boarding house for dervishes – a *khanaga*. They faced each other across the pool and the pointed arch of the *khanaga* was reflected in its surface. The madrasa was set back a little way behind some willows, with two white mosaic birds above its gateway. In among the willows there was a statue of Khodja Nasreddin, who robbed from the rich to give to the poor in the tenth century and thereby qualified as a Communist hero in the twentieth. To the north there was another madrasa, older, bigger and plainer than the Grand Vizier's. To the south there was a row of shops.

The *khanaga* had become a gallery for tourists. In the dormitories of the madrasa you could exchange dollars for rubles and rubles for ice-cream. But Lyab-i-Khauz bore no scars of Soviet experiments. On the contrary, the stone terrace by the pool was the most delightful place for tea in all of Central Asia.

The morning after eavesdropping on McAlister of the *Boston Globe* I went there for breakfast, arriving out of breath having exhaled all the way up Sovietskaya Street to avoid smelling its dark blotches of pee.

It was nine o'clock but the best seats were already taken. (Not seats, actually, but low wooden daises with moulded rails like bedsteads at each end.) The desirable ones were away from the edge of the pool in the shade of the willows. They were staked out by sun-dried Uzbek men in skull caps and quilted robes and soft leather boots. The youngest of them looked about eighty. None had a full set of teeth. Most had white whiskers. They talked, played chess and filled their bowls of tea from china pots with wired-on tin spouts. With each new arrival and departure all those on a given dais would solemnly cup their faces in their hands. It was a rolling party and looked like rolling on till dusk.

It was tempting to cast these wizards as retired *Basmachi* who once had ambushed Red platoons along the Golden Road to Samarkand. But the red and silver medals pinned to the quilting over their hearts suggested that, in the Great Patriotic War at any rate, they had been good Soviet patriots.

There were three counters in a wall on the north side of the pool. One served *shashlyk*, one *plov* and one noodles. Stacks of *lepeshki*, unleavened bread, were being carried down some steps from the boot of a Lada parked behind the kitchens. They were still warm. I bought one, and a pot of tea, and six *shashlyk* draped with raw onion and dripping with vinegar and their own mutton fat. I found a vacant dais, took off my shoes, got comfortable and stuffed myself. For the moment anyway, Heuerbach was welcome to Tajikistan.

In the days when Bukhara had a *khauz* for every mosque and *khanaga* they were used for washing as well as for the domestic water supply. When the Soviet authorities filled most of them in they dealt a serious – but not fatal – blow to the city's ancient custom of public ablution.

For unnumbered generations Bukhariots had regarded bathing as a mainly social activity. They would gather up their robes, descend the stepped side of the *khauz* to the water and slosh it on their necks and hands and feet without ever being separated from the seamless conversation that was always there around the pool whoever happened to be taking part. They were not about to retreat behind the doors of Soviet bathrooms and spend the most convivial hour of the day in white enamelled isolation.

Instead they entered an unsigned doorway, between the jewellers' and cap-makers' bazaars on Frunze Street. From here a dark corridor led to a dim, domed changing room. My eyes took a moment to adjust. Naked bodies came and went via a narrow stone staircase that arrived in the middle of the room from somewhere underground.

Someone tapped me on the shoulder. A boy held out a tin basin containing soap, back scrubber, a towel and a plastic bubble of shampoo. That would be five rubles. A medicinal massage by the resident doctor would cost extra. The boy nodded in the direction of an old man undressing across the room to reveal a well-muscled body and a very long penis.

I had come with the idea of just looking but just looking already felt like cheap voyeurism. I took the basin, got undressed and entered the underworld.

The stone steps were worn from three and a half centuries of continuous use. A heavy mist hung in a stone doorway at the bottom, clinging to the naked bodies passing through it and to the glistening stone walls of a vaulted chamber beyond. By faint steam-filtered daylight from a single hole in the roof you could make out stone benches round the sides of the chamber, stone archways to more chambers, and bodies of all shapes and textures.

Two young men lay writhing in lather on the floor of an alcove. Older ones sat on the benches staring into space, or at the backs of their eyelids, or down at their navels. I wondered what the procedure was, and what stage in it these gentlemen had reached.

Splashing sounds were coming from the next chamber. I followed them, trying to jettison self-consciousness.

There was no procedure, of course. In another alcove big brass taps protruded from the wall and I joined a short queue to fill my basin half with scalding water and half with cold. I poured this over my head, washed, rinsed, sat down on one of the stone benches and began to relax.

The doctor's physique had been exceptional. Most of the older men had shrivelled genitals, largely hidden beneath the soft, ballooning bellies that in these parts denote a steady income and a conscientious wife. The young men tended to be hung like bulls. I could not help noticing.

Nasreddin put his hand on my bottom just as I was leaving.

'Where do you come from?' he asked in Russian as we surfaced in the changing room.

'England.'

'I love you.'

This was friendly.

'*Nye tochna?* (Is that not right?) *Pa Fransuski, zhoo voo zeim.*'

'What?'

'*Zhoo voo zeim.*'

'Ah. *Je vous aime.* I love you too.'

So we got off to a friendly enough start, me and Nasreddin. He had an odd face, with a short nose that lifted his top lip to reveal his gums. He had close-cropped hair which by the time he had finished dressing was covered with a skull-cap. He said he traded Kara-Kul fleeces and drove taxis on the side. It might have been the other way round but he seemed to know that a foreigner would find the fleece-trader part more exotic.

We took tea, which was included in the price of the tin basin, then wandered back to Lyab-i-Khauz. After the session in the baths I felt less of a tourist and more of an old Bukhara hand.

Perhaps it had been a ritual of sorts after all. Perhaps you do have to go naked to go native.

Nasreddin's lime-green Zhiguli was parked in the shadow of the madrasa with the white mosaic birds. We climbed in and drove to the eastern edge of the city, where he and his extended family seemed to own an entire street. On the way there it emerged that fleece-trading and taxi-driving were but necessary evils for a roving mind. Nasreddin's vocation was world politics.

He reaffirmed his love for me (as a concept; an Englishman) then sounded off about the harm done to Uzbekistan by Soviet imperialism and the harm soon to be done by an American-owned multinational corporation which had bought the Zeraf-shan gold mines two hundred miles north of Bukhara in the middle of the Kyzil-Kum. Joint ventures Nasreddin could take. Outright purchase of national assets he could not.

We came to a stop outside a wooden door, the middle one of three in a long white wall. Nasreddin's older brother lived on the left. His younger brother lived on the right. He honked. The doors in the wall opened and we fell to a three-pronged attack by dogs, men and children. Two of the children, a girl and a boy, seemed from their short noses and lifted lips to be Nasreddin's.

The girl was spun round and despatched to tell her mother there would be company for *plov*. The boy clung to his father's leg like plaster of Paris. I gave him a red plastic propelling pencil and he spent lunch drawing Zhigulis.

We ate in Nasreddin's big front room where I was installed on a sofa next to a Tartar summoned from across the street, apparently to bridge any cultural chasms that might appear between Europe and the Orient. Nasreddin sat facing us, crosslegged on a Turkmen rug. He and I did argue briefly about the end of the Cold War. For him it meant inflation, hardship and the imminent threat of real war ignited by sparks from other former Soviet Republics already ablaze. Moldavia, Georgia, Azerbaijan, Tajikistan. (Tajikistan! I felt a visceral tug. Heuer-bach would be in the thick of it by now.)

Georgians never used to fight each other, said Nasreddin. They were the friendliest people in the world. Whenever two of them happened to meet outside their homeland – in Bukhara, for instance – you could count on them to kindle a party. Now they were tearing each other to pieces over a couple of Black Sea resorts. So much for the New World Order.

I tried taking an optimistic line on the newly empowered United Nations. With America and Russia voting together for the first time in the UN's history, the blue berets would put the world to rights in no time. Nasreddin's smile said succinctly that such hopes were as naive as his fears were justified.

A news bulletin was in progress on the television in the corner of the room, under the collected works of the fifteenth-century epic poet Alisher Navoi. Cotton bushes were being uprooted and replaced with apple saplings in the Termez oblast near the Afghan border. Nasreddin and I could agree on this at once. Apple trees need no artificial irrigation. You can sink your teeth into their fruit (whereas sinking your teeth into balls of cotton belongs in the same category as blackboard-scratching). And apple trees are givers of shade whereas cotton plants are stunted, spoilt, ugly and ungrateful. Never mind the need for cash crops in a developing economy. Some worthy international body with an Anglo-Saxon acronym would have to make a compensatory grant. Apple trees in Termez were a good thing.

'What do you expect?' said Nasreddin. 'We are Uzbeks. We know our land.'

He picked me up next morning from my hotel and took me to the railway station to catch a train to Samarkand.

Bukhara's station is eight miles south of the old town at Kagan, because the Emir refused to let the Trans-Caspian railway bring its dirt and noise and Christian contamination near his walls.

Nasreddin had dropped me at the hotel the previous evening. On the way to Kagan he described how, leaving the hotel, he had intercepted a Russian prostitute heading for my room. He had told her I was one of a growing army of British muslims who would sooner roast in hell than sleep with a Russian whore. Nasreddin laughed. I winced, wishing he'd let her through.

Entering Kagan we passed a beautiful old Russian church. Its white stucco had been well-preserved by the dryness of the Kyzil-Kum, but its doors and windows had been boarded up.

'That *was* the Russian church,' said Nasreddin.

'What is it now?'

'It's empty.'

'Not a church, then?'

'No. The Russians have cleared out. This is Uzbekistan.'

I lacked the stomach and the vocabulary – and probably the experience – for a discussion on the difference between patriotism and spiteful chauvinism. As the train from Ashkhabad pulled in we shook hands and Nasreddin said, 'We'll meet again.'

The weird thing was, we did.

Samarkand

~~~~~~

The train from Ashkhabad continued eastwards, parallel to the ancient caravan route that inspired James Elroy Flecker's most famous couplet.

'For lust of knowing what should not be known,' the poet wrote while dying of TB the year before the First World War, 'We take the Golden Road to Samarkand.'

Frederick Delius later put the lines to music. The SAS adopted the couplet as its motto and the world at large dolloped on to the already semi-mythic city of Samarkand a new surfeit of high-cholesterol mystery and romance.

Flecker never saw this road and from close up it didn't seem particularly golden. It was an interminable grey asphalt causeway between cotton fields. There was the beige of the earth on either side and the dark woody green of the cotton shrubs, but nothing that glistered. The railway ran parallel to the road and at regular intervals it passed walled cotton yards with conveyors sloping up to points in the sky which in October would become the tops of cotton hills.

It was June and even hotter than the Kara-Kum had been in May. In a month I had crossed nearly a thousand miles of desert which at times had felt as though it had been robbed of life and interest by Mongol invasions, Soviet experiments and its daily session in the solar furnace. But there was no shortage of life on the train to Samarkand, which was filled with the thick smell of sweating bodies and ripe picnic bundles. Its metal was hot to the touch. A dull haze covered the sky. I sat in a third-class wagon, ignored the quick brown eyes staring at what they probably thought was a Balt, and tried to read. It was thirsty-making prose – an interlude in *War and Peace* on the nature of history. I looked up. The eyes looked away.

A crippled veteran carrying a plastic bag shuffled past, drew level with the seat opposite and stopped, panting. He looked like a walk-on Bolshevik in *Battleship Potemkin*. He took off his thick grey jacket, hung it on the peg above the seat and sat down. From a jacket pocket he took a plastic mug. From the plastic bag he took a thermos flask, a twist of newspaper, a lump of liver sausage and a small round loaf. He produced a penknife to cut up the sausage, which he ate with wedges of bread. He dropped some green tea into the plastic mug from the twist of paper, then poured hot water over it from the thermos. He chewed methodically, moistening the cud from time to time with sips of tea. I gave up reading.

Across the aisle a man who later called himself a *mujahed* was lying on his stomach on a middle bunk. He had a black beard but a benevolent expression. His blue eyes were about eighteen inches from my head and focused on it. On the opposite middle bunk a younger man who turned out to be a traffic police cadet was asleep. On the bottom bunks lay two young women travelling together. One was awake. The other was waking up, stretching under a single sheet as she came to the surface. The *mujahed* watched me watching her.

We pulled into Navoi. A dervish in sash and turban strode the platform incanting prayers at full power, glancing to the left and right to stroke his beard for those who cupped their faces in their hands, and stuffing the notes they proffered down his shirt.

The police cadet and the woman under the single sheet woke up. She and her friend rolled away their bedding and invited everyone to tea. They were from Alma-Ata, which made sense. There was big city sophistication in their tight jeans and 'Chanel' T-shirts, and their brazen invitation. One was twenty-six and married, the other twenty-five and single. They had been visiting friends in Nukus. The police cadet sat next to the 25-year-old and took off his shirt. She laughed and later went with him to the restaurant car.

So romance lived on the Golden Road. Or chemistry on the steel one. Mm. I wrote that down, and the *mujahed* asked what I was doing. Writing a book, I said.

'Then you must read the Koran. It tells us how to live and how to build. If you study it for three years you will understand and write a very good book.'

He had heard from an Indian visitor that in Britain the Koran had all but superseded the Bible. I said that as far as I knew the Bible still had a certain following.

'Do you think fundamentalism is good?' he asked. I said if fundamentalism told people what to believe then I thought it was bad. He smiled and touched me on the shoulder.

'I also think freedom is good. If everyone is free to study the Koran there will be Islam in every country, freely.'

As we pulled into Samarkand I felt as if I'd drunk too much coffee. It must have been the excitement of knowing that brochures were about to be obliterated by the real thing, like queuing for Wimbledon for the first time.

Samarkand. Maybe it was the name; those evenly weighted syllables, impossible to confuse and easy to say wherever you come from. Maybe it was the situation; last stop for west-bound caravans before the desert, last stop for east-bound caravans before the mountains. Maybe no one knows the original reason for Samarkand's fame, which was noted but not invented by Herodotus. In the end it makes no difference. People tend to have heard of Samarkand.

I dumped my rucksack in the Hotel Sayor, near the station, and headed for the Registan. The bus down Karl Marx Street was packed (which was perhaps not surprising; this was the second city of Uzbekistan, population 600,000, king of the cotton belt). The bus stopped outside the Intourist Hotel. Manoeuvring towards the door I glimpsed something huge and very grand, half a mile away across a shallow valley. More people shoved in. The door closed and the bus headed down into the valley.

The snapshot hung there in my head, petrol blue and glinting, unbelievable in the most literal sense.

The bus stopped again directly opposite the Registan. I got out, crossed the road and tried to take in, broadside on, the most magnificent man-made sight on the Silk Route.

The Registan is a square formed by three huge medieval madrasas, each one smothered in mosaic. The Honourable George Curzon MP saw it in 1888 and knew exactly how extra-ordinary it was. 'No European spectacle indeed can adequately be compared with it,' he wrote, 'in our inability to point to an open space in any western city that is commanded on three of its four sides by Gothic cathedrals of the finest order.'

The ceramic cladding is what makes these buildings exorbitant. Here you have the intricacy of a Persian carpet and the fragility of an antique dinner plate, but you have it by the acre. It speaks of unlimited money and man-hours, of the irrelevance of bottom lines and the pricelessness of awe.

A couple of caretakers were fiddling with spotlights for the evening sound and light show. Otherwise the place was deserted. I sat at the top of a tier of plastic seating on the open side of the square and soaked it up. No captions. No points of detail being pointed out. This was a purely sensory experience.

The façade of the Tilla Kari madrasa is the one that meets new arrivals from the bus stop. The other two confront each other in a face-off that silences most mortals, whom wide-angle lenses have not prepared for the way they dwarf the space between them. Curzon was used to an instinctual hush inside a Gothic cathedral. At the Registan the hush is on the outside.

Stephen Graham pretended at first not to be moved by it.

'I spent the May of this year,' he wrote in his most casual tone, 'in what is particularly the land of Tamerlane, a sort of Russian India on the northern side of the Hindu Kush, a country with a majestic past but with little present.'

Samarkand had been in steady decline since the Uzbek Khans made Bukhara their capital in 1599, so it is probably true that the mosques and tombs and seminaries built by Tamerlane and his heirs were in disrepair when Graham saw them. But they had lost none of their power to impress. Graham's own photographs give it away, especially one of Russian military cadets in bright white hats and tunics, dwarfed by the massive side-walls of Gur Emir, Tamerlane's mausoleum. In the photograph the building is still standing despite three centuries' worth of earthquake cracks which snake like forked lightning from its fluted dome to its foundations.

Sure enough, within a page, Graham senses 'a strange atmosphere of mystery and melancholy.' He cannot help but 'linger in the romantic idea of all the splendour that has passed away.'

So he lingered and jotted down his thoughts. Then he pressed on to Tashkent.

Within a few years Soviet power was declared in Samarkand.

Mystery, melancholy and romance were banished. Splendour was to be contemporary and real or not at all. The result was the exact opposite of Communism's impact on Bukhara. There the Bolsheviks neutered a rival political and commercial centre. Here they built one of their own around the ruins of its fabulous medieval predecessor. While they were about it they rebuilt the ruins too.

There is probably a file in an archive somewhere setting out precisely why they bothered, but anyone can guess that Tamerlane (c. 1330–1405) lived long enough ago not to be seen as a threat to Soviet power; that his monuments were considered if anything potentially useful symbols for the nation-building that began when Soviet Uzbekistan was born in 1924; that the Bolsheviks may actually have liked the geometric abstractions of Islamic art and architecture. They were certainly keen on archaeology, which is, after all, an attractive discipline for Communists, since it turns up hoards of jewellery and pots which seem to show that wealth was always concentrated in the coffers of the very few.

Then there was the money to be made from foreign tourism. For whatever reason, Samarkand's monuments got the treatment. Teams of scientists arrived from Leningrad and set about replacing every fallen tile, every peeled swirl of gold, every carved terracotta faience panel sogged by rising damp or pulverized by heat and termites. They re-learned all the old techniques. Where Azeri painters had used arsenic and sulphur for their colours, so did the Russians. Where Khorezmian glaziers had stoked their furnaces with saxaul for one glaze and cotton twigs for another, the People's Academicians did likewise.

Purists complained, preferring authentic ruins to authentic reproductions, but I thought the Registan was fabulous.

Back in the hotel I latched on to an English group that was being given a guided tour of the principal monuments the next day. It was a small group. There was David and his wife Elizabeth, Anna from Vienna, and Walter.

David had three letters before his name and several more after it. He knew prime ministers and presidents by their first names. He was balding, an occasional smoker, exigent as to travel arrangements, immensely clever and possessed of a honeyed baritone. He was the natural leader of the group, not to mention much of HM's government. One of the first things he confided to me was his very low opinion of journalists. He and Elizabeth made a formidable couple.

Anna had emigrated to Australia and spoke with a hybrid accent that sounded South African. Walter was slim, not tall, a former county rugby player and eighty-six years old.

I joined them for dinner. Deafening Turkish music and engrossing Turkish belly dancing ruled out conversation. Walter outlasted everyone, including the belly dancers. Later I found him stalking the lobby.

'Thought I'd have a beer before bed,' he said. There was no beer, but we talked three-quarter moves over instant coffee.

In the morning three Volga saloons swept us back to the old town. We doffed our sunhats to the Registan, having all admired it already, and followed an athletic Russian woman called Ina down Tashkent Street to Bibi Khanym.

Ina was a tour guide hired from the Intourist hotel. Bibi Khanym was both a person and a place, she said. The person was Tamerlane's senior wife and probably Chinese. The building was a mosque she commissioned as a surprise for the warrior king while he was away butchering Hindus by the hundred thousand in northern India. When completed in 1404 it was the biggest mosque in the world, but Bibi's engineers were not equal to her vision. The giant blue dome was already showing cracks when Tamerlane died the following year. It had never been structurally sound and no one prayed there now. Soviet restoration money dried up before the Soviet Union ended. A tower crane stood idly over the ruined gatehouse.

David, Elizabeth and Anna used the allocated fifteen minutes for a conscientious scrutiny of tiles and squinches. Walter found a block of stone to sit on in the shade and reminisced about climbing trips to Switzerland between the wars. Then we piled back into the Volgas for a short freewheel to the necropolis of Shah-i-Zinda, a street of tombs on a bare brown hillside in Afrasiab, the ancient Samarkand that Alexander knew. Afrasiab was founded in the eighth century by a descendant of the Prophet who was beheaded by a band of brigands while at prayer. The holy man picked up his head, jumped down a nearby well and has stayed there ever since.

David and Elizabeth showed backbone at Shah-i-Zinda. Its tombs boast round their doorways some of the finest ceramic art in Asia, Ina told us, but David and Elizabeth already knew. They had read up on it. Even as the sun beat down and Walter panted with thirst they asked for more time. Even as Anna took Walter back to a Volga to sit down, David and Elizabeth peered at priceless decorative panels and fired questions at Ina about faience and majolica and which was which.

Not wishing to be outswotted I stayed with them, baking, scribbling and forming a worthless theory about faience *and* majolica. The theory was that all the dazzling blue ceramic art of fifteenth-century Samarkand held the same appeal for contemporaries as chrome bumpers did for 1950s Californians: shininess, extravagance and artificiality. As we drove in the Volgas to Gur Emir I nearly shared this theory with David and Elizabeth, but thought better of it.

The mausoleum of the Great One stood on a quiet street behind the Intourist hotel. Its cracks had been closed up since Stephen Graham's visit. Our fellow visitors were not Russian military cadets but a large group of half-interested Uzbek women.

We filed round the edges of a tall chamber naturally lit by sunlight pouring through grilles of delicate carved brick let into the drum at the base of the dome. Arranged on the stone floor were seven coffin-sized tombstones. In the crypt beneath the central tombstone, which appeared to be black, lay the remains of the most merciless killer born into the human race until it begat Hitler.

Timur-the-lame, crippled early in his career by an arrow wound to his right thigh, wanted to be a second Genghis Khan. His empire was never as big as Genghis Khan's and it did not last as long, but he killed at least as many people to create it. He served his apprenticeship as a highwayman on the road over the western end of the Zerafshan range between Samarkand and Shakhrisabz, the town where he was born and later built his biggest palace. In the 1370s he ransacked Gurganch, which had been profiting from Silk Route trade at Samarkand's expense since the Mongols had destroyed the Route's southerly variant 150 years earlier. Later he honed his talent for slaughter on campaigns to the Caucasus and southern Russian, Baghdad and Anatolia. In 1397 he crossed the Hindu Kush, killed 100,000 Indians for resisting him at Delhi, and 100,000 more on his way home. It is said that not a bird moved in northern India for months after his departure.

By this time his fame had spread to Europe. The King of Spain despatched an envoy, Ruy Gonzales de Clavijo, to treat with Tamerlane before it was too late. Clavijo reached Samarkand in 1404 to find the warlord slight and wizened but hospitable. The feast of the age was in progress. Tamerlane and his horde were encamped in silk tents outside the city on the banks of the Zerafshan river, making music, playing games and eating mutton by the herd. Tamerlane also found time to dispense justice, ordering corrupt officials to be hung up by their feet to die.

Shortly after Clavijo headed home (his request for a written treaty having been turned down at the last moment), Tamerlane set out for China on what was meant to be his greatest campaign and the fulfilment of his destiny. But he died before crossing the Tien Shan, and as he died he whispered, 'Only a stone, and my name upon it.'

No ordinary stone was chosen, but the world's largest jade; the black cenotaph in front of us. Its true green shows only when the sun first strikes it in the morning. Tamerlane's body was placed in a stone box in a separate chamber ten foot below the floor, and a mason etched inside its lid: 'If I am roused, the earth shall tremble.'

Tamerlane was not disturbed for five and a half centuries. Then, on the night of 22 June 1941, a Soviet scientist opened the box to study the ancient skull. Within minutes an assistant ran into the crypt with the news that Minsk was being bombed. Operation Barbarossa, the invasion of Russia by Nazi Germany, had begun, and would not end until the Battle of Stalingrad.

The story of Tamerlane's curse is ideal for an Intourist-trained guide: a spine-chilling yarn for hard-to-please foreigners and an incidental reminder of the event in World War Two that became the principal justification for the next fifty years of Soviet Communism. Ina said afterwards she had been looking forward to telling it, but David, whose background reading knew no bounds, got there first.

He and Elizabeth and Anna and Walter left the next day for Bukhara and I missed them as soon as they had gone.

From Samarkand Stephen Graham continued north-east up the Trans-Caspian line to Tashkent. He never ventured into the mountain fastness to the south, the wild region bordered by Afghanistan and China which was then known as Eastern Bukhara and in 1929 became Soviet Tajikistan. I nearly didn't either. Ina had said gravely that Tajikistan was in a state of war and that to try to go there was lunacy. David had agreed, citing the latest Foreign Office intelligence. Most discouraging of all, someone took $1500 in cash from my room in the Hotel Sayor. This left me with twenty dollars to last about four months. Feeling slightly sick, I reported the theft to the police, who said there was not much they could do. Then I went to the Intourist Hotel for a cup of coffee and a think, and used up my luck ration for the entire trip by bumping into a British television producer making a travel programme about the Silk Route. He gave me a life-saving wad of twenty-dollar bills in exchange for an English cheque. Having been a ruble millionaire I was now merely rich, and reckless to boot. As I left the hotel McAlister walked in, McAlister of the snappy war-corr vernacular, last seen in Bo-kha-ra heading for Du-shan-be.

I asked if he and his compatriot had made it to Tajikistan and he replied, a touch defensively, that their driver had been turned back at the border. They had turned back with him. (Foiled! I tried not to betray my glee.) That did it. I'd heard that trains were getting through on the main line from Moscow to Dushanbe, which crossed the desert a hundred miles west of Samarkand and stopped at an oasis called Karshi. In the afternoon I went there on a bus.

War in Tajikistan

~~~~~~

After the warnings and prevarication, getting to Tajikistan was easy. I was assigned a bunk in a compartment on an evening train passing through Karshi on its way from Moscow to Dushanbe. There was an hour before dusk to stand swaying in the corridor and watch the slow mauve sunset.

For most of the night we trundled in a wide arc through the flatlands of Surkhandarya, like a wise old anaconda circling its prey. The train was full: Russians coming home from staying with relatives.

'Coming to see our war?' said a woman in my compartment. Her husband, in the standard Soviet travelling garb of tracksuit and flip-flops, talked at length about who was fighting whom. Most of it went over my head but I picked up that Baltic sniper mercenaries were making a killing along the road from Dushanbe to Kurgan Turbe.

Later I learned a little more. The war in Tajikistan was apparently between former Communists hanging on to power on the pretext of keeping fundamentalism at bay, and Islamic rebels seeking power on the pretext of cleansing the country of corrupt former Communists. These labels camouflaged a clan war between Kulyabis from Kulyab (on the side of the old Communist regime) and the natives of Kurgan Turbe, a stronghold of Islamic rebels due south of the capital.

The Kulyabis had allies in Khodzhent, formerly Leninabad, regional capital of a northern lobe of Tajikistan in the Fergana Valley. The Islamic rebels of Kurgan Turbe had kinsmen in the Garm Valley, which runs east from Dushanbe into the High Pamirs.

Wedged between former Communists and rebels were several mighty Russian garrisons under orders from Moscow to protect themselves and ethnic Russians and the country's international borders. Their hardware was coveted by both the warring clans.

In addition there were three bit-players: the Ismailis of Badakhshan (also known as Pamiris because Badakhshan comprises most of the Pamirs), who seemed adept at filling important posts in the former Communist regime while at the same time seeking a form of independence for their remote and spectacular homeland in the eastern half of the country; the democrats, very few in number, nervously allied to the Islamic rebels; and the Afghan Mujaheddin, pursuing their jihad against Communism by smuggling guns across the upper Oxus.

Rakhman Nabiyev, the former Communist leader, had recently been taken at gunpoint to Dushanbe airport by a group of thugs called Tajik Youth and forced to stand down. Dushanbe remained mostly in the hands of former Communists and was reported calm though cut off from the outside world except by train.

Whatever was happening in Tajikistan, it did not seem to be fulfilling Stephen Graham's prophecy that 'Central Asia is likely to remain for a thousand years one of the most peaceful places upon earth'.

Neither did it seem coincidental that the first corner of Central Asia to blow up in the Russians' faces when they relaxed their grip was also the last to be subjugated by the Bolsheviks. Enver Pasha recruited his fiercest *Basmachi* guerrillas in Kurgan Turbe and fought a rearguard action with them against the advancing Red Army until his poetic death by a mountain stream near the Afghan border in the summer of 1922.

Bloodstock had to be a factor. Among former Soviet Central Asian peoples, Tajiks are the odd ones out. Like Afghans they speak a Persian language while Uzbeks, Turkmens, Kirghiz and Kazakhs speak Turkic ones. Like Afghans they are of Indo-European descent while the others are Altaic. Why should this not translate into temperament? Afghans have a good claim to being the most irrepressible nation in history. They defeated British India twice in the nineteenth century before humiliating Soviet Russia in the twentieth. For their Tajik cousins to pass up the chance of a scrap with the infidel would have been a betrayal of their very souls.

Bloodstock, then, and geography. On the map, Tajikistan is all frantic shading. Tajikistan is where the deserts leap into the air, break open into chasms, grow glaciers, sprout forests, gush waterfalls and terrorize lowlanders with yaks, yetis, palpitations and oedemas. Tajikistan is nine-tenths mountain.

On the train to Dushanbe I had several aims in mind, including to see a war, to see the High Pamirs, and, of course, to be somewhere McAlister had failed to get to. I also wanted to locate the final resting place of Enver Pasha. This was a matter of conjecture among western scholars, since Tajikistan's frontier zone had been closed to foreigners throughout the Soviet era. It would have been intriguing to find out whether the burial place was marked or widely known, since, besides being an anti-Soviet rebel and therefore presumably due for rehabilitation, Enver was a Turk who died on Tajik soil and a *Basmach* whose memory had been systematically suppressed by the Soviet authorities. But I never did find his grave, for a variety of reasons: a crucial bridge had been blown up, an armoured convoy heading in the right direction left Dushanbe without me, and a journalist with whom it turned out I had once shared a flute teacher put his foot down.

At about midnight we paused near the Afghan border at Termez before turning north-east up the Surkhandarya valley. It was still dark when we pulled into Dushanbe.

The cavernous station hall filled instantly with agitated families, but the city beyond it was chilly and empty. Not wishing to take chances with Baltic snipers I took a taxi straight up Lenin Prospekt to the Hotel Tajikistan.

Lenin Prospekt was broad, tree-lined, deserted and immaculate. The hotel's windows were all dark but a side door pushed open and I snoozed on a leather sofa in the lobby until roused by reception.

The manager, with pursed lips and exaggerated politeness, accepted my Uzbek accreditation and directed me to a room on the seventh floor. It too was immaculate, with olive green bedspreads, clean-cut Scandinavian-style furniture and a balcony with a view of uninterrupted trees.

The morning was fresh and sunny. I stood on the balcony and felt wildly exhilarated.

There was a knock at the door.

'Barry?' said a voice.

It was Superman, the journalist whom I had last seen in Ashkhabad collecting contacts so he could hit the ground running when the big story broke. Perhaps this was it, the big story. Perhaps he was running. One thing was certain: he had grown a moustache since Ashkhabad, making him look more like a nineteenth-century Russian army captain than Superman. He was looking for Barrv of the World Service.

'No. I'm Giles.'

We went in search of Barry.

Barry was sharing a room with a bewitchingly cool Reuters correspondent in an even more luxurious hotel a few blocks further up Lenin Prospekt. They had both been shot at a few hours earlier near the front line, south of the city, and he was using her portable satellite telex machine to send a story on the incident to London.

Superman had been an agency hand once, so he talked shop with Mademoiselle Reuter while Barry concentrated on his keyboard and I concentrated on not making a fool of myself. Presently we returned to the Hotel Tajikistan, where Barry and Mlle Reuter were met by a burly Russian gangster type who took them off in a Volga to an undisclosed location to discuss helicopters. Superman and I ended up lunching with Alfred, an Armenian-born photographer with a thick French accent who was on assignment for a glamorous Paris picture agency, and Mike, originally from California, now working for the *Moscow News*.

No one seemed to understand the war. Barry had said the scoop was down on the Afghan border but had not invited anyone besides Mlle Reuter to join him on his putative helicopter ride. Alfred said the scoop was a mullah named Khadji Akhbar Torajonzoda who would sooner or later turn Tajikistan into a fundamentalist Islamic republic but knew exactly how to play the international press and for the time being was pretending to be a democrat. Torajonzoda was in town and Alfred, a rounded rogue with a worldly turn of phrase and a towering reputation earned during the Iran–Iraq war, had spent the morning trying to persuade him to be photographed preaching. Mike said the scoop was in Kulyab. 'I gotta get to Kulyab,' he said. 'I'm gonna *die* to get to Kulyab.' It was all right. He was going there in an armoured convoy the following day. Superman said with a mysterious twitch of his moustache that the scoop was wild sheep in Badakhshan.

(That evening the world's most awestruck foreign correspondent *manqué* wrote in his notebook: 'The work of a foreign correspondent beats that of a film star, having roughly equal exposure and being concerned with reality. It beats that of a sports star, not being confined to a sports ground. And it rivals both for pay since it consists of travelling to the world's most exciting places, staying in the best hotels there and phoning home every night, all at someone else's expense. Foreign correspondents are spies, explorers, writers, orators and experts rolled into one. They are the last breed of adventurer in a less and less adventurous world. They work alone, but are powerful out of all proportion to their solitude.'

I was wrong but sincere. Stephen Graham had a more considered view: 'In our country,' he wrote in 1916, 'a certain glamour overspreads the personality of the polyglot who writes of foreign Courts and foreign policies, but as an observer of the Press for many years I can give it as my opinion that, as a nation, we do not gain much from the pens of those journalists who run in and out of chancelleries and are well known at foreign Courts.')

Day two in the war zone dawned as bright as day one. Superman went off in a taxi to where Barry and Mlle Reuter had been shot at and I chatted with Sher Ali, an amateur historian on the hotel staff, about Enver Pasha's grave. Mr Ali said the grave was eighty kilometres east of Dushanbe near the village of Baljuan on the road from Kangurt to Khovaling in the oblast of Kulyab. But the bridge over the Vakhsh river at Nurek was down, dynamited by Islamic rebels from the Garm valley. There

was no way to Baljuan except under armed escort via Kurgan
Turbe.

I remembered Mike's mention of a convoy, thanked Mr Ali
and walked the half mile from the hotel to the gatehouse of the
former Red Army's Dushanbe garrison. It was a futile sortie.
The duty officer told me to wait across the street. From there I
watched camouflaged lorries for an hour before being told the
convoy had already left.

The news at the bus station was more hopeful. Despite vigi-
lante checkpoints down the road and categorical assertions at
the hotel that no buses were running to Kurgan Turbe, buses
were running to Kurgan Turbe.

'When?' I asked of a frazzled-looking driver whose face was
darkened with grime and lightened with grey stubble.

'How should I know? When they're ready.'

He hooked his thumbs into worn belt loops under his belly
and turned away.

'Is it safe?'

'Safe? Yes, it is safe. No, it is not safe. *Maladoi chelavyek*, what
do you want me to say? Don't you know we have a war?'

He turned away again. A long line of stalled passengers
listened from their patches of concrete floor. He turned back
again.

'Usually, *daibok*, it is safe.'

Daibok. God willing. A Russian expression which some
Muslims seemed to prefer to inshallah, though often, as in this
case, they laced it with more than a hint of mockery.

The bus station was on the western edge of the city, tidy and
monumental as befitted a Soviet republican capital. Here the
valley of the Surkhandarya was wide and the mountains on
either side were far enough away to be obscured by haze.

I took a taxi back into the city centre and got out at the bazaar.
The alley leading to the main hall of meat and produce was
lined, comfortingly, with the usual kiosks selling Turkish sweets
and cigarettes and lipstick, and with stacks of plastic basins and
brush-heads made from twigs. Trade was brisk, especially in
brush-heads, which made sense because Dushanbe was meticu-
lously swept.

Across the road two dark-eyed Tajik women dressed in

western business suits were boiling water for tea behind the counter of the hard currency shop in the foyer of the Ethnographic Museum. I failed to engage them in conversation, admired some Tajik musical instruments and a carved wood *chilim* designed for the smoking of raw opium, and walked east along Ismail Somoni Street to Lenin Prospekt.

At the junction, Russian grandmothers in floral headscarves talked among themselves, waiting for a trolleybus. I took tea and *shashlyk* upstairs at the Chaikhana Rokhat, which had a roof but no walls. Down on the Prospekt there was little traffic. But for the warmth and the colour of the tea leaves, which were green, this could almost have been Volgograd.

The bus driver's war seemed a million miles away. Having more or less decided to take a bus to Kurgan Turbe the following day, I strolled back to the hotel.

Superman had returned from the front line. Like Barry and Mlle Reuter the previous day, he had been shot at. He was not hurt but he was angry. He could easily have been killed and he knew that if he had been it would have been pointless. At dinner that evening he and Alfred exchanged a grim sort of dialogue.

ALFRED: This is a stupid war.
SUPERMAN: Right. Dead right.
ALFRED: Sometimes you don't calculate the risk. You forget your wife and kids. But here there's nothing to get killed for.
SUPERMAN: In the Lebanon I could see Israelis lining up to shoot at me but I didn't care. Here I do.

I mentioned that buses were still running to Kurgan Turbe and asked if there was a serious chance of getting hit there, at which point Superman rounded on me.

'Yes, yes, yes. They're shooting. Shooting for the fun of it. You're not going there.'

The sound of gunfire near the hotel a few minutes later settled it.

'Cleaning their guns,' said Alfred, and we headed for the basement bar and Johnnie Walker at six dollars a shot.

There was already a gathering down there in the gloom. People leaned forward from Intourist's finest chrome-and-leather armchairs pooling information, withholding information, smoking. Barry was back. He had the scoop after all. His chopper ride had dropped him in on peace talks being brokered by the Kirghiz deputy prime minister. Hence, apparently, Dushanbe's two-day period of calm which had just ended with the news that the talks had failed.

Barry was being quizzed by a Pakistani feature-writer in a blazer and a man from *Newsweek*, recently arrived. Also in attendance were two consultants from the European Commission, one fat, one thin, whom Alfred said were spies.

Superman stayed out of the fray. We talked about England and it turned out we had played the same instrument in the same school orchestra, five years apart. We had both been second flutes.

It also turned out that he was serious about wild sheep in Badakhshan. Marco Polo sheep, to be precise, with tremendous curling horns and lungs that let them run for days at 15,000 feet. In the secluded wastes of the Eastern Pamirs, closer to China than to Dushanbe, they had thrived throughout the Soviet era. Now western millionaires were being helicoptered in to hunt them and were paying $18,000 to export each trophy. It was big business, and it would make a damn fine magazine piece.

Superman wanted to join a hunt. I wanted an excuse to visit Badakhshan. Neither of us wanted to hang around in Dushanbe now the truce was over. In the morning we went to the Foreign Ministry.

The Foreign Ministry seemed to be staffed entirely by Pamiris. In the Protocol Department they rhapsodized about their mountains: higher than the moon, colder than the Arctic, more exquisite than Scheherazade. The Minister for Badakhshan phoned the Mayor of Khorog, the chief town of the Pamirs, and told him to expect us. (I had visions of a radio telephone ringing in a wind-whipped Nissen hut.) A Khorog visa was stamped and slipped inside my passport, but before a second one could be prepared for Superman we were called before the Foreign Minister.

He asked for our credentials. They had not been issued by the Tajik Foreign Ministry, he said. He spoke into a telephone long enough for Superman to say through his moustache, 'This does not look good.'

We tried to make light of red tape but the minister turned pale and showed us the door. He muttered a few words to an assistant in the outer office. The trip seemed to be off. For our own safety, a secretary said. There had been shooting on the Khorog road.

Our passports were returned to us. The Minister for Badakh-shan apologized to Superman. To me he said nothing, but he looked at me intently as he put the passport in my hand. Back in the sun on Lenin Prospekt I looked inside and let out an involuntary yelp. The Khorog visa was still there.

Badakhshan

～～～～

The Foreign Ministry's story about a shooting incident turned out to have been true, ruling out travel to Khorog by road. Taking aim from across the River Piandzh at Kalaikhum, Afghan guerrillas had killed five CIS frontier troops. Forty Afghans had been wounded in the ensuing skirmish and the Pamir Highway was closed until further notice.

The fuel shortage had hit road traffic anyway. In Dushanbe a lorry park for Pamiri vehicles had become a refugee camp. Most drivers had been stranded there for at least a fortnight, listening to their radios, buying *shashlyk* twice a day and drinking beer from preserving jars.

For several days cloud in Khorog had ruled out flying there too. Once, feeling trapped, I had given up on Badakhshan and paid a taxi-driver called Ibod seventy precious dollars to take me to the Kirghiz border by the direct but little-used Garm Valley road. It was a 250-mile drive. Ibod had vodka on his breath when he woke me at six in the morning and he drove very fast all day. Once in the valley we climbed steadily for three hours, hugging a long series of inlets and headlands on the north side of the grey silt plain created by the river. On the south side rose the Pamirs; a series of perfect, sharp, laundered white peaks so high they ought to have left vapour trails and so foreshortened they looked climbable in a day. The tarmac ran out at Lyakhsh, where Kirghiz men in white felt hats were digging up potatoes. The plan was to walk from here to Kirghizstan proper and get another ride there. Ibod was confident the next village was less than three hundred kilometres away. I had relished the idea of a long walk, but, faced with the reality, stayed in the car. We gave an Afghan a lift back to Dushanbe. He claimed to have entered the country on foot via China and Kirghizstan. He had a gun and a wild look about him, and said he was going to kill the government. Mindful of this, Ibod accelerated instead of slowing down as we approached a government road block on the way out of the Garm Valley. Fortunately the militia men didn't shoot.

That night, my last in the Hotel Tajikistan, a Russian woman knocked at the door of my room and asked if she could come in. She wanted to talk about something. She was younger than me, with dyed blonde hair, magenta lipstick and a steady stare. Sitting on the bed, her hands between her legs in the folds of a cotton skirt, she asked if I would like to have a maiden. I pretended not to understand.

'Don't you want sex?'

'N-no.'

'Excuse me, then.'

She got up and left and the questions came crowding in. (What – with you? Now? How much? For how long? Would you go straight on to room 702 afterwards?) I realized I could feel my pulse in my throat.

The sky was clear the next morning so I rushed to the airport and by paying dollars made sure of a seat on the only plane going to Khorog. It was a forty-seater but by the time the gangway under the tail was pulled up, there were sixty people in the main cabin and seven in the cockpit.

According to Aeroflot the 45-minute flight from Dushanbe to Khorog is the most dangerous scheduled passenger service in the world. It ends with a dive into the gorge of the upper Oxus, which forms the Afghan border and is known locally as the Piandzh. The runway at Khorog is on landfill on the Soviet side of the river. There is only one way to make the approach and no way of aborting it once begun. The pilots are paid danger money.

It took for ever to get airborne. The Yak used the whole of the runway and for several minutes seemed certain to be snagged by the trees and telephone wires on rising ground east of the airport. The co-pilot let me share his seat and admitted the plane was overloaded.

'But we'll get there?' I said.

'*Daibok.*'

Below to the right was the Nurek dam. A giant reservoir

pushed back from it into a tangle of thirsty brown ridges. Straight ahead the mountains were white rather than brown and they were at eye level. The pilot pointed a biro at the highest ones: Peak Revolution, Peak Communism, Peak Frunze. Still climbing, we banked to the right, following the border. Peak Lenin. I couldn't make out Peak Lenin. It was two hundred miles away at the back of a spreading crowd of mountains.

The Pamirs are a massif rather than a range; the hub of Asia, with the Tien Shan, the Himalayas, the Karakorams and the Hindu Kush for spokes. From a mile or so beneath the cramped cockpit, deep valleys formed by tributaries of the Piandzh began their long eastward climb to the hub of the hub, the Fedchenko Glacier, Badakhshan's ice-cap. By now the Pamirs lay to the left. The Hindu Kush, the gaunt spine of Afghanistan, strode up from the right to the edge of the Piandzh as if to grab a wing-tip.

A tiny fan mounted above the instruments ruffled the flight log on the pilot's knee. We were within Tajik airspace, but not by much. Keeping to the left of the canyon cut by the river we cleared a high pass by a few hundred feet. It was thick with ice and heavily crevassed. Now the plane was flying straight at a mountain. A bell rang in the cockpit and we banked sharply to the right and the nose dipped. The co-pilot was reading numbers off a check list. We flew out of shadow into the sun over the river and banked again, to the left, with the nose still down. The co-pilot pointed out pale green poppy patches on the right-hand side, the Afghan side, but they were gone in a few seconds. I saw a pale strip of runway much too far below us, shoe-horned into the bottom of the canyon next to the river. The nose dipped some more. Being in it was beginning to feel like skiing. The co-pilot began counting down the height from two hundred metres. It must have looked as if we were going to crash. One hundred metres. Eighty metres. I noticed two helicopters parked at the far end of the runway, coming closer very quickly. Sixty. Forty. Still over the river at ten metres the nose came up and the pilot throttled back. We hit the ground and he slammed the joystick forward and that seemed to do the trick. The mountains on either side stopped screaming backwards and the helicopters stayed where they were at the end of the runway.

'You take the bus from across the road,' said the pilot. 'Welcome to Khorog.'

The Yak parked opposite a miniature terminal building surrounded by trees. A line of tense hopefuls had formed behind a policeman on the tarmac, waiting to scramble for seats on the flight back to Dushanbe.

Thinking the Foreign Minister might have someone looking out for me I avoided looking people in the eye and walked into town instead of catching the bus. I needn't have bothered. The petulance of unelected egos in Dushanbe counted for very little 532 kilometres up the Pamir Highway on the edge of the Roof of the World.

The air was cool and so dry that I could practically feel it sponging the saliva off the inside of my mouth. It was midday and a strong sun struck the bottom of the gorge. The road was lined with yellowing poplars. On the far side of the runway the Piandzh raced northwards to its next deep corner, gouging remorselessly into the earth's crust. Above it, huge dark mountainsides seemed to cast a spell of general stillness over the space between them. Nothing moved except the view from the road, and that only at walking pace.

Across the river in Afghanistan snow was visible high up. On the Tajik side the slopes were bare and the tops too far back to see. I whistled as I walked, smug to have got here and clinically intoxicated, as any normal mountain junkie would have been.

After about half an hour the road swung abruptly eastwards and Khorog appeared on both banks of a tributary called the Gunt. The capital of Soviet Badakhshan had a main street and two filigree suspension bridges, one of them for walkers only. They linked the civic centre to a tidy ribbon of bungalows beneath a curtain of brown scree on which white stones announced in letters twenty feet high: *SLAVA ORDENONOCY-OMU PAMIRU* (The word 'Pamir' makes us proud).

Neatly arranged along the main street was the standard apparatus of Soviet administration and enlightenment: post office, telecom building, museum of local studies, 'university' (a brand new structure in glass and concrete, locked), regional Party offices, regional Soviet, regional KGB headquarters. The hammer and sickle still flew from the Soviet building and Lenin stood in front of it, waving at the mountain opposite. The poplars continued up the pavements, buckling them in places. They cast stripes of shade in which the burghers of Khorog ambled unbusily about their business. Most of them wore cheap Soviet clothes – flat caps and headscarves, zipped acrylic jerseys, straight-cut frocks and scarecrow-style jackets. The older men wore grey felt Homburgs. Skull caps did not seem to be their style.

There was a creaking guesthouse by the river and tea in a *chaikhana* round the corner. The sun was already angling down over the Hindu Kush as I set out on foot for the village of Bidur, on a quest for petrol.

The path to Bidur was actually the Pamir Highway. It followed the Gunt upstream, turning north once clear of the town. A silver ibex on a boulder the size of a house seemed to indicate the end of Khorog and the beginning of the wild country. But then the road entered a series of concrete avalanche shelters. At the entrance to one of them there was a blue and white mosaic of a cosmonaut, space-walking. I think I got the message; if Soviet engineering could conquer the cosmos then it could conquer the Pamirs too. But there was still a petrol shortage and it threatened to pin me down in Khorog when what I'd hoped to do was follow the Pamir Highway to its eastern terminus at Osh. On my map the highway was a lovely orange line that meandered temptingly through the mottled mass of mountains.

The road and the river performed a grand sweep to the right and squeezed into a defile. Above it on the left a steep slope had been terraced and planted with potatoes and dotted with stone huts. An old man picking his way down a stream bed with a skinny bundle of firewood said that Karim lived at the top.

The top was a long way up and clearly the fashionable end of Bidur. The stream bed led to a jeep track which had left the main highway beyond the defile and wound its way up over easier terrain. The jeep track twisted on past large adobe dwellings with clean mud yards enclosed by fences of woven sticks. It stopped at the principal residence of the village. A boy ran out and took me to his father, Karim, who was with a crew of villagers putting up green railings round a cemetery behind the house.

Karim was taller than the rest of them. He was heavily built, with a floppy black moustache and an easy laugh. He listened with a broadening grin while I explained how an associate of the Minister for Badakhshan had sought me out at the Hotel Tajikistan to say that, in the circumstances, Karim, not the mayor, would be the one to help with onward travel from Khorog.

It was the end of the day. The crew of railing-builders was dispersing. Karim bade them goodnight, handed me an apple from a convenient tree and led the way indoors.

His house was one enormous room lit by a central skylight. As dusk turned to night this turned from grey to blue-black. A paraffin lamp was brought to a small table where we ate dry biscuits and more apples and drank tea and then Tajik port. It was a split-level room, like a pub theatre, with raised sleeping dens off three sides of the eating area and a kitchen off the fourth. Karim had seven brothers. One of them sat at the edge of the light and joined in the conversation. (The others were spread across the former Soviet Union.) Karim's wife, son, daughter, aunt and father stepped forward to be introduced, then retreated to the gloom to watch. They laughed a lot and made scuttling noises when Karim called for more refreshment.

The conversation was mostly about hunting. Karim was the front man for a commercial Marco Polo sheep hunting operation whose clients were liable to offload forty thousand dollars on a two-week trip, most of it paid locally for export licences for horns. Forty thousand dollars was more than the entire staff of the regional government could hope to earn in their collective lifetimes, which made Karim something of a player.

He was still hard to pin down on the subject of petrol. He hadn't had a hunting client this year because of the war. Everything was scarce, including influence.

He preferred to talk about previous seasons, with fifteen clients and a permanent base camp a day's drive east, three and a half thousand metres up on the edge of Lake Yashyl-Kul. Here hunters acclimatized and saddled up for a three-day ride to Yul Mazar near the headwaters of the Bartang river. Anything louder than a horse would scare off the sheep for weeks. Even from Yul Mazar it could take five days of stalking and five freezing bivouacs to line up a single shot.

Karim reckoned there were about eight thousand Marco Polo in the Pamirs. A maximum of thirty could be shot legally each year.

I asked about snow leopards.

'About two hundred,' he said.

He had never seen one. He had seen 'only the dead Marco Polo with its throat missing'.

There were snowmen out there too, he added after a slight pause. *Snezhni chelavyeki.* His guides had seen them on the glaciers and he had no reason to doubt their word. It took me a while to register that he was talking about yetis, but what with the flickering light and the big floppy moustache it was hard to tell if he was serious. I was falling asleep and wished I could have curled up then and there in one of Karim's sleeping dens, but he seemed to think only the guesthouse would do.

He gave me a lift back into town in his jeep and said he would try to arrange onward transport the following day. The chances were fifty fifty, he said. Only the military had fuel. There was a moon somewhere behind the mountains and by its diffuse light, through the mosquito-netting over the window in my room, I could see the River Gunt shimmering past the poplars on its banks. The room itself was cramped and cold, with a narrow bed and a bare wood floor. Any more luxury would have been out of place, but I still dreamed of warm white towels and thick Swiss duvets.

It was not quite true that only the military had fuel. In the morning we attended a strange ritual at the petrol station. Every vehicle and adult male in Khorog seemed to be there, yelling and honking. I pulled out my camera but Karim was embarrassed and said photography was not permitted. At ten o'clock the pumps came on for two minutes and in an unseemly frenzy a lucky few filled buckets and jerry cans which they then auctioned. Bidding on my behalf, Karim got enough petrol to power a jeep a hundred miles up the Pamir Highway with a little left over for its return (most of which could be freewheeled). Karim said the remaining four hundred miles to the Kirghiz city of

Osh, over the bleakest, loneliest territory in Central Asia, were in God's hands. At least he was honest.

The driver for the first stage of the journey was to be Davlat, an *okhotnik*, one of Karim's hunting guides. He was red-faced, with straight, dark hair. He looked like a Russian or a Tartar but described himself as Macedonian; a descendant of the soldiers left behind by Alexander the Great on his all-conquering march to India in the seventh decade of the fourth century BC.

The important thing just then was that he had a healthy jeep and a full tank of gas.

Those first pre-paid miles with Davlat were also the most beautiful. Beyond the Bidur defile we climbed gently up the broad valley of the Gunt, crossing and re-crossing the river, threading through self-possessed villages of flat-topped houses, some with haystacks on their roofs, most with skylights like Karim's. There were apple orchards, precious patches of wheat and potatoes, tethered goats and boys on bicycles. Beside a half-built dam intended for the electrification of the valley a line of railway tankers had been turned into workers' cottages.

The upper slopes were of harsh sunburned rock unrelieved by streams or alps. As we gained height we saw snow but it was a miserly dusting, a concession forced by altitude. By this time the villages were behind us, the road more serpentine, the engine note keener. Davlat was not a great talker. He kept his foot down and leaned forward over the wheel.

After a sequence of hairpins between converging buttresses the valley opened out again. It seemed to be closed at the far end by a smooth grey bowl that dwarfed a scattering of low buildings.

'Dzilandi,' said Davlat, nodding at them.

I got to know Dzilandi quite well.

It had a canteen, a bunkhouse, a permanent population of perhaps twenty, a small army camp which they called the *zapravka* and very little traffic.

Davlat left me there and returned to Khorog.

I waited a day and a half for a lift, reading *War and Peace* on the side of the road. I was taking my time over Tolstoy and savouring his every ballooning metaphor. Pierre by this time was dabbling with Freemasonry. I disapproved, but somehow trusted he would give it up before it got him into trouble. It was hot for an hour or two either side of midday but bitterly cold the moment the sun eased its angle of attack. After dark I watched for headlights from a room in the bunkhouse which a shuffling cross-eyed Russian caretaker kept warm with a coal stove.

There was a gallery of pin-ups above the registration desk: real officers from Badakhshan divisions of the Red Army, with names like Vasili, Vyechyslav and Valery, from a series of cut-out-and-keep portraits called 'We Are Internationalists', published by an army magazine.

The canteen served tomato soup and rationed Russian bread. There was nothing else. The tomatoes were grown in polythene greenhouses built by Russian frontier troops no longer stationed here, and superheated by piped water from a hot spring a mile down the valley.

The Russians had also built a bath-house on the grey slope beneath the spring. It smelled of pure sulphurous pollution but the water was deep and blissfully hot. I went and lolled in it on the second evening, invited by two Uzbeks from the canteen. Our damp hair froze solid on the way back up to the bunkhouse.

That night I began to feel stranded. The little that there was of Dzilandi had already gone a long way.

The caretaker shook me awake at seven the next morning. Two army trucks were pounding up the smooth grey valley from the hairpins. By the time I had scrambled outside they were turning off the road into the military compound. I found the two drivers and two Russian officers travelling with them tucking into a mouthwatering breakfast of tinned meat and oats heated over a primus. They had left Khorog at five and had a long day ahead. They were making for Osh, four hundred unusually rugged miles away, with no overnight stops.

Did they have space . . . Would they consider . . . ?

They did. They would. They even let me share their breakfast. By half-past seven I was straddling the gear stick of a road-eating Zil 434 V8 monster, delirious to be moving again.

Hell hath no desolation like the East Pamir plateau. What appeared over the pass behind Dzilandi was a very different sort of Central Asia from Stephen Graham's paradise. It was a caramel-coloured moonscape where a freshly potted geranium would have lasted maybe twenty minutes. Maybe more. That is for geranium experts. But this was not a fecund place. We slogged across the bottom of a shallow pan of hard sand and up the other side to a second pass from which the view was bigger but just as dry. Beyond a pair of salt flats which could each have been the size of Sussex the world seemed to fall away. In a sense it did fall away, to Afghanistan's Vakhan corridor, established in 1895 to keep the British and Russian Empires apart. Until then the two superpowers had surveyed and coveted this territory, the Russians with a view to sending armies over it, the British with a view to stopping them. But it would have been a cold, debilitated Russian force that stumbled off the Pamirs into Hunza, and anyway it never came.

The Soviets staked out the Pamirs with their trusty T-section fence, and later, with early warning stations. I saw one between the salt flats, an eerie white bubble full of radar. I was about to take its picture when Sergei shook his head and put his hand over the lens.

Sergei was going home to Russia. The truck was full of his furniture, which from Osh would trundle back to the motherland in a railway container. He was a *pogranichnik* – a frontier guard. Sasha, in the other truck, was his commanding officer. The garrison at Khorog was being pared down in preparation for the day the frontier became the Tajiks' problem. Sergei's severance pay was the loan of the truck and three hundred litres of fuel.

He was full of tales of Afghan cowardice – of *mujaheddin* shooting unarmed *pogranichniki* from behind, then throwing up their hands in instant surrender when combat troops came for revenge – but he seemed to be using a kind of army rhyming slang and the tales stopped coming when he realized I wasn't picking up their nuances.

Except where scarps and ridges intervened, the road ran straight as a die. So much for wriggling on the map. Strangely often, faint tracks would depart from it at right angles and vanish into the mountains. Who used them and where they led were mysteries to which the Pamirs offered few clues, though we did pass a single village set on a plain of short, dry grass being grazed by distant yak. The landscape called for a Tibetan monastery, but the village consisted mainly of white prefabricated huts; winter quarters for the yak herds, or so I guessed. I had to guess because we didn't stop. We thundered on and soon the huts had merged back into the plain behind us.

Around lunchtime we began slaloming. The driver, whose name was Alikhan, was dozing. I touched him on the arm and asked if he was OK.

He snapped awake.

'Yes. OK. Without a problem I drive for three days without sleep.'

He dozed off again. It was hard to be sure because he had lizard eyes that were already squinted against the sun. But yes. He had gone back to sleep. Next time we veered right off the road. He woke up in time to stop the truck turning over, but looked a little shaken.

'Talk to me,' he said, so I asked the standard questions. Did he have a mother, a father, children? How old? A house? (He had them all.) Then we did coffee. We talked gallons of it; steaming, very black and very sweet. I described America's greatest invention, the refill. I talked longingly about bottomless coffees in roadside diners. It was a form of sado-masochism. Coffee was the only thing scarcer in Tajikistan than petrol.

Alikhan heard me out, then said that coffee was actually for civilians. Army drivers needed something stronger. He pulled from his pocket a very hard cheese ball, bit it in two, gave me half and ate the other. It was inedible but it worked for him. He indicated with bony fingers that the horizon was exploding before his very eyes, and drove on unwaveringly for fourteen hours.

Gradually the road turned north, leaving the plateau and lining up for the two high passes which smuggle it into Kirghizstan between Peak Lenin and the Chinese border.

We ate two more tins of meat and oats 4200 metres above sea level in the army *zapravka* at Murgab. The Red Army reached this chilly haunt of secret agents and geologists in 1922, approaching from the north and driving the last free Kirghiz nomads before them. It was a significant piece of claim-staking by the world's most vehement anti-imperialists and I suppose in a two-bit way I was witnessing their retreat exactly seventy years later. But if anything I was too late. Beside us and some big black choughs labouring in the thin air the *zapravka* was silent and deserted.

Sergei said the largest ruby ever found had come from a long-abandoned mine somewhere in the mountains to the west. That had been before the revolution, when Murgab revelled in the name Pamirski Post. The ruby had been commandeered for a Tsarina's crown.

In the late afternoon the south wall of Peak Lenin appeared on the right of the windscreen and inched across it to the left. In the foreground a crater lake called Kara-Kul, formed by a rogue asteroid ten billion years ago, mirrored the snows of what for a geological blip had been the Sino-Soviet watershed.

This place was almost too fantastically remote and grand. It was too much, anyway, to take in at forty miles an hour from the cab of a V8 Zil. I had skirted the war and was skirting the Pamirs. I had missed the grave of Enver Pasha and failed to see a single Marco Polo sheep. If I wasn't careful the mountains of Central Asia would begin to shun me as a lightweight. There had to be a way to get in among them, properly.

I did have the beginnings of a plan. It centred on a piece of Soviet machinery I had first seen many weeks earlier from the window of the train to Baku, trailing dust as it bounced along a rough track beside the railway.

The idea was never more appealing than as we skirted lake Kara-Kul, climbed to the Kizyl-Art pass and descended to Sary-Tash, the first town in Kirghizstan. At Sary-Tash the road to Dushanbe via Lyakhsh and the Garm Valley – the road whose western end I had explored with Ibod the taxi-driver – left the Pamir Highway heading into the sunset. The sunset also gave the grand north faces of Peak Lenin and its neighbours a haunting, luminous look. I would have given anything to putter up that road, master of my own departure and arrival times, and camp beside a stream on one of the long green flanks leading to the snowline. But Alikhan's truck seemed to be the only thing leaving Sary-Tash in any direction and I resisted getting out. By a miracle – the miracle of the cheese balls, perhaps – he stayed awake for six more hours of arduous night driving through the

Alai mountains, which ran east–west between the Pamirs and the Fergana.

We reached Osh at two in the morning and dozed in the cab outside another *zapravka* until dawn, when I took the first of a series of buses down the valley to Tashkent. Hoping to return to both the valley and the city via the mountains of Kirghizstan I did not spend long in either, and went straight to the railway station to buy a ticket to the Kirghiz capital.

To Tash Rabat

In the marble-floored concourse of Tashkent's central station there was an information booth where I asked about tickets to Bishkek.

'Two rubles,' said a fat-faced Uzbek woman. Two rubles was incredibly cheap.

'Where from?'

'Two rubles.'

'But where are they sold?'

'Two rubles.'

I paid.

'Next door. Under the Hotel Lokomotif.'

Under the Hotel Lokomotif it was mayhem; a wrestling arena for hundreds of unfortunates seeking tickets west along the Trans-Caspian line, north-west up the Syr Darya towards Moscow and north-east up the TurkSib towards Siberia. As a form of torture chamber it was familiar from Astrakhan and Krasnovodsk, only bigger.

One wall consisted of a line of ticket windows, half of them closed. The open ones were obscured by mooing herds of human livestock off which sweat rose like steam. I stood at the back of a queue for an hour. No one joined it behind me but plenty of people joined it in front. When the *dyevuchka* behind the window took an hour off for lunch some of them seemed to give up. When she returned, so did the mob.

A young man in a blue tracksuit said there was a train to Bishkek in two hours. He was making assaults on the front of the queue from a well-victualled camp set up by his wife on some moulded plywood seats in the middle of the arena. I asked why he couldn't queue properly and he said, 'My place is at the front.'

I lacked his spunk. Instead I simmered in a silent, impotent, bigoted, peppery broth of indignation at this obscene mockery of the divine right of the consumer, and at these rancid barbarians for being unable to apply roll-on or wait their turn. I had been on the road for two months but just then it seemed much longer. Never did a closet service addict crave so ardently a false smile and a well-trained 'Can I help you?'

Beyond the scrum, behind the window, there was a computer. Ticket requests had to be entered in it but the printer was down so the *dyevuchka* snipped and folded tickets by hand. The longer the journey the longer the ticket. Those to Novosibirsk at the end of the TurkSib line took a quarter of an hour to issue and seemed to require a black belt in origami on the part of the *dyevuchka*.

Eventually Blue Tracksuit got his tickets and even I made some progress. Half an hour before the train was due to leave only six people stood between me and the window. With ten minutes to go I reached the front, and was told the last tickets to Bishkek had been sold.

I wandered away in a daze. Perhaps this was a sign. Perhaps I should have been walking; when Stephen Graham reached Tashkent in 1914 the railway stopped and with hardly a backward glance he walked the remaining thousand miles to Siberia.

All thoughts of walking evaporated when Blue Tracksuit slunk over and said that by a happy chance he had a spare ticket if I could pay in dollars. Still, as we ran for the train, I vowed to find a way round queues.

From Tashkent the train crossed the flat eastern end of the Kyzil-Kum, then wound into the Karatau Hills, which were big but not exactly tall. They were smooth and curved and covered in grass; understated, but still a natural frontier.

We were leaving the desert and would come down on to steppe. We were leaving the hot country once squabbled over by Bukhara and Kokand and would come down on to the ancestral pastures of Kazakh nomads. We were leaving the lands taken by Russian generals to keep other Europeans out, and would come down on to those settled by Russian peasant farmers who knew heavenly homesteading country when they saw it.

The train was blessed with many broken windows. Some enlightened vandal had levered them half out of their seals, bequeathing fresh air to a generation of fellow travellers. After dark I sat on a splintered sill for a bit, leaning out towards the black hills and crooning at the stars. There was some distant lightning, which was fitting. Stephen Graham had seen lightning and been moistened by a shower as he lay by the road in his sheet 'sewn three ways round' on his first night north of the railhead.

Supper consisted of vodka and hard-boiled eggs at the invitation of Ibragim, Artik, Rafshan and Khursa, Kirghiz traders taking apricots from Osh to market in Bishkek. It rained overnight. Rain and the wonderful smell of rain-dampened dust came into the compartment.

At Bishkek station, 350 miles north-east of the Tashkent sweat-box, the early morning air was clean and mild. The city sloped unspectacularly away to the north, mostly hidden by trees. The forecourt was dark with damp, and the gardens between the empty carriageways of Bulvar Erkindik were drenched with dew.

There were mountains close by. You could feel their airconditioning. You could sense them in the tilt of the earth, which rose to the south as it dipped to the north. Hildebrand's trusty 1:3,500,000 map of the western Soviet Union showed them starting on the very edge of the suburbs. But you couldn't see them because the cloud was down.

I got a room with a high ceiling and a wrought iron balcony in a solid-looking grey hotel opposite the station. An opera singer was practising upstairs. The dining room was a study in measured Soviet grandeur, with dull gold frillies round the mirrors on the walls and plastic jugs of apple juice on the tables.

Under my balcony, surrounded by beds of ornamental mountain mosses among trees at the top of Bulvar Erkindik, there was a statue of General Mikhail Frunze on a horse. Frunze was born in Bishkek before the revolution and gave his name to the town after becoming famous for leading the Bolshevik conquest of what became Uzbekistan. Frunze the place reverted to Bishkek in 1991. Frunze the man had not yet fallen to post-Soviet, anti-Soviet image-wrecking. Mothers and prams skirted him placidly. Clear mountain water gurgled down each side of the gardens in concrete ditches. One of them had become blocked, forcing the prams to skirt a comely little flood too.

I went for a walk. The air took some getting used to. It slipped demurely off the skin leaving goosepimples, whereas in the deserts it had been an assailant. I turned left on Kievskaya Street and followed it to the bazaar, where tobacco was being sold in heaps graded according to strength and an eager salesman with wayward white whiskers gave me a cigar-sized sample of his most pungent blend, rolled in newspaper.

A travelling circus from Osh had set up a tight-rope in front of the bazaar's entrance. A man in purple velvet knickerbockers with a padded crotch was jumping off the rope on to the padding and bouncing back up again, keeping time to the melancholy beating of a single leather drum, watched by an enraptured oval of what I took to be mainly Kirghiz shoppers. But many of those thronging the bazaar could equally have been Uzbeks, Kazakhs, Turkmens or even Uighurs (the Turkic natives of Xinjiang, China's westernmost province). I had learned that Central Asia's capitals are cosmopolitan places as far as the region's porous internal borders and not-so-porous international ones allow. More especially, all these races are Altaic as distinct from Indo-European. Their early generations fished together from the same gene pool as the Mongols, with the result that a Uighur can no more reliably tell a Kirghiz from a Kazakh, without listening to them, than an Englander can tell a Dutchman from a German. The only people who stood out unmistakably were the men in pointed hats of white embroidered felt. Only the Kirghiz wear the *al-kapak*. With their flat cheeks and eyelids and their skin weathered beyond brown to the reddish tinge of rosewood, these men were locals.

Ibragim the apricot trader was in the audience. He had already tired of selling apricots and knew the funambulist from home.

'*Kak?*' he said. ('How?' It was his standard greeting.)

'Very well,' I said.

'*Kak aktyor?*'

He called his bouncing friend an actor.

'Excellent. Strong here,' I said, pointing between my legs.

'*Kak* Kirghizstan?'

'Also excellent. Better than Uzbekistan.'

He offered me a bag of apricots for having said the right

thing. Osh's Kirghiz and Uzbek communities frightened Soviet authorities by killing two hundred of each other in street fights in 1990. If Ibragim was anything to go by they were still not getting on.

I asked him where the Heavenly Mountains had got to, the famous Tien Shan, and he waved vaguely as an Australian might when asked the way to the Outback.

'Between Bishkek and Osh is all mountain.'

He mimed some exaggerated corrugation then stuck a half-eaten apricot in his mouth to free his hands for applause as his friend finished bouncing and leaped fifteen feet to the ground.

Not just between Bishkek and Osh. I knew from Hildebrand that between Bishkek and China there were five – *five* – majestic mountain ranges, two of which cradled an inland sea called Issyk-Kul. From the Alpine Club in London I knew that none of them had been properly explored by a westerner in the twentieth century. From the writings of those who had glimpsed Kirghizstan's interior since the Russian Revolution there were grounds for hope that it was a unique and wondrous place, not modernized by cable cars and ice-cream signs on the one hand, nor by smokestacks, tractors, demagogues and nuclear testing on the other. If the idyll had survived – the paradise of Sarts and horses' milk and brooks and berries that had been upland Central Asia as interpreted by Stephen Graham in the imperial summer of 1914 – then it was surely to be found among the clouds behind the tight-rope and the railway station.

Ibragim retired to a caravan with his bag of apricots and the funambulist.

In the afternoon I walked north to the bus terminal on the edge of the steppe and ascertained that buses ran to Lake Issyk-Kul but not to many other places in the mountains.

The Tien Shan finally made their appearance as the light was fading. I was leaving the bus terminal by a footbridge over a car park full of cigarette vendors and idle taxis, heading south and staring straight ahead. There was a breeze but the darkening heaps of cumulo nimbus beyond the city were oddly static. In an instant of revelation that deserved backing from a symphony orchestra I realized this was because they were not clouds at all, but mountains. I sat down and swore breathily at them for about five minutes.

This view was the one that told Russian colonists arriving in the later nineteenth century that their trek across the steppe was over. It was a banner in the sky that marked the end of the grinding transition from Europe to Asia and the limit of the Tsar's ambition. It was their promised land; their Manifest Destiny. They must have jumped off their wagons and hugged each other and smeared tears of relief and excitement across their dusty faces.

I bought a packet of filterless cigarettes and smoked one in a macho sort of way despite the nausea and the headspin. The occasion had to be celebrated somehow.

The next morning I visited a company called Dostuk Trekking, which an Intourist representative at the hotel had said was run by 'very mountain specialists'. A shy young Russian woman called Vica ushered me into a room with two desks and a display of rock samples in a glass-fronted cabinet. Vica spoke English and explained to a hunched man sitting under the rock display that although I was no mountaineer I was anxious to explore the Tien Shan, having heard they were the wildest, most beautiful mountains in all of Asia.

'It is true,' said the hunched man, whose name was Valery Georgevich.

'It is true,' said Vica, translating.

Valery Georgevich gave me some large-scale maps of the central Tien Shan and a packet of postcards of the interior. One of the postcards was of Tash Rabat, a medieval granite caravanserai three hundred miles up the high road to China. Standing alone against a backdrop of steep green pastures, it made a surpassingly pretty picture. I asked how to get there.

'Valery Georgevich says it is difficult,' said Vica. 'If you have much money you may take an excursion with Intourist. The other possibility is *avtostop*.'

Avtostop was hitch-hiking. That would have to be it, then.

'There is one other thing,' I said as I got up. 'I was hoping to buy a Ural.'

Valery Georgevich listened while Vica translated. When she had finished his face brightened. I had expected him to laugh and that to be the end of it but he had a keen eye for a deal, and a Ural in mind.

He spoke to Vica.

'Valery Georgevich says the Ural is very strong. On it you may see our whole republic.'

'Including Tash Rabat.'

'Including Tash Rabat.'

We agreed a price, to include a helmet, a jerry can and help with documentation. Valery made a call and announced that the machine was ready for viewing at once.

A Ural is a type of motorbike. A 650 cc, 36-horsepower shaft-drive flat twin that sounds like an old cargo plane and comes with a side-car whether you want one or not. It weighs a metric tonne and consumes more petrol than an average family saloon. Standard equipment includes spoked wheels and two huge black rubber saddles. Designed by BMW for German staff officers in the Second World War, replicated by the million over the next five decades in the Russian city of Sverdlovsk, it is beloved of Central Asian police forces, easy to ride, hard to roll and devilish handsome. I craved one – to get into the mountains, to avoid ticket queues at railway stations and for the sheer throbbing fun of it. Valery Georgevich knew of one for sale and we rolled out of Bishkek in his jeep to find it.

He was a former submariner and champion alpinist. He had bumped the bottom of the Atlantic, surfaced in the Gulf of Mexico and climbed every seven thousand-metre mountain in the Soviet Union by every possible route without oxygen and with heavy loads, which was apparently the reason for his hunched back. The rest of him was slight but springy. He walked in battered trainers on the outsides of his feet and could grin like a leprechaun. It is true that he stood to gain from the motorbike deal but he was still much kinder to me than I deserved.

Since independence he had gone into partnership with a geologist and fellow-climber called Nikolai Nikolaevich. Dostuk Trekking was the result; a travel agency with grand plans and limited resources. They employed Vica as interpreter and secretary, and owned a broken-down bus. Their office was in a rented bungalow between the railway and the mountains.

We drove through fields of maize to the vendor's house. The vendor, a friend of Valery's brother's, had a stern expression and odd zips round the bottoms of his jeans. He wheeled the Ural out into the sun from a stable and I practically swooned. It was magnificent. The petrol tank and side-car were blue. The tyres were so little used they were still shiny.

The vendor kick-started it and demonstrated forward and reverse, lifting dust and straw into the air as he let the clutch out and lurched towards us, backwards. He skidded to a stop with the merest hint of a grin and turned the engine off.

'Do you know how to ride one of these?' he asked.

'Yes.'

'Do you have a licence?'

'Yes.'

Both lies. My English driver's licence allowed me to drive, in addition to a car, a track-laying vehicle and a mowing machine but not a motorbike, and, anyway, it was only provisional. I was counting on officialdom not reading English.

'Do you know mechanics?'

'Not much. I would like a lesson.'

It took two seconds to shake on the deal and a week to get it approved by the traffic police. Valery did the cajoling. He stood for hours in queues at police headquarters, occasionally giving me forms to sign and reporting each evening that progress had been made and everything would be *normalne*.

When the stern vendor found out I had lied about knowing how to ride a motorbike he said if I wasn't careful I'd find myself in prison, so I took lessons with Valery's brother's girlfriend's son, Grigori. These became crucial when the police told Valery I would need a Kirghiz licence for which a practical test had to be taken. But Valery worked away at the underlings in their uniforms, making little jokes and eventually winning us an audience with a chainsmoking departmental head to whom he presented my English licence as if it were a diamond-encrusted Fabergé egg. The departmental head listened to Valery's mild entreaty, took a stamp, placed it on a form, performed a neat karate chop on top of the stamp and showed us the door.

We returned the following morning to pick up a blue card in

lieu of a Kirghiz licence, and a yellow diplomatic number plate: *ФЦЯ0225*.

Meanwhile Grigori had excelled as an instructor. Along the leafy back streets round his home I had learned the Russian for throttle, clutch and brake, and to be gentle with them. The key was low revs. Grigori would sit in the side-car and calmly twist his wrists forwards when I let the engine roar between gears. Bliss was it in Bishkek to be alive, but to clunk smoothly into fourth and duck the willows along the tow-path of the Chu canal was very heaven.

Grigori also demonstrated how to charge the carburettors before starting and how to change a wheel in the event of a puncture or snapped spoke. The spare wheel sat on the lid of a small boot at the back of the side-car. Inside the boot there was a tool kit in a waxed canvas bag with separate compartments for spanners, allen keys, a spoke tightener and a hammer.

The day we got the number plate Grigori's mother, Lula, invited everyone round for *laghman* to celebrate. *Laghman* is the Kirghiz national dish, a soupy sort of noodle bolognese, but this was an all-Russian gathering. It was strangely solemn, even when Valery poured out *shampanski* into vodka glasses. (Lula disliked having bubbles up her nose and drank a homemade balsam liqueur instead.) There were toasts to Grigori's grandmother (the oldest present; she had come south from Novosibirsk as a child), to peace in Kirghizstan and to my journey. Then the clouds opened and the men stood in the back porch to smoke, watching the vegetable patch get a soaking and a water butt fill with the run-off from the roof.

Valery gave up yet another afternoon to help me track down tanker lorries selling petrol. We found one by a roundabout in a desolate industrial suburb. The petrol ran out as we reached the front of the queue but Valery persuaded the driver to siphon twenty litres out of his own tank.

That was enough to get to Rybach'ye at the west end of Lake Issyk-Kul. Here the brother of Valery's partner, Nikolai Nikolaevich, lived and was expecting me. He would provide a fill-up for the next stage to Naryn, the principal town of central Kirghizstan. Here another geologist associated with Dostuk Trekking had a friend who worked at the fuel depot. I had his address too, typed out by Vica on a piece of card.

On my last day in Bishkek I went to the State Fine Art Museum. It was full of People's paintings of the highlands, with slender snow-capped peaks, broad green alps, bus-loads of city-dwellers joining their rural kin for folkloric festivals, and helicopters bearing Soviet doctors to treat the Kirghiz children of the revolution in their mountain huts and yurts, howsoever remote. The canvases were big and crude, and mouthwatering. I decided there was nothing wrong with socialist realism – it was no more propagandist, after all, than your average orthodox ikon.

In the same indulgent frame of mind I visited the Lenin Museum, a tremendous marble shrine set in a wide open space flanked by government offices and the parliament building at the very centre of the city. Inside, on two levels linked by a monumental mulberry-coloured marble staircase, a dazzling exhibition of bas-reliefs, lithographs and brass-framed manuscripts told the story of the Russian Revolution and the building of the Soviet Union. The exhibition had occupied a third level too, but up there the conversion of the Lenin Museum to a museum of Kirghiz history had begun. The first new display was of lists of names – with photographs where they were available – of Kirghiz dissidents executed in the purges of the 1930s. Their skeletons had been exhumed from a mass grave in the foothills of the Tien Shan the previous year.

Saying goodbye to Valery, Nikolai and Vica at the offices of Dostuk Trekking, and riding east out of town with my rucksack and a picnic in the side-car, I felt as if I had been given the freedom of Kirghizstan.

A policeman pulled me over within a mile.

'Document.'

I presented the blue card.

'Document,' he repeated, as in 'come on you smug Balt, show me your licence'. I did. He tried to read it and did not seem impressed. He came to 'provisional'.

'Professional?'

'Yes.'

I rode on, hoping he had not been typical.

The road to Lake Issyk-Kul ran above the plain and below the mountains, dead straight for miles at a time. The strong sun fried my arms but Boris (I had not given much thought to its name) created a steady anaesthetic wind. The road was rough. The steering was heavy. The engine was loud. The aluminium cooling fins round the cylinder heads near my feet were very hot and my chinless helmet kept slipping back off my forehead. Freedom was no pushover.

Still, with wheat and apple trees beside the road instead of cotton bushes, and two-thirds of a tank still sloshing between my legs, it was hard not to feel that God and Allah were in their heavens and all was right with the world.

I had lunch off the road under a tree yards from a burnt brick tower that is all that remains of the tenth-century Karakhanid city of Balasagun. The top of the tower gave a view of six white villages neatly spaced along the foot of the mountains among squares of green and yellow cultivation. At the bottom there was a map of the Silk Route from Antioch to Xi'an, with Balasagun in the middle.

The Silk Route, which had become *avtodoroga* 365, entered the gorge of the Chu beyond Balasagun and climbed between mountainsides strewn with loose black schist to a broad saddle which held in the lake. I took the gorge at about thirty m.p.h. Halfway up it another Ural overtook doing at least sixty with a passenger in the side-car, which is when I began to suspect that Boris might be sick.

Up on the saddle the road to Naryn and China took a right fork and climbed into arid, dun-coloured mountains to the south.

The gradient eased. At the entrance to the Issyk-Kul Nature Conservation Area there was an emissions check which Boris's tailpipe passed. (My mouth wouldn't have: it was burping unburnt petrol fumes after a failed attempt to re-fill the tank by siphoning from the jerry can.)

At last the climb became an easy roll along the flat. The mountains stood unctuously aside. The horizontal became a gentle descent and the lake came into view.

The scale of the scene was hard to grasp. You could see per-haps the first fifty miles of water, after which its blue surface merged with a heat haze, which merged with the sky. Along either shore ran mountain ranges whose imperfections had been edited by distance. Each was a row of regular rounded pyra-mids, green and brown at the bottom and white at the top. It was a view of a lake fringed by mountains that a child might have drawn. To the north were the Kungey Ala-Too, the sunny mountains, separating Kirghizstan from Kazakhstan. To the south were the Terskey Ala-Too, the shady mountains, separat-ing the lake from the fastnesses of the central Tien Shan.

For three hundred years the lower slopes of these ranges gave the nomadic Kirghiz some of the lushest livelihoods in Central Asia. Some Kirghiz even gave up being nomads, their mi-grations condensed by the magic of height differential. Villages and vegetables grew up on the lakeside, where winters are mild because the lake, being slightly saline, never freezes. In summer the animals and able-bodied men and women would trek up to the *dzhailoo*, the high pasture.

Then the Russians came and took the best land in the name of their god and their Tsar. At first they bothered only with what was easy to farm and close to the lake, leaving the *dzhailoo* to the Kirghiz. But by the time Stephen Graham trudged along the far side of the Kungey Ala-Too they were ploughing up the slopes as well.

In 1916, hearing of a rebellion against the Tsarists in Tashkent, the Kirghiz launched their own revolt and killed two thousand settlers. Russian troops did roughly what Boer or British ones would have done in equivalent circumstances; killed a pro-portion of the natives on suspicion of being ring-leaders, deported the rest and burned their villages to the ground. Partly as a result, third- and fourth-generation Russian immigrants still lived in their grandparents' whitewashed houses in the main towns on the lake. Also partly as a result, they were frightened of the newly independent Kirghiz.

Vladimir Nikolaevich, Nikolai Nikolaevich's brother, was one of those Russians. He lived with his wife and two young sons in a modest walled compound two streets up from the beach at the east end of Rybach'ye. The compound was his castle. Within it were three bedrooms, a garage, three pigs, a hutch of rabbits, self-sufficiency in vegetables, a well, a strawberry patch and cherry trees for fresh fruit and *kompot*. The town had its mayoral office block and its ninety-foot grain silo but neither obscured his view of the lake and the Terskey Ala-Too. He had climbed most of them. He had climbed and mapped most of the Kungey Ala-Too and spent much of his working life protecting its flora and fauna. He loved this place. He had been born here and returned after national service. His parents had built the rabbit hutch. But if he could have got his hands on thirty thousand rubles for the railway container he would have packed it all up and gone to Russia faster than you could say *natsionalizm*.

Natsionalizm had been growing for two years. The Kirghiz were trying to ban Russian and make their own language the official one. The Kirghiz would not consider Russians for posts in the police or the government or at the bus or railway stations. (What did they expect his sons to do? Herd sheep?) The Kirghiz wanted to replace the Russian way of naming people with some ancient tribal system which had no need of surnames; just 'ulu' between the first name and the patronymic.

'Ulu!'

Vladimir got up and left the television room. Real or imagined, *natsionalizm* was getting to him. The subject had arisen because of a long news report on fighting in Moldavia. The camera had stared as if mesmerized at the mutilated dead bodies of ethnic Russians.

Vladimir returned with more cherries.

'We do not yet have war in Kirghizstan, therefore people say we never will. Idiot people including Russians. Friends. They think Kirghizstan will not be like Moldavia and they are fools.'

We walked down to the beach. Some Kirghiz boys were swimming. A white steamer had left the Rybach'ye jetty perhaps twenty minutes earlier, heading east. Its wake had more or less subsided. Beyond the swimmers half a dozen fishing canoes were drifting, each with a single torso upright in the middle, some with lamps. Wavelets trickled in over the coarse sand. Across the lake, between the water and the *dzhailoo*, the lower ramparts of the Terskey Ala-Too had a soft grey colour in the fading light.

Vladimir saw a piece of litter, walked over to it and picked it up.

'No culture,' he said.

It was a *transcendentally* beautiful evening.

I spent the night in Vladimir's spare room, which doubled as a larder, overflowing with jars of cherries on the floor and a fridge full of home-made pork salami. In the morning his wife scrambled eggs for the three of us (the sons were visiting their grandmother in Bishkek), and gave me a tiny Russian translation of Shakespeare's sonnets. The goodbyes were brief. No addresses exchanged. No pledges to keep in touch. Not from Vladimir.

From Rybach'ye a minor road left the lake heading south. The River Chu fell in alongside as it had the previous day. Up on the saddle, the river had seemed about to lose its way. Now it swept decisively out of a V in the mountains, flowing like broadsheet from a printing press and cutting a turquoise swathe through the tussocky brown earth. Yesterday's mystery had been why it did not flow out of the lake. (Issyk-Kul is fed by eighty rivers and drained by none.) Today's was why it did not flow into it. It just didn't. The vast topography of Kirghizstan no doubt held other mysteries too.

The road squeezed into the V and then peeled off up a long alluvial ramp. The slopes on either side were red. The only vegetation was a straggly shrub that perfumed the air as I tried to decide between second and third. From the top of the ramp the road skirted a reservoir that was only half-full and re-joined the main highway to China a few miles before Kochkorka.

Kochkorka lay in a big green bowl with mountains rising above the snowline on three sides, and had a lucky feel about it. The main street had been saved from through-traffic by a by-pass. It was lined with tall deciduous trees, then by broad verges ideal for the tethering of motorbikes and horses, then by neat painted bungalows with picket fences. There was a horse for every bicycle and at least two of each for every car. It was a Kirghiz town. I did not see a single Russian face there. Its central business district consisted of a line of incongruously modern shops and a bazaar. Looking forward to a night out with a camp fire, I hoped to buy a pot, and the first shop in the line sold pots exclusively. For a dollar's worth of rubles I bought a general purpose aluminium cooking pot with a lid and handles, and filled it with salami and *lepeshka* from a canteen down the road. A lucky feel, as I say.

Valery Georgevich had circled a place called Son-Kul on the map. It was another mountain lake, higher than Issyk-Kul and much smaller. I was expecting an ordinary alpine miracle with steep wooded shores, a glade for a tent, a jetty made of stepping stones and perhaps some trout to tickle, but Son-Kul was not like that.

Son-Kul may actually have been sacred. No one said it was, but it had an aura which was either intrinsic holiness or something even stranger. For one thing it was very remote. There was still some way to go and Kochkorka already seemed a long haul from Bishkek, not to mention London.

The road climbed out of the green bowl and into a ravine. There was no rival traffic about and Boris felt quite sprightly. There was a new river for company; a frothing white one crossed occasionally by footbridges. At the head of the ravine, beyond a truck-stop called Sary-Bulak where I bought a small sack of dry biscuits to add to the salami and *lepeshka* in the pot, there was a signpost up a dirt track to Son-Kul, ninety kilometres away. The track began with a steep climb and Boris slipped noisily out of second. That part of the gearbox never really recovered.

The first hill was short. It led to a pass at the end of a long, high valley whose sides and floor were all pastureland. At the foot of the pass were the farmyards and machines of the local collective, and an oddly empty village of breeze-block huts. Beyond these the track continued for two easy hours to another hill which proved altogether tougher for second gear. The hill was a long series of hairpins up a deep notch in the south side of the valley. I should have taken them all in first but was too impatient.

We ground to a halt several times, with horrible tearing noises coming from under the saddle. Having no clue about motorcycle maintenance beyond what Grigori had taught me I had no choice but to treat Boris as if he were a horse. During one of his rests I saw a shepherd on a real horse trotting down the far side of the valley beside a stream towards a tent. The sky was a blemishless blue. The grass shared the soft turf with millions of tiny flowers. The cool air ruffled them but the silence was total. It wasn't a bad place to have to stop.

In fits and starts we wound on past the snowline, through a herd of black yak and over a high pass that revealed the lake.

I turned off the engine and stared. Son-Kul was hardly a lake at all. It was more like a prairie emerging from a swim. It was a distant oval mirror twenty miles across and still ten miles away, ringed by mountains, floating on a billiard table. It was God's *aide-mémoire* to remind him what the world looked like after the great flood. It was very quiet. It had been quiet below the pass but if silence has an address it would be Son-Kul. I began freewheeling down towards the water.

The first yurt appeared almost at once, in a dell below the track with a wisp of smoke coming from the hole in its roof. I took its picture in a rush in case it disappeared. A yurt! A real yurt in the wild, on the *dzhailoo*! More of them appeared every few minutes: round, white, soft and sturdy, hiding cleverly in the contours like so many mushrooms. The design had not changed in a thousand years and its oldness came as a mild sort of ambush.

The track skirted the lake eastwards to a low bridge over a stream swollen with the afternoon's melted snow. The stream's banks were made of soggy grass. Grass covered the long, shallow slope to the lake, all the way round it. Grass carpeted the mountains all the way up to the snow. Grass was everywhere, evenly cropped and watered, ready to eat.

On one side of the stream there was an empty row of stables, on the other a yurt and a caravan with a red cross between its windows. This was the closest thing to a village for three hours in either direction. Valery Georgevich had lent me a musty tent-shaped tent with room for two, called a Pamirka. I rode up the slope beyond the stream and pitched it at the foot of a knoll, using tools and stones instead of tent pegs. The afternoon ended very gradually.

That night I lay on the grass in a down-filled jacket, also lent by Valery, and watched the stars.

One of them moved. An aeroplane. London–Singapore? Thirty-nine thousand feet? Something like that. Businessmen and stewardesses. Bone china and vintage wines in Club. In-flight entertainment, briefcases full of photocopying, suitcases full of suits, minds full of schemes and rackets and anxieties. I doubted if a single one of them had anything to do with Kirghiz-stan. I doubted if a single person in that aeroplane would ever even hear of this bewitching sanctuary below them. We were separated by a few thousand feet of air but we might as well have been in different centuries.

Contrary to the Soviet version of the history of the Kirghiz people they have not inhabited the Tien Shan for two thousand years. They came here from the Far East in the sixteenth century having been driven there from south central Siberia in 1293 by Kublai Khan.

Like the Mongols, with whom they inter-bred for at least two hundred years around the time of the crusades, the nomadic Kirghiz were totally dependent on their horses – for transport, leather, food, fun and intoxicating liquor. Kirghiz babies lived the cliché and rode before they walked. Kirghiz adolescents chased each other for their kisses in a horseback mêlée called *kesh kumai*. Kirghiz shepherds rode for days to find lost sheep, or just to get some peace. Kirghiz elders measured wealth in horses and supervised their breeding. When horses died they were eaten. As they lived they were milked. Some milk was drunk fresh, some fermented into *koumis*. On working days *koumis* was drunk in moderation; on feast days in excess.

I woke to a feast day.

A doctor in a tweed jacket and fur hat came over from the caravan with the red cross and stood on the far side of the stream with a pair of binoculars in a leather case in one hand and a flask of *koumis* in the other. The binoculars stayed in the case. They seemed to be his credentials.

He beckoned me over. The melting had stopped overnight and the stream was easily jumped. Back in the caravan we drank the *koumis*.

Stephen Graham thought *koumis* 'a pleasant drink', which was an oddly neutral reaction. It smelt of sweat and triggered a sequence of not obviously related associations on hitting the palate: sweat, salt, beer, milk, bubbles, stilton, beer, salt. At least it was strong. After six glasses it was, if not pleasant, then persuasive.

The doctor looked about eighty years old. He had been trained after the war in Tokmak, near Bishkek in the valley of the Chu, and had fifteen thousand patients, most of them yurt-dwellers, all within two days' ride. They did not seem to be taxing him too much. The surgery contained four bunks, three of them empty, the fourth covered with drying meat. He said he only drank *koumis* for breakfast on special occasions, and I confess I thought he was referring to my visit.

Burping and unsteady, I set off up the mountain behind the caravan. The summit looked close but still took two-thirds of the day to get to and the other third to get down from. It gave views of much of central Kirghizstan: the back of the Terskey Ala-Too and the mountains behind Bishkek; the Fergana range to the west; maybe even a hint of the monsters of the Central Tien Shan a hundred and fifty miles to the east. Maybe not, but I had learned not to trust clouds.

On the way down, tired from having sunk a long way into the snow, I happened on the feast. Men in dark suits, the doctor in his fur hat among them, were milling around the door of a yurt. It was one of three yurts pitched in a choice position above a stream and far enough below a rounded spur to be protected from the wind. Women wearing long-sleeved cotton gowns in reds and oranges and sober woollen waistcoats as overgarments were sitting on a huge rug laid out on the grass. They were singing a round that came up towards me over the stream more as an ululation than a melody. Horses grazed on the spur, not tethered but not going anywhere. Beyond the spur was the lake.

As I approached the yurts a young man came up to meet me and offered tea. He was the only one not formally dressed, though he did have on an *ak-kalpak*, the traditional white felt Kirghiz hat. He plucked a woman from the group on the rug and once we were installed in the largest yurt she brought the tea. As the guest I sat at the back facing the door, leaning against a bed. The only light came from a hole in the middle of the roof. It took several seconds to make out, in the gloom, the red wooden frame and the rowdy felt hangings stretched over it, and the hundreds of bright woven straps holding everything together. In the middle of the floor there was a mound of fried dough balls and a bowl of butter. The young man sat across the corner of the mat and introduced himself as Sultan. He invited me to eat.

'We have had a wedding today,' he said.

The dough balls were better than they looked. I said it must have been a splendid wedding and asked where the bride and groom were.

'Here,' said Sultan.

He looked up at the young woman pouring the tea.

'This is Gulna.'

Gulna smiled very charmingly. Sultan asked my opinion of the yurt and I tried to make up for my gaffe with all the Russian words I knew for 'excellent' and 'beautiful'.

'It is my wedding yurt,' he said. 'I invite you.'

What seemed at first to be a general welcome turned out to be a specific invitation to share their wedding night. I did not accept at once. They laughed and said there would be six other people anyway, excluding children. Friends had ridden over from the far side of the lake and could not be expected to ride back at night after so much *koumis*. Besides. Gulna put down the tea-pot and fished a sleeping baby out from under the bed behind me.

'Our first,' she said. 'One year.'

There wasn't much left to be consummated so I said I would love to stay the night. *Koumis* was brought. With it came Sultan's father, who called me Jack London and took me for a spy. His son said to take no notice.

Before the light went everyone gathered on the rug outside and I took the wedding pictures. Then those who lived nearby saddled up and rode off into the sunset. I walked down to fetch Boris. There was apparently a track up to the encampment suitable for wheeled vehicles, but it was hard to make out. During an attempt to cross the stream Boris sank up to his axles in a bog. No amount of revving would budge him. I raced back up to the camp for help.

'Problem. Motorcycle in river. Sorry.'

Sultan was snoozing but Su-un Bek, his little brother,

grabbed a halter and ran out on to the spur. So did everyone else, eventually, pulling on coats and whistling at the horses. A bevvy of giggling sisters in galoshes spread out into a semi-circle to head off runaways. The father stood near the yurts cracking open walnuts with a knife and shouting 'Mister Jack, Mister Jack'. Sultan, still sleepy, emerged with a basin of oatmeal and lunged when his horse came within reach. Su-un Bek scampered everywhere but not quite fast enough.

Sultan's horse would not be caught. It would take another one to catch it. The sun had sunk below the mountains but by an orange glow left in the eastern sky the departing wedding guests could be seen riding slowly down the great green slope towards the lake. I whistled frantically. Sultan's father yodelled, but into the wind. They didn't hear. I pictured Boris sinking out of sight.

Then a miracle rode up out of the dusk; a rodeo king with dark eyes and a hare-lip, mounted on a sweating stallion. He took the halter from Su-un Bek and set off after the riderless horse, round and round the circle of spectators, cheered on as he broke from a canter into a gallop, leaning forward, legs forward, whirling the rope like a cowboy, silhouetted against the orange as the orange turned to mauve and the mauve to purple. Even if Boris had sunk without trace it would have been worth it for this.

Boris hadn't. The renegade was caught and Sultan rode down to the bog with the miracle man, who turned out to be his other brother, Alik. They considered harnessing the horses to Boris's front forks but it seemed too much trouble and they ended up heaving him out with their bare hands. I had walked down with the sisters. Three of them climbed on to the side-car and Alik gave them a lift back up, taking an impossible route at an impossible speed and shredding what remained of second gear.

There was more *koumis* before bed, but not much more. Everyone was tired. The bed at the back of the wedding yurt had been made up for me with thick striped quilts. The other guests slept on blankets on the floor. There was a screen to give Sultan and Gulna some token privacy, but it seemed to be enough. As I stared up at the moonlit hole in the roof and listened to the happy couple coupling I realized that the idea of finding a patch of Central Asia untrammelled by the twentieth century was no longer merely an idea. It had taken shape. It was this yurt, this sagging bed, the animal smell of the quilts under my nose and the sounds of snoring and copulation a few feet away. It could not have been more wonderful, and it was close enough to paradise for me.

We were woken in the morning by the sun coming in through the hole in the roof, and by hundreds of sheep tramping past the yurt on their way up to higher pastures. For breakfast we finished the wedding food and washed it down with tea to which Gulna added *koumis* even though it curdled it.

I gave her the biscuits I had bought in Sary-Bulak, and Sultan some cigarettes. After warm farewells and earnest promises to send the wedding photos to an address in Kochkorka where Alik would pick them up I rode carefully back to the lake-shore road, avoiding bogs.

A track left the lake and followed its outflow, zig-zagging where the water plunged over waterfalls and re-joining the main road between Sary-Bulak and Naryn. Tash Rabat was a strenuous day's ride beyond Naryn, and Boris would never have made it there but for the sharp eye of Alik Mulukbaev and the steady hand of his brother.

Alik was the man from the fuel depot at Naryn whose name Vica had typed on a piece of card. He saw petrol dripping from a carburettor and took it apart. His brother, a dentist, peeled off a perished rubber seal and cut a new one from a vinyl floor tile with a pair of nail scissors. I was to prevail on their kindness again, too soon.

After a night as Alik's guest, I took the road to Tash Rabat over a ridge behind Naryn and down in the last high valley before the last high range of mountains before China. That was if you looked south. If you looked east or west there were more rising pastures, more clefts of juniper forest, more granite sentinels, more snowfields and hanging glaciers. Kirghizstan's mountains were inexhaustible. There seemed to be a new, perfectly formed, alluringly untouched line of mountains the length and breadth of the Pyrenees for every weekend of the year.

The one that hid Tash Rabat was called the At-Bashi range and I bumped along the bottom of it for most of the day, heading south-west. The road was unpaved. Jeeps and lorries on their way to China sent up choking clouds of dust. Occasionally bees feasting on the nectar of poppies along the valley floor slapped me in the face.

The road climbed imperceptibly so that by the turn-off to Tash Rabat the mountains to the left seemed to have shrunk. Boris took them on bravely; in third.

Ten miles off the main road the little side valley turned a corner and opened out to the width of a meadow, where the track ended in a car park. A car park. I might have known. Someone had made a postcard of Tash Rabat, after all. At first I was dismayed, but in the two days I camped next to it no one else used it and I went back to feeling like a pioneer.

Beside the car park stood the caravanserai, half-embedded in the slope, welcoming occasional Intourist clients as it had welcomed silk traders through a huge fortified gateway made of horizontal slabs of granite.

It had been discreetly restored. Behind the gateway there was a dome of the same granite slabs, now stuck to each other with trowel-fulls of cement where they had begun to cave in. The mud-floored space underneath was as big as a barn. It was dark and cool all day and smelt of the cows which strayed in there at night. Tash-Rabat had not yet stooped to electricity or captions.

The cows belonged to Meelis, a gamekeeper and hunting guide who lived with his parents in a tiny white house across the car park from the caravanserai, next to the stream.

Once he got used to the idea of an *Anglichanin* Meelis seemed glad of the extra company. He lent me a horse and led the way up one of the few still-unpaved sections of the Silk Route to Asia's continental divide. We left the *dzhailoo* far behind and looked down from thirteen thousand feet into China, almost. In fact the bleaker, lower mountains which marked the western edge of Xinjiang were blurred by haze, though through the telescopic sight of Meelis's rifle (he had hoped to bag an ibex) we could make out a lonely lake called Chatyr-Kul whose far shore was the border.

Meelis said Marco Polo had come this way a hundred years

ago. Marco Polo actually came a rather different way seven hundred years ago, but Meelis's foreshortening of time seemed fitting.

On the way down he described hunting wolves in winter, which he did to protect the cattle. Winter was the only time the wolves left traces but the temperature routinely fell to minus forty. The horses were shod with spikes and sometimes had to fight through two metres of snow. I asked what he wore to keep warm and he said he had a complete suit of inside-out sheepskin. I asked how the horses kept warm and he said they breathed hard.

Back at the meadow by the car park he couldn't resist tinkering with Boris, tightening his spokes and pumping up the spare tyre. It was kind, but not sufficient.

Halfway up a long hill on the way back to Naryn the engine stopped communicating with the rear wheel. There was no movement to be had in any gear. Just an ugly grinding noise. It sounded terminal.

Heavenly Mountains

❧❧❧❧

The driveshaft was the problem. It was a case of excessive torque, soft alloy and mechanical sex. Where the toothed male end of the driveshaft entered the gearbox the female hole that was meant to drive it round and round had stripped it. Eaten it alive.

Alik Mulukbaev and his brother came to the rescue. They stopped what they were doing and worked on Boris until he was mended and there was nothing I could do to repay them.

'You are a long way from home,' Alik said. 'You have a problem, so we help.' That was that.

Fortunately the hill on which the driveshaft went was the last before Naryn. I did not realize this and feared that Boris might be stolen while I was away getting help. But a jeep gave me a lift and I found myself at the fuel depot within a quarter of an hour.

Alik was signing for half a million rubles in cash. He stuffed the bricks of new notes in his briefcase and we roared back to Boris in his Lada.

'You're rich,' I said.

'I have to buy a train of petrol,' he grinned. 'Maybe half. Five hundred tonnes.'

He was leaving for Bishkek by official Volga before dawn the following day. There he would make some inter-city calls and fly to Samara (above Volgograd on the Volga) or Krasnovodsk, depending on where there was fuel to be had and at what price. Such was the reality of economic collapse. The mission would have been unthinkable the previous year.

We towed Boris to the top of the hill. Alik freewheeled all the way down to his house on the motorbike while I followed in the car. With much banging the driveshaft was removed.

'Novyi cardan,' said Alik, clucking. New driveshaft (needed). It was a phrase I learned. He phoned Al-Akbar, his brother.

Al-Akbar stopped halfway through a crowning job and told the patient to come back later.

People need petrol and people need teeth. Alik and Al-Akbar were well-placed in Naryn's barter economy and Al-Akbar, who happened to be better-placed than Alik in the matter of driveshafts, drove with me to the police chief's house. The police chief directed us to a police cadet's caravan. The police cadet listened to Al-Akbar and cheerfully dismantled his own Ural to provide us with a *novyi cardan*.

'He won't have to wait next time he needs his teeth done,' said Al-Akbar on the way back to Alik's house.

Boris's new driveshaft was installed in a five-hour operation that ended after midnight. I tried to help but was no use and was put in the sauna instead. After that Alik's nephew Rustam, who was visiting from Fergana, ushered me into the sitting room for a screening of *Terminator 2: Judgment Day*, with Arnold Schwarzenegger dubbed into Kirghiz.

Between washing the engine grease off his hands and departing for Bishkek Alik hardly slept. I thanked him, hopelessly.

'When you come to England . . .' I began, and he interrupted with a huge laugh.

'If I ever come to England it will be as a gangster. I will be so rich you will have to be my guest in a hotel.'

Once mended, Boris attracted attention in other more dangerous ways. Nikolai Nikolaevich, the geologist-mountaineer who was Valery Georgevich's partner in Dostuk Trekking, would be in Kara-Kol at the eastern end of Lake Issyk-Kul in two days' time and had suggested I meet him there for an expedition to the central Tien Shan. Returning to Kochkorka I pulled off the road into a large lay-by from which a short path led to a roadside restaurant in the style of a chalet. The restaurant nestled among trees in the bottom of a gorge and the lay-by was on a slope. I walked up the path. The restaurant was closed. Back in the lay-by Boris had disappeared and been replaced by a furious young man in an *ak-kalpak* who berated me in Kirghiz before switching to Russian.

'You are a BAD MAN without intelligence. I was sleeping and almost I never woke up.'

He pointed to some bushes. Boris was embedded in them. He held his two trembling index fingers an inch apart. An inch seemed to be the amount by which Boris (Boris of the 1000 kilograms) had missed his head while rolling into the bushes. I gave the man a lift back to his village and took great care over parking after that.

Beyond Kochkorka, zooming along in the dappled shade of the tall trees which both heralded the town and bid you farewell on its behalf, we were stopped for speeding, which felt rather glamorous, but the traffic police refused to fine a foreigner. Instead they asked if I had any sunglasses for sale.

'I'm so sorry. This is my only pair.'

'No problem,' they said. 'Good road in our beautiful republic.' And on we zoomed, immune.

The sunglasses were stolen the next day by a sharp-eyed teenager who gave me a push-start halfway along the south shore of Issyk-Kul. The road was made of teeth-chattering, shoulder-shaking rippled tarmac. I had stopped for a rest and been unable to get Boris started again. The sunglasses were actually prescription glasses with clip-ons and their loss was more irritating than the thief could know, but it was hard to be irritated for long beside Issyk-Kul.

Up to the right were steep wooded valleys, like the dark bits in nudes, and glimpses of glaciers. Every few miles streams rushed out of the valleys and under the road. Down to the left was the lake, vast and dark blue and majestically deep. It was far too big to have remained secret from Soviet resort-builders and, sure enough, the choicest headlands and beaches were adorned with concrete blocks with lake-view balconies and adjoining concrete balneotherapy centres. But even they were easy to ignore. Lake Issyk-Kul was that grand.

The rendezvous with Nikolai Nikolaevich passed off according to plan. It took place in a muddy yard full of six-wheeled geological survey trucks outside Kara-Kol. I had to ask directions only once, of a telephone engineer. He didn't know where the *baza geologov* was but reckoned his colleagues back at the exchange would, so he strapped a pair of steel jaws on to the insides of his feet, walked up the nearest telegraph pole and asked them. By way of thanks I tried to make a joke about the superfluousness of mobile phones when you have a pair of steel foot-jaws handy, but he didn't get it.

Nikolai was hard to miss in a fluorescent red jersey. In Bishkek he had worn the anxieties of business more heavily than his partner, Valery Georgevich. His humour there had been rationed, his smile thin, his deliberations formal. He was Vladimir's brother, after all. But in his bright red jersey, away from the city among old geology friends and hardware, he was positively *animé*.

Nikolai took me to see another lake, named after a Bavarian geographer called Merzbacher who discovered it in 1903. It filled the entrance to the North Inylchek valley, twelve thousand feet up near the junction of the Kirghiz, Kazakh and Chinese borders. Nikolai had explained that for most of the year it was held in by a passing glacier but that every summer an ice plug in the glacier melted and the lake drained in three days, like a bath.

He was taking me there gratis in the hope that I would tempt others to pay him to take them there. He was also escorting six Spaniards to Dostuk Trekking's own base camp on the glacier above the lake, from which they hoped to climb Kirghizstan's highest mountains.

The Spaniards were snoozing in one of the geology trucks. They were *Madrileños* who sang a lot, slept a lot, ate a lot and shaved very little. Between them and their dozens of barrels of equipment they filled the truck, so for the next stage of the journey I stayed with Boris.

We entered the mountains in convoy at the extreme eastern end of the Issyk-Kul basin. The road was smooth at first. The views were straight from chocolate boxes and the air was scented by stately Kirghiz pines. Then it started raining. A memorial bulldozer appeared on a boulder. The hairpins began. The rain turned to hail. The hail turned to snow, the alp to scree, the tarmac to rubble, the scree to landslides-in-waiting. I was very cold and wished I was in one of the yurts beside the road. Boris chugged on, overtaking the truck. At the top of the pass the truck caught up and Nikolai barked at me to keep going or I'd catch hypothermia.

The word 'Inylchek' was somehow redolent of Eskimos and

ducklings. I was hoping for tents, huts, woodsmoke and the sound of chopping, but Inylchek turned out to be a disused mining town. The ore was tin ore, Nikolai said, but it had not been touched since the invention of the plastic bag. Later someone said the closing down of Inylchek had been political; a Moscow move to thin out Kirghizstan's industrial base. It was an eerie place on a wide, flat valley floor where two grey rivers met.

We spent a night there in geological survey huts. It was cold outside but Dostuk Trekking rustled up a casserole of longhorn sheep, and Nikolai provided alcohol to wash it down. Neat alcohol. The Spaniards declined it, saying it would give them headaches at this altitude, but I tried some and so did the expedition nurse. It stung my chapped lips, to which she afterwards applied some cream.

The helipad was a grass shelf fifteen miles up the same wide valley and the helicopter was an Mi-8 MTB, with five rotors and a big orange pod and twin turbines that could shatter a geological era's worth of accumulated peace in a nanosecond. It had 'Aeroflot' in blue on each side and kerosene smudges like thunderclouds below the two exhausts. It was the Lord of the Skies. The Dominator. It was a drug and I duly became addicted to it.

That first trip lasted half an hour. (On a mule it would have been a week.) We flew for fifty miles up the Inylchek valley with the cabin shaking and the windows open. Nikolai picked coolly at a box of cherries while the rest of us stuck our heads out to be deafened and re-coiffed by a freezing hundred-mile-an-hour wind. Halfway through the flight we heaved over the monstrous grey snout of the Inylchek glacier, and smaller, cleaner glaciers began to tumble down the fearsome cliffs on either side.

We landed in a strange world of blizzards, avalanches, masochists, potato soup, and saintly women in pink duvets. The base camp, Svyezdochka, was on the glacier's north lateral moraine beneath the fluted snow walls and black rock fins of Peak Maxim Gorky. It consisted of a dining hut and half a dozen tents, the biggest of them housing a military two-way radio on a trestle table. There was also a half-built sauna beside an icy pool filled by a lost trickle of meltwater. Across the glacier, set back at the head of its own cwm and resembling a colossal slice of baked Alaska, was the north face of Pik Pobieda – Peak Victory. It was so high that when blocks of ice the size of small hotels broke off the top they could take three minutes to rumble down into the cwm. Instead of subsiding there they would send up clouds of powder snow that threatened to advance into the main valley and engulf us but somehow never did.

The head of alpine operations at Svyezdochka was a hulking protégé of Nikolai's called Sasha; a champion climber in his blond, musculatured prime who had built most of the camp by way of relaxation between training sorties along the sharp and unstable 21,000-foot-high ridge of which Peak Maxim Gorky was a part. He was lurking Achilles-like in his tent when we arrived on foot having landed in the middle of the glacier and picked our way in training shoes through a web of crevasses to the moraine.

Nikolai told him I would need a place to pitch my tent. He leaped up the slope above the dining hut and produced a neat ledge the size of a Pamirka in five minutes of Stakhanovite boul-der-heaving. He put up the tent too, for good measure, in a flash, securing the guy ropes with more boulders, leaving the canvas drum tight and perfectly symmetrical. It was exhausting to watch.

The women in pink were Lena the nurse, Vica whom I knew, and Nastia. Nastia had come from Moscow to interpret for the Spaniards. Their lipstick-coloured feather-filled overcoats were provided by the company. The Spaniards were not used to hav-ing women on their expeditions and at first considered them a distraction. Later, one by one, they fell in love.

Nikolai intended that I walk down the glacier to Lake Merz-bacher with some Siberian climbers who were staying at the camp. The plan was delayed by their ascent of Khan Tengri, and by their condition on their return.

Khan Tengri looks innocent enough in postcards: a beautiful marble pyramid which climbers usually approached from a safe col to the west. But the summit was still twenty-four thousand feet above sea-level and the Siberians had been stuck below it in a blizzard for three days without much oxygen or any food.

They were all but dead on arrival. They had swollen, purple faces and lips like barbecued king prawns. For three days they lay silently in their tents, venturing out only to shuffle like ghosts to the dining hut, where Lena would tend their black frostbitten toes with a pair of scissors, a bottle of antiseptic and a saucer to catch the dead blood.

'We suffer to live and we live to suffer,' Nastia explained.

The Spaniards lived to enjoy themselves and the contrast was so blatant it was almost embarrassing. They had space age techno-clothes which ruled out frostbite. They had walkie-talkies that could bounce them to Madrid off any passing satellite when they were homesick. And their barrels were full of *salchichas*, *chorizos*, *jamones*, *bonbones* and other flavour-enhanced, vitamin-enriched, vacuum-packed rocket boosters which were meant for high-altitude assault camps but started to appear in the dining hut when the deluge of potato soup showed no sign of letting up.

One afternoon, while the Siberians recuperated, the Spaniards walked up the glacier to the advance base camp for Khan Tengri. They let me go with them even though the most suitable footwear I could muster was a pair of walking boots called Dickies from a shop in Oxford Street. The camp was a village of geodesic dome tents out on the ice, busy with Swiss and South Korean expeditions from a separate base camp on the other side of the glacier supplied from Kazakhstan. The Swiss and Koreans had even groovier equipment than the Spaniards. It zinged with corporate logos and its owners eyed us disapprovingly.

'*Somos los mas gordos aquí*,' said one of the Spaniards, sitting on a rock and taking off his boots. 'We are the fattest people here.' It was true. We laughed, a tad nervously, and trudged back for more potato soup.

While the Siberians' recovery continued the Spaniards set off in earnest for Khan Tengri. Rather than be at a loose end I followed them, in borrowed boots, as half of a hastily organized two-man team which had Nikolai's blessing to go 'until the motor has enough'. The motor was apparently my heart. My guide was Sergei, another protégé. He was less of a statue than Sasha, with a limp and a mangled nose. But he was super-fit, inured to pain, in love with the mountains and possessed of a few words of French.

Our equipment was old-fashioned and user-unfriendly; the bare minimum for survival. I told myself it was not foolhardy to be using it, merely rugged. We left the advance base camp before dawn and before even the Koreans had stirred. For four hours we slogged up a twisting ice-fall towards the west col. Sergei imagined I'd be slow but until elevenses I managed to surprise him, concentrating only on the next step. Khan Tengri itself was no distraction. It is said to be the most perfect mountain in the Tien Shan but was lost in cloud. There was a quiet snowstorm in progress.

'*Ça va le motor?*' Sergei would ask.

'*Ça va,*' I would reply, trying to ignore the thumping in my throat.

Then Koreans in neon yellow centrally heated Spandex salopettes started overtaking and the route reached a steep pitch during which the thumping became so loud that I could not breathe fast enough to drown it out. At the top Sergei built a snow seat and made tea.

'*Ça va le motor?*'

All of a sudden I felt sleepy.

'*Ça va pas.*'

'*On descend?*'

'*S'il vous plaît.*'

Discretion was the better part of valour that day. (We were also lucky; the following year four British climbers were killed by an avalanche near where we had stopped for tea and wise-after-the-eventers said the traditional route to the col should have been abandoned long ago because of avalanche danger.) The next day it was the other way round. Three of the Siberians had recovered and were ready to head for Lake Merzbacher. We left at eight in the morning with what Nikolai said was an easy six-hour stroll ahead of us – down the main glacier, past tributary glaciers with absurd names like Komsomolskaya Pravda and Proletarskaya Turist, to Zilyoni Polana (Green Meadow), the campsite for the lake. Ten hours later we were still out there on an endless snaking ridge of loose stones in the middle of the ice leviathan which had formed this harsh, vertiginous, monochromatic mountainscape, which made ants of the humans doomed to walk in it. At dusk we were still miles from land, exhausted, anxious, slowed down by a foreigner complaining of a damaged knee, then of a strained heart, then begging them to stop even as dusk turned to darkness and the heavens opened and the going became slippery as well as blind and riddled with crevasses that had to be crossed to reach the campsite, which, with each passing hour of night, remained 'just two kilometres ahead' until the foreigner stopped believing in it and cursed his guides for seeming not to suffer, and eventually stopped caring about anything, and saw a light.

It was ten o'clock.

Under an orange awning in the middle of Green Meadow some schoolmasters from Westminster were downing digestifs and playing chess. They looked up as we entered.

One said: 'Have a jellybaby.'

Another offered Earl Grey, English Breakfast and Assam. The Siberians stood silently behind me, dripping. We went for English Breakfast with a dash of lemon.

It would have been an even more peculiar encounter had it not been planned. As it was, the imperturbable and friendly Westminstonians were expected up at the Svyezdochka camp later in the week. They were on a Dostuk Trekking trek that ended there. In the mean time they hoped, like me, to see Lake Merzbacher. Nikolai had brought us together in a piece of transmontane troop deployment worthy of the closing chapters of the Great Game.

The lake eluded us. It was on the far side of the glacier and the next day we got close enough to see icebergs drifting sail-like across the blue-black water between the dark jaws of the North Inylchek valley. But physical contact – the dipping-in of toes – depended on the arrangement of crevasses in any given year. This year they were ill-arranged. The schoolmasters had their own Russian guide who said, when we were one hundred yards from the shore, that it might take two days to find a way through.

We had tortellini and ragu for lunch (the schoolmasters had brought their own supplies) and ambled back across the glacier during the afternoon, pushing boulders into crevasses and talking about England.

By this time the glacier was not simply the glacier. It was the sodding glacier. I had had enough of ice and the shifting grey geo-debris that encrusted it and the constant fear of being swallowed by a giant blue slit-mouth, then killed, frozen, compressed to parchment thickness and deposited a century later twenty miles down the valley. I told the schoolmasters that walking back up to the base camp was going to be hell and I didn't want to do it with them. Not if there was an alternative.

The alternative arrived the next morning, heralded by its unmistakable throb. In the whole world of engineering there is nothing closer to a mating call than the sound of an approaching helicopter. This one came down the valley, not up from Inylchek. It paused over Lake Merzbacher, then turned to look across the glacier. It may have been persuaded by our frantic waving or it may have been coming anyway. As it dipped its nose and charged towards us over the waves of ice and moraine, and the throb crescendoed and re-echoed off the mountains into an apocalyptic bellowing, I packed. The schoolmasters helpfully threw at me things they didn't want to carry up the glacier. The helicopter waited a foot above the flattened glass and the pilot tut-tutted.

As I ran for the door he slid open his window and flipped down his microphone.

'WHERE TO?'

'SVYEZDOCHKA. UNDER MAXIM GORKY.'

'IMPOSSIBLE. I CAN'T LAND THERE.'

The wind from the rotors made it hard to stand up.

'YES, YOU CAN.' (Sasha had built a helipad below the dining hut.) 'I'LL SHOW YOU.'

'I'M GOING TO KAZAKHSTAN FIRST.'

'THEN WHERE?'

'HOW MUCH?'

'TWENTY.'

'TWENTY WHAT?'

I thought for a second.

'POUNDS. BIGGER THAN DOLLARS.'

He nodded and flipped the microphone back in position.

Aeroflot. Number one in the Tien Shan for value, customer service and thrills.

The main cabin was empty bar four groggy-looking climbers and their equipment. To get to Kazakhstan we spiralled up a steep cwm on the far side of the valley, thundered over the sculpted icing of the Khan Tengri ridge. Then we descended gradually over lesser ranges to a roadhead where a cook and cardboard boxes of supplies were waiting to be ferried to the Kazakh base camp on the glacier. We returned there by a not much less spectacular route and, having dropped the cook and cardboard boxes, proceeded with a few sudden swerves to Sasha's new helipad.

It was a memorable morning. At one point, on the way down into Kazakhstan, the pilot had seemed about to land on a lonely sweep of *dzhailoo* but instead hovered inches above the grass for five minutes while the co-pilot picked wild mushrooms. Such was the strangeness of subsistence-living in a former super-power, where the official helicopter charter rate was four hundred dollars an hour.

The Spaniards were on Khan Tengri. Sasha was on Peak Maxim Gorky. Vica and Nastia were bored. Lena had found a boyfriend in the Kazakh camp. Sergei was busy finishing the sauna. Nikolai was busy keeping everybody busy getting ready for the Westminstonians. I was enjoying (and probably abusing) his hospitality and was secretly tempted by the idea of another day or two of Blighty banter with the schoolmasters. But whatever staying on might add up to it would not have much to do with Kirghizstan. I decided to start the long journey back to the real world, and took the next helicopter down to Inylchek.

On cue, Merzbacher began to drain.

'You were destined to miss it,' said a pigeon-chested dervish dossing in one of the geology survey huts. When I arrived he had been standing motionless in his porch dressed only in swimming trunks, staring at the sun. I tried not to disturb him but he slid out of his pose like a mime artist.

'I am Saïd,' he said.

'Hello.'

He touched my bottom lip, which was chapped.

'Does it hurt?'

'No. It's fine. It was worse but it's much better.'

He tried exorcizing my bad karma by looking grimly at the lip and holding up to it the fingers of his right hand. Every few seconds he would point them towards the ground with an odd rustling noise.

He wanted me to take my clothes off, pointing to the white skin under my shirt and explaining that my soul was a snake frustrated by the refusal of its urbanized human body to slough.

Boris started first time, which was a relief. The river carrying the meltwater from the Inylchek glacier was in thunderous, angry spate. Nikolai had said it rose ten feet within an hour of Merzbacher's ice-plug giving way. The road to Issyk-Kul crossed it. Heavy grey waves pounded the bridge, which seemed sure to disintegrate and join the water on its suicidal journey into the Takla-Makan, the Chinese desert that is supposed to devour every man and droplet fool enough to enter it. But the bridge stayed in its pilings. I shivered briefly in Lake Merzbacher's chilly spray, then rode back over the high pass where Nikolai had told me not to stop in the snow, and down past the yurts and the memorial bulldozer and through the pinewoods above the floodplain of Lake Issyk-Kul, and at length to the town of Kara-Kol where two weeks earlier the telephone engineer had strapped on his steel jaws.

Kara-Kol was supposed to be Kirghizstan's Geneva. President Askar Akayev, a physicist without a Party past and with a real yen for markets and voting, wanted Kirghizstan to be the Switzerland of Central Asia. It was not yet clear what Kirghizstan would export, nor whether it could manage Swiss-style inter-cantonal harmony. The fighting between Kirghiz and Uzbeks in Osh in 1990 had not been a hopeful start. But the geography was all in place. Like Switzerland, Kirghizstan was mountainous and landlocked with four larger neighbours. Its Lac Leman was Issyk-Kul. Its Geneva was this cool colonial outpost at the gateway to the high Tien Shan.

Kara-Kol had its old town. Not Calvinist old on the one hand nor Kirghiz old on the other, but Russian old; a bazaar made of long wooden sheds divided into shops, with steps up to ver-andas that also served as sidewalks and broad eaves for shel-tered shopping in all four seasons. The straight streets rising from the bazaar towards the mountains were lined with wooden homes, some with two storeys and even grand carved lintels, all in the shade of evergreens.

It was the first week of September, and there was light rain every afternoon. Each time it came I was reminded that even in the deserts the big heat would have passed by now. It was somehow satisfying to know that I had been in Central Asia long enough to see a season come and go. But before that season was replaced by the opposite extremes of winter I had to return to Tashkent and from there follow the last third of Stephen Graham's route up the eastern edge of Kazakhstan, with the steppe on my left and the Tien Shan on my right, to the Altai.

I found a room in a comfortable hotel where Valentin, a former motocross trainer, ran a travel agency. He took Boris for a spin and diagnosed further carburettor trouble besides the non-existent second gear. He put me in the side-car and with much revving and skidding piloted us to a garage. He bought a cog and wrote out the address of the master mechanic on the north side of the lake who would fit it. There would be nothing to pay. Valentin's name would guarantee red-carpet treatment. As for the carburettors, he dismantled them and ripped from each a metal pin which he said had been restricting fuel supply. Boris would now do 120 kilometres an hour, *vizzout prablyem*.

The master mechanic on the north shore charged a thousand rubles to explain that the cog was a third-gear cog and therefore useless. The fuel supply was freed-up as Valentin had promised, but with no obvious effect on Boris's top speed. His fuel consumption simply doubled.

Along the north shore there were plenty of holidaying families with petrol cans whose contents could be bought, if not for rubles, then for dollars and the promise of a photograph from England. But away from the lake life on the road became an endless hunt for petrol.

It was a windy afternoon when I rode through Kochkorka for the third time. Instead of following the Naryn road I turned west, hoping to improvise a high-level route to Tashkent. The change of direction made the wind a head wind. The road gained height steadily, up a long green valley like the parallel one leading to Son-Kul, and the head wind became a cold wind.

The tank was less than half empty. I crouched over the handle-bars to save fuel and keep warm. A desperate-looking Kirghiz couple stranded beside the road with another Ural flagged me down and begged for some petrol. As a test for God, to see if he existed, I gave them five litres which they siphoned into a clever collapsible container that looked like a wellington boot.

He did! God was up there in the fast-moving grey clouds above the long green valley in the lonely heart of Kirghizstan. (I had suspected it at Balasagun, and again on first entering Kochkorka's beautiful bowl, and again at Son-Kul.) He arrived in a gleaming Toyota in the person of a Kirghiz businessman who had stopped at the pass at the head of the valley to stretch His legs and admire the view. He opened His gleaming boot to reveal the mother of all back-up petrol tanks, from which He filled Boris's tank and my jerry can, refusing all payment. On the way down the far side of the pass I felt the glow of the Good Samaritan rewarded.

The glow was enhanced further on by a policeman who was so surprised to see a yellow number plate that he gave me mutton and *divinosti shest* for the road. This was Nikolai's drink, 96% proof spirit. The policeman asked if he could get a job as a policeman in my country and cruelly I raised his hopes by saying sure he could, as long as he went easy on the *divinosti shest*.

Boris and I wriggled on through the Heavenly Mountains. We stopped that night at Chayek, where thirteen bank inspectors on assignment hosted a vodka and spring onions party at the hotel, and the next at a truck-stop called Ot-Mok, where it snowed, and the next at the town of Kara-Kul, where I had a mild existential crisis.

I sulked in my diary: 'Writing in the completely unsignposted Hotel Turist in Kara-Kul, with the almost unbelievably uninterested Russian woman in charge, in the suburb of a thousand yapping dogs. I don't feel as if I'm in Central Asia or the Soviet Union or the former Soviet Union or near China or quite near India. I feel nowhere. Not the back of beyond – there are people, roads, streetlights – but nowhere. Astronauts experience weightlessness. I am experiencing placelessness.'

Hunger might have had something to do with it. The uninterested Russian woman had responded with a blanket *nyet* to requests for food or information about food and my aluminium cooking pot was empty after a twelve-hour-day in the saddle.

The last four hours had been spent skirting every inlet of a large reservoir fed by the Naryn river. Kara-Kul, not to be confused with Kara-Kol, was separated from the reservoir by a forbidding bare mountainside. The town was built from scratch in 1970 to provide homes for workers on the dam that was to harness the Naryn and bring hydro-electricity to Kirghizstan. Their work was long since done. Some now had jobs to do with electricity. Most did not. The dam was somewhere near but out of sight. Kara-Kul felt like a washed-up ship whose crew had stayed aboard for want of anywhere to go.

That was the evening I arrived. The next morning was less bleak. The director of the hydro-power *kombinat*, a white-haired Kirghiz gentleman with an enormous desk and a bank of chunky telephones, wrote out a *propusc* granting access to the *Ma. Zal*, whatever that was.

Power lines could be seen leaping up the forbidding mountainside from a transformer station on the outskirts of town, so I rode there and was directed to a tunnel. An elderly caretaker who later claimed to have been duped inspected the *propusc* and let me in. The tunnel was dark and chinklessly black, with a dripping roof. Sloping downhill slightly, it continued for three kilometres and came out on the top of the dam. The scene was instantly recognizable from huge canvases in Bishkek's Fine Art Museum of Kirghiz mountaineers swarming the cliffs of the Naryn gorge in hard hats and shorts, drilling holes for dynamite, bolting catwalks to the rock, pouring concrete, bending reinforcing rods and in a few cases of painterly fatigue apparently abseiling for the fun of it. The building of the Toktogul dam had been a landmark in the history of Soviet Kirghizstan.

The mountaineers had gone but the catwalks and concrete were still there. The concrete filled to a depth of 215 metres a ravine so deep and narrow that the God of Balasagun, Kochkorka and Son-Kul had clearly meant it to be plugged sooner or later.

Below, boiling blue water emerged from the turbines and

surged away down the ravine. Above, broken brown cliffs framed the sky.

It turned out that I had strayed out of bounds. An engineer giving two dignitaries a guided tour ran over when he saw Boris roll out of the tunnel, and asked what the devil was going on. He seemed satisfied by the *propusc* and let me join the tour. We went down in a series of lifts and staircases to the turbine room, where four 300,000 kilowatt generators looking like giant daleks imprisoned up to their waists in concrete hummed under the gaze of V.I. Lenin. Next to Lenin's head on the wall was one of his sayings on the significance for Communism of the electrification of the Soviet Union. This was the *V.I. Lenin Mashin Zal*, partly buried within the broad base of the dam, partly hewn out of the cliff. The engineer shouted above the noise that it could withstand a direct hit from an atom bomb. The dignitaries nodded soberly.

While we were having tea in the engineer's equally atom-proof office he received a telephone call from the caretaker at the end of the tunnel and said perhaps I should go and see him.

The caretaker had become suspicious and raised the alarm. He locked me in and called security. Security arrived promptly in a minibus and accused me of spying.

I scoffed nervously.

'In your country can you walk into power stations like a tourist?' said a beefy Kirghiz type in dark glasses.

I wasn't sure. British Nuclear Fuels were certainly keen to show people round Sellafield. The question turned out to have been rhetorical.

'No. Here also no. Here is not Issyk-Kul. Here is strategic.'

A thin-faced Russian looked up from my passport.

'Do you have links with the intelligentsia?'

'I have been a student,' I said, determined not to understand. 'I have attended university.'

'Do you have links with the military intelligentsia of your country?'

'No. Completely not.'

'What were you doing on the dam? Now you have secret information to sell abroad, yes?'

This was genuinely baffling, but the Russian continued helpfully, 'For example, how much water is in the lake. The Uzbeks always want to know.'

'Did you take photographs?'

'Only of Vladimir Ilyich.'

'Shall we take his film?'

I pleaded. There is something brutal about confiscating film, even from a hopeless photographer. They told me to follow them to the director's office and not even to think about escaping. The director asked why I hadn't just gone to the *Ma. Zal* as agreed, and I said the whole thing had been a misunderstanding.

'Do you apologize to us?'

'It's not my fault if your colleagues look at your *propusc* and let me through.'

'Do you apologize to us?'

'Yes.'

Everyone relaxed. They even sold me some petrol. It was not nice to be accused of spying, but it turned out to have been useful practice.

From Kara-Kul the road followed the Naryn gorge to the Fergana Valley. It stayed high above the river – there was no room next to it because a series of lesser dams had half-filled the gorge. The tarmac was good. Lorries were abundant. *Shashlyk* stalls lured them off the road wherever there was room. The sophistication of Uzbekistan seemed to encroach a long way up into the highlands from the valley floor.

I wasn't ready for too much sophistication, though. Instead of rolling out into Fergana's heat and haze and making straight for Tashkent, I clung to the foothills on the main road from Bishkek to Osh, turning off it for a last look at the mountains at a place called Arslanbob.

Arslanbob was famous for its walnuts but I ended up associating it with honey. It was a Kirghiz village in a high amphitheatre of walnut groves said to have grown from nuts brought all the way from Macedonia by followers of Alexander. The nuts, two waterfalls, the fresh air and a link I never fathomed with a Muslim saint made it a haunt of holidaying Uzbeks, including Nasreddin the Kara-Kul fleece trader from Bukhara, whose parting words had been 'we'll meet again'.

Boris was only firing on one cylinder. The long climb through the walnut groves had been a sad ordeal; the flogging of an ill if not dying horse. I got a bungalow in the *turbaza* where tourists seemed to stay and went in search of spark plugs.

Nasreddin saw me heading for the bus park.

'Mister DZHAILZ!'

For a second I couldn't place him. The short nose and top lip were unmistakable but the skull cap had gone and he'd grown his hair. He was blending with the holiday hordes in a Chinese tracksuit.

'DZHAILZ! Nasreddin! Bukhara!'

But of course. We embraced like reunited refugees.

'*Nu kak?* How are you?'

I said I was well, and fond of Kirghizstan, at which he lowered his voice.

'This is Uzbekistan.'

'Arslanbob?'

'Of course. This is an Uzbek holy place. We come here every year. Stalin gave it to the Kirghiz but we will get it back.' He paused. 'Do you like honey?'

Nasreddin knew the source of the finest honey in Central Asia and hoped to pay for his holiday by reselling it in Bukhara. Transport was his only problem. I gave him a lift in Boris down through the walnut groves to the bee farm and was rewarded with unlimited bread and honey. It was good stuff. The honey was dribbled straight off blocks of honeycomb on to the bread, and tasted of golden syrup. Nasreddin bought sixteen kilos of it in one-and-a-half kilo jars. On the way back up to the *turbaza* he kept both cylinders working by cleaning the spark plugs with match-heads every few minutes. He also purloined two spares.

Juggling plugs, cleaning plugs, praying for flat roads and petrol tankers, I limped on round the head of the Fergana Valley to Osh. On my first morning there Boris shook when I tried to start him, which was a hopeful sign. But as men and children ran out into the street I realized it was not a hopeful sign. It was an earthquake.

The bungalows shook for about ten seconds.

'Can you feel it?' asked the nearest father, laughing as if at a village idiot and comforting the baby on his arm. 'Not big. The big ones make you fly.'

At the fulcrum of the Pamirs and the Tien Shan earthquakes are a way of life. This one briefly made the headlines not for its Richter reading, which was only four, but for toppling unsafe buildings and killing twenty people.

There were aftershocks throughout the morning, which I spent at the Ural garage of the military police. Mohammed, the chief mechanic, was a grey eminence on motorbikes; all-knowing, much-consulted and grey-haired. He was to Urals what Valery Georgevich had been to mountaineering. When I arrived he and his staff of two were sitting on upturned crates, smoking cigarettes and chuckling at the rumblings of the earth.

They chuckled at Boris too, and took him apart. Mohammed dismantled the entire gearbox, gave it to his apprentice to wash in a bath of diesel, and rebuilt it with new cogs for third as well as second. His Russian deputy chief mechanic was a clutch specialist so he replaced the clutch. The apprentice, when he had finished with the gearbox, tightened the spokes, corrected the timing on the distributor, refitted the driveshaft and bashed out a dent caused by a collision with a lorry at Ot-Mok.

They worked, whistled, cracked jokes and broke half-hourly to smoke under an awning next to a barnful of yellow and blue skeletons of cannibalized militia Urals. I was in raptures. I felt as if I was watching a friend undergo life-saving surgery.

The tremors trembled on into the afternoon and Osh's sang-froid was at times alarming. At lunchtime the bazaar was teeming underneath a concrete roof that shook with every aftershock. 'If it falls, it falls,' said an Uzbek selling pastry bundles filled with minced mutton. Across the road the circus with the tight-rope act was back from Bishkek and the man in purple knicker-bockers was bouncing on his crotch, apparently unbothered by the idea of the pylons shifting and the rope between them snapping while he was in mid-air.

Maybe this was faith at work. Osh's Muslims live under the life-giving gaze of Suleiman Gora, a long hill and holy place that overlooks the bazaar. They say its silhouette looks like a preg-nant woman on her back, and that barren women who go up there to pray at dawn will have a child within the year. I went up and stumbled on a group of women praying, though not apparently for children. Most already had them; dark-haired, brown-skinned cherubs charging around a terrace of crazy paving ignoring the prayers and their mother and pulling down telescopes to look up (without coins) in the black afternoon sky.

This did not in itself confound the story of the barren women, and later that day I thought for a moment I was meeting one.

The *turbaza* Ak-Buura, in the foothills behind the city, had almost everything necessary for the rest and recuperation of the proletariat (I had learned the essentials in Arslanbob). Stirring wake-up music rent the air before breakfast. The air itself was fresh, to relieve the endemic respiratory ailments that tend to accompany forced industrialization. Accommodation was in rustic cabins. Meals were taken at fixed times in a single cavernous dining room and the whole complex was connected up by a network of delightful wiggly paths through dense shrubbery inhabited by strange silver statues of Communist children in gym slips. My cabin was so rustic that it had birch-forest wallpaper.

All that was missing was the proletariat. The holiday season was over and the only people in the dining room, lost in a distant corner, were two women. I was seated next to them and we were each given a bowl of *laghman* and a fried egg.

One of the women was Russian, from Barnaul, north of the Altai in Siberia. She came every year to be with her Kirghiz lover. The other I assumed was Kirghiz but later that evening she knocked quietly and crept into my birch forest with a water-heater and a bowl of fruit. She was not Kirghiz, she explained in a deep, soft voice. She was a Buryatin.

Her name was Liubi. Her family had been transplanted to Fergana from the Siberian Buddhist Buryatin city of Ulan Ude in 1937 by Comrade Stalin.

She continued swiftly: 'I must tell you a tragedy before you go. That is why I have come. If the nightwatchman finds me here he will think I am immoral, but I must tell you this.'

She wore a denim waistcoat and skirt, and dark glasses which she did not take off despite the dim light from the weak bulb above the bed. She plugged in the water-heater to make tea and gave me an apple. She could only be one thing: an infertile woman on a pilgrimage to Suleiman.

'Which route will you follow to Tashkent?'

I hadn't thought about it.

'Take the low route. Do not take the pass if you want to live. Three years ago my son and husband took that road. A Kamaz – you know a Kamaz? Forty tonnes. It killed them both and threw them to the bottom of the valley and drove on. The driver did not stop. My brother had to go to Tashkent and hire professional alpinists to get the bodies. It took five days and cost three thousand rubles.'

Her low voice did not falter and her timing seemed practised.

'My heart has given pain since they died. Twice I have been to clinics in Tashkent and once to Novosibirsk. The doctors could not help me so I come here, to a medicine man in Osh, who says I must eat only fruit. Here –'

She offered me another apple then froze as the nightwatchman passed the window. His steps receded. She leaned forward and put a hand on my knee.

'Tell me you will not take the pass,' she said, then unplugged the heater and left.

I could hardly take the low road after that.

To Baikonur

~~~~~~

Boris fairly purred out of Osh after his militia make-over. Along the flat floor of the Fergana Valley the going was smooth and fast. We may even have topped eighty k.p.h. Every house was using its front garden to grow grapes or dry tobacco leaves, which were suspended in their thousands, individually, from rows of strings. The *kolkhoz* land behind was used for cotton, and space had been found somewhere to grow the heaps of melons being sold and sometimes squashed beside the road. After the rampant wilderness of Kirghizstan it was a shock to see homo sapiens so firmly in control.

The high and low roads to Tashkent divided at Kokand, where I stopped for the night. The hotel sent me to the police station to get a visa stamp and having got one I had a conversation with one of the policemen, sitting in his car.

'The Soviet Union will be back, you'll see,' he said.

'With a central government in Moscow?'

'Yes. Ninety per cent of people want the Union back and it will happen.'

'But surely not with the Baltic states.'

'No.'

'Ukraine?'

'Yes. They want it back. You'll see.'

'And of course the Central Asian states . . .'

'Of course.'

'But many Central Asians don't like Russians.'

'Nonsense. They are idle talkers. It is true the Russians brought us prostitution and taught us how to drink but we learned to live together. The Union will be back. You'll see.'

'Communist?'

'Of course. Eighty per cent of what Comrade Gorbachev said was right. Everything Boris Idiotovich Yeltsin says is rubbish.'

'You're the first person I've heard say anything nice about Comrade Gorbachev in nearly four months.'

'Ninety per cent of people in Central Asia want the Union back. It will happen. You'll see.'

He managed half a smile in half an hour of barked pronouncements and percentages, but was kind enough to be giving me a lift back to the hotel.

It was dark and cold outside; a single misty evening that announced the start of autumn. We sat for twenty minutes with the engine running and the headlights on, not going anywhere. The engine seemed to have to be red hot before it moved. The lights shone through a tall fence into the grounds of the palace of Khudayar Khan, projecting on to its façade the giant shadow of an airliner. A Yak 40 – I recognized it from Dushanbe.

The façade of the palace was dazzling even in the weird light, with mosaic covering every inch of it and slim round turrets over the main gate. The rooms behind it, I discovered the next day, were orgies of decoration with as many twirls of gold and painted plaster per square foot as any in Bukhara. The palace was a proud monument to the upstart Central Asian power of the early nineteenth century – the Khanate of Kokand – and it posed (and answered) an intriguing what if: what if Kokand had not challenged Bukhara and taken from it the Fergana Valley and Tashkent?

What if General Kaufmann, the Tsar's chief empire builder in the Central Asian theatre, had faced a united Uzbek empire in his campaigns of the 1860s instead of two squabbling khanates turned easily against each other? Would he have conquered Central Asia with hardly a struggle? Would the Bolsheviks have managed any better? Might they not have left the whole thirsty, unfathomable place alone?

Whatever might have been, Kokand did challenge Bukhara. Kaufmann did conquer Central Asia and General Frunze did reconquer it for Lenin. One result was the Yak 40 in the headlights. Its shadow on the palace was somehow succinct.

The high road to Tashkent headed north-west from Kokand, crossing the Syr Darya then climbing into the Catkalski range, a southern spur of the Tien Shan that crimps the neck of the Fergana valley. Boris took the long ascent beyond the river with such gusto that at the pass I gave away a spare spark plug to a broken-down Volga. The descent to the west must have been where Liubi's menfolk came to grief. There was no need of a Kamaz to push you off. The road was so narrow that any old distraction would have been enough – an itch, a passing bee – and the long scree below would have done the rest.

We got down safely and continued into the night along the gorge of the Angaren river, one of several that supply Tashkent and its factories with electricity and water. The air was cold, the moon strong, the road a roller-coaster. Boris was on song and his rider, frankly, felt like a TT hero on the Isle of Man. But our relationship was doomed. At Angren, where I spent the night, the driveshaft broke again.

Months earlier, over instant coffee in a cramped office with the mid-morning traffic of Moscow's inner ring road thundering outside, a journalist in corduroys had described peering through a tinted window in a bunker on the Kazakh steppe at flame pouring from the engines of a Russian space rocket.

'It's a must-see,' the journalist said. 'A real once-in-a-lifetime.'

He had witnessed the blast-off of the mission on which Helen Sharman, a British scientist, became the first foreign cosmonaut in Soviet history. It had marked the arrival of the Soviet space programme in the era of *glasnost* and the foreign press had been invited to Baikonur, the Soviet Cape Canaveral, the cosmodrome from which Gagarin launched the human exploration of the cosmos.

I had seen a documentary about Baikonur: Soviet footage with an English voice-over. It had shown fully formed rockets edging out of tall sheds on a vast and otherwise empty plain. It had shown the Soviet super-elite, the *wunderkinder* of the most prestigious physics institutes of Leningrad and Moscow, cosseted in a secret city in the middle of a far-off forest, shaping stabilizers, plotting curves and detonating solid fuel mixtures. It had shown gantries, catwalks, cockpits, countdowns and the billowing controlled explosion of a space launch. It had shown Gagarin in his orange suit, before and after his historic flight; the embodiment of a generation of Soviet pride. It was a spooky and seductive film about a quintessentially unvisitable place. Yet the man in corduroys had been there and where a journalist had led might not a *picatyl* follow? I had no idea. Hildebrand showed Baikonur in tiny print at a lonely junction of unpaved roads five hundred miles north-west of Tashkent, but one thing was clearer by the day: Boris would not make it.

In Angren I introduced myself to the police. They questioned me and fined me for not having an Angren visa, and finally introduced me to a Russian lawyer with a friend who claimed to know where he could get a *novyi cardan*. I paid him twenty dollars. He towed Boris away and two days later brought him back, fixed, almost. He had another new driveshaft but now the right-hand cylinder was playing up again. With a heavy heart I resolved to find my great blue temperamental steed a good home and leave him there.

Valentin, the former motocross trainer in Kara-Kol, had given me the name of a lecturer in Ural maintenance at the Tashkent Road Transport Institute, whom I set out to find.

Tashkent had an excess of road transport: Zils, Ladas, other Urals, Volgas, buses, Kamaz trucks and Zhigulis. I spent the morning getting hot about the feet and breathing their emissions, crawling northwards on a four-lane highway through a dusty cottonscape, then through cotton holding yards, then shunting yards, then factories, then blocks of flats.

The centre of Tashkent was more congenial than the fringes, being an oasis with a famous canopy of shade. Bold works of late Soviet architecture pierced it, and the Road Transport Institute was one of them. Outside it a huge yellow dumper truck with a cargo of green glass bricks reared up on a pedestal like a circus elephant.

The women in the secretarial pool all knew of Sasha Silienka. He worked elsewhere though, under the law faculty near the Karl Marx monument.

The law faculty was a stately old building, statelier and older than the Soviet Union by the look of it. Clad in dark red stone, it curved round a peaceful plaza in which Marx stood among trees. It was shut. A fried chicken restaurant at its right-hand end knew nothing of Mr Silienka. I tried a side street. A gate-keeper at the entrance to a car park pointed down a ramp to the law faculty's cellar, from which came the sound of machine-gun laughter and a radio. I opened the door and there he was. Sasha Silienka in his lair, naked to the waist, glistening, flirting with a woman called Irina, talking much too fast to understand.

I introduced myself.

'YoutheBritishwritermotorbikerValentintolmeaboutonnatele-phone?' Something like that.

'Hello.'

'Wherethehellayabeen? MistaSilienkabeenexpectinyouaweek-siddown.'

'My Ural . . .'

'SiddownyouwannacocacolathisisTashkentwegoteverything.'

'Slowly, please.'

'Hedozzenevenunderstandthebeau-ti-ful Ru-ssian language. So. You wann a co-ca co-la?'

The room was plastered with posters of Lamborghinis and Czechoslovak motocross stars. Down the middle there was a long glass-topped table and under the glass were more Czecho-slovak motocross stars. On top of it was a mouthwatering heap of Ural parts. Forming a T with the table was Sasha's desk. He sat behind it. Irina sat on it. From a neighbouring room came occasional bangs. Sasha's partner in Ural motocross racing was tuning something up.

'Meet my friend, Irina. My student, and my friend. Notmy-wifehahanonomywife'sthirtyfiveIrina'sonlyeighteenandvery-beau-ti-ful.'

I said hello to Irina and asked Sasha if he would like to have Boris.

'Buy?'

'No.'

'What?'

'Have.'

'Give?'

'Yes.'

'Are you mad?'

'No. I want to go to Baikonur.'

'Mad then. Hahaha.'

He said of course he could find a use for Boris and in return I should be his guest and watch *dyevuchki* with him on the Playboy Channel. I lied that I already had a hotel room, and went out to be with Mr Marx.

Karl Marx's statue seemed at home in its little arboretum; grateful for the privacy. Gravel paths led through the trees to a clearing where some wooden benches offered quiet contemplation of the bearded German philosopher. His was a soothing presence, whereas Lenin usually made you wonder anxiously what you had done wrong.

Marx's predecessor here was General Kaufmann, on whose monument Stephen Graham noted in 1914 the words:

> I pray you bury me here that everyone may know that here is true Russian earth in which no Russian need be ashamed to lie.

True Russian earth. I sat down on one of the benches and looked at it: scuffed gravel, trodden grass and scattered, fallen leaves.

In fact, it took a salvo of earthquakes to launch the real Russification of Tashkent. They came on May 2nd, 4th and 5th, 1966 with aftershocks continuing throughout the year. Three hundred thousand were left without homes. According to the propaganda machine volunteers came from all sixteen republics of the USSR to help their Uzbek comrades construct a new capital, which in a sense was true. Workers were shipped in from wherever there was surplus labour, and were not paid.

The strong quakes hit the city from directly underneath, bouncing most buildings but leaving them repairable. A sideways shrug of the earth would have been far more destructive, but the builders of the new society had their pretext and chose not to waste it. A small portion of the old town, a labyrinth of unpaved streets and blind mud walls round the bazaar, was left standing to remind Soviet Tashkent of the medieval conditions from which they had been saved. The rest of the city was rehoused in suburban *micro-raioni* – a grid-system of rows of plumbed and electrified apartment buildings linked to the brave new centre by trams and trolleybuses. The new ministries, museums, concert halls and hotels were set among parks and esplanades and ringed around with fountains – not decorative dribbles, but walls of water designed to take on the heat of July and August with their spray.

Then came the crowning honour and a mighty new responsibility: the city was given the Order of Lenin and turned its face outward to the world. Having been transformed into the model Soviet Asian city, it was given the task of wooing the non-aligned millions of that unhappy post-imperial holding pen known as the Third World. Tashkent's became the only international airport in Soviet Central Asia and its street signs the only ones transliterated into English. Ethiopians, Indians, Vietnamese, Namibians and Angolans arrived in Ilyushins and Tupolevs to stay in very large hotels and attend conferences on the miraculous Soviet leapfrog from feudal colony to modern industrial economy without the trauma of capitalism.

I wondered what Mr Marx would have made of it all. He looked a bit smug behind his beard – but then he didn't know what happened next. The miracle collapsed and now the hotels were full of foreigners giving instruction on development instead of taking it.

The Hotel Uzbekistan towered over the trees and the law faculty like a colossal piece of angle iron. The diplomatic Fords and BMWs outside were unfamiliar and intimidating. Inside, the lobby was abuzz with real western business types and tour groups with smart wheeled suitcases and clucking multi-lingual minders. Upstairs, suites served as temporary embassies and airline offices and import-export bureaux. There was a hard currency sushi restaurant on the 22nd floor. Downstairs at reception they took credit cards. Rooms were $120 a night.

Feeling poor and grubby I tried the even taller Hotel Chorsu (formerly the Hotel Moscow) at the other end of Tashkent's central axis, and found it half the price but just as full, this time with businessmen from Pakistan. A conference of Turkic-speaking transport ministers was taking up the Hotels Tashkent and Dostlik. There were rooms at the Rossia, but also giant roaches. I ended up with Sasha Silienka and the Playboy Channel after all. As a result, for an unsettling day or so, Tashkent became a city of breasts.

Sasha spent most of his waking hours not lecturing nor even philandering, but moonlighting for private clients on two rhino-sized lathes in the rooms, whence the banging had come, next to his grotto.

'*This* is why I am rich,' he had said, showing them off. On these lathes he could not just rebuild engines, he could grind cylinder heads from scratch. (It was like picking mushrooms with helicopters; you were as rich as the piece of public property you happened to operate.) He was still down there boring holes in magnesium alloy wheels when I returned roomless from the Hotel Dostlik.

Irina had gone but Sasha said she wanted to show me round Tashkent in the morning. He broke off drilling for a moment and lifted his visor.

'You like her? You like women?'

'She seems . . . I really don't know her.'

'You don't have to know her to like her,' he said, leering like the devil and groping the air in front of his pectorals. 'Hahahahaha.'

He scooped up a double armful of magnesium alloy shavings, carried them up the ramp into the car park, dumped them in a heap and lit them with a single match. They went up with a whoosh in a pillar of white flame and Sasha laughed manically again. I asked if the fumes were noxious and he said pshaw it's a big country, plenny of air.

We drove in his Lada to a cluster of new tower blocks close to the centre where his wife was waiting up in a pristine sixteenth-floor flat.

Sasha had insisted in the car that Irina was not his *dyevuchka*; that they absolutely did not 'sexualize'. I didn't believe him. Meanwhile he introduced his wife as his *Karalieva*, his Queen. She had a smooth, pale face and a tiny permanent frown. After a supper of meatballs and beer the three of us sat in a line on a large red sofa with the twinkling lights of Tashkent beyond net curtains, sixteen floors below, for three-quarters of an hour of breasts, lips, buttocks and, er, beavers.

A parade of bodies that had been sculpted, toned and oiled in the gyms and professional undressing rooms of southern California sashayed down their tops and peeled up their bottoms as they writhed in water, rolled in mud, danced in cages and draped themselves over gleaming Harleys.

They all arrived in the room by cable, which lent some weight to Sasha's earlier announcement that 'thisisTashkentwegot-everything'. Tashkent had cable! Sasha was delighted with it. He absorbed the Playboy Channel rather seriously, repeating every now and then the four syllables 'be-oo-ti-ful'. His wife said nothing.

I had not seen anything like it in years and had to cross my legs. When I realized Sasha might be thinking that a session of soft porn was part of an average adult's recommended daily cultural intake in the free world, I said pompously, 'The West is not all like this. This is fantasy.'

'Yes,' said Sasha. 'But it's real fantasy.' And with that he may have captured the true loin-grabbing fascination of pornography. It may be about second-guessing fantasy but some lucky photographer, somewhere, has persuaded a real woman with real breasts to strip and pout for real. It happened behind closed doors in front of fake backgrounds in unmarked studios God only knew where, but it happened.

Irina was not bad at second-guessing fantasy either. She clip-clopped into the grotto in the morning in high heels and a flouncy cotton skirt and a lime-green top undone almost to her navel, revealing the inside halves of two large golden bosoms pushed upwards and against each other by a black bra. She wore pink lipstick, mauve foundation and perfume that might as easily have been fly-spray. Her birchbark-coloured mane was frozen with industrial-strength lacquer into an outrageously voluminous bouffant. Sasha seemed to make a joke at her expense, which she parried with a real pink blush and a succulent glotto-labial put-down. (Russian can be desperately arousing.)

'Come on, Giles. Are you ready for your tour?'

She took my hand and led us up the ramp out into the fresh, goose-pimply autumn morning.

We walked down Karl Marx Street away from the statue and the Hotel Uzbekistan towards the foreign ministry where, on my brief visit from Nukus, I had been flattered with accreditation.

There were not many people around and no cars – Karl Marx Street had been pedestrianized. Young Uzbek men in white coats tended big blackened dishes of *plov* and chickpeas set up over gas flames beside pavement eateries. The smell of food and the smoke from slow bonfires of fallen leaves and Irina's perfume more or less cancelled each other out. Clip clop. The men in white coats whistled at her and she ignored them, used to it. We passed, on the left, an enormous concrete box which she said was the city's largest restaurant, the Zerafshan, run by the Armenian mafia; and on the right an ice-cream and gooey cake emporium famous locally for its roof of blue plastic domes, which made a change from Samarkand's ceramic ones.

We turned right on Alleya Paradov, formerly Lenin Prospekt, the city's ceremonial jugular. It had been sealed off to traffic except for the occasional ministerial Volga, and was very peaceful.

'Say me your biography,' Irina cooed as we walked past a plinth from which Lenin had in Soviet times watched May-day march pasts. He had been replaced by a globe.

'You know,' she continued. 'When born, where born, mother, father, brother, sister.'

I told her all that.

'Do you have a wife?'

'No.'

She laughed nervously and said she was happy I wasn't married. She had worked up a fever the night before thinking about today. She knew what I thought about her and Sasha but it was not so. He was a great man, a great trainer, and she wanted to be his first champion motocross pupil. That was all.

'You are all plus and not minus,' she said rapidly, for which I thanked her, wondering where our tour was leading.

It was leading to the tomb of the unknown soldier, where, Irina explained, newly-wed couples came to have their picture taken. A guard of honour of uniformed Uzbek boys goose-stepped round the eternal flame. I tried not to stare at Irina's cleavage. What did she want? Sex? Marriage? Visa support? She probably just wanted to show me round, but I felt like a sailor on shore leave.

In the afternoon we found ourselves in Sasha's Lada while he scurried into an office block to meet a client. The day had warmed up. Irina had hitched up her skirt – so as not to crease it, she said. The cotton folds hung between her bare legs, which were the same golden colour as her breasts, which had almost freed themselves from the black bra. A pink plastic naked mannequin hung and jiggled from the rearview mirror. Irina asked if I liked it and I said sure. I wondered what she would have done if I had slid my hand up her leg at that moment. I didn't. Sasha returned and we drove to the Road Transport Institute, where Irina said innocently she wished our tour could have gone on longer, then got out and disappeared into a throng of fellow-students.

That evening Sasha offered more of the Playboy Channel or a double bill of *Emmanuelle* and *9½ Weeks*, both of which he had on video. I passed on all three but the breast-fest continued in the morning with half an hour of non-stop Black Sea toplessness on Russian breakfast television, to go with the tea and pancakes provided by Sasha's long-suffering *Karalieva*.

I didn't begrudge Sasha his flesh deluge and I didn't exactly fight it off myself. But with the collapse of the Soviet Union porn had rushed into Tashkent like air into a vacuum and Sasha seemed to think that it was most of what democracy and freedom stood for. Feeling primly ashamed on the West's behalf I escaped after breakfast to wash my mouth out with a visit to the Museum of Decorative and Applied Art.

The museum was edifying enough. It was a turn-of-the-century Russian diplomat's villa done out like a mosque, with carved *karagachi* hardwood columns round the courtyard and tiled squinches and *mihrabs* inside. The applied art was a modest collection of reproduction antique silks and jewellery and Koran-holders. But for purifying power none of this was in the same league as the metro station.

Tashkent had a cut-and-cover metro system and the station nearest the museum was called *Kosmonavtov*, the station of the Cosmonauts. It was quite unlike the other stations on the network, which were smothered fetchingly in motifs from Central Asian history and carpets. *Kosmonavtov* was more than a metro station. It transcended both mass transit and terrestrial culture. It was a huge underground shrine to the most glamorous achievement of the Soviet military-industrial complex, the space programme that beat NASA to every landmark in the space race except the moon. The Registan at Samarkand had been a monument to totalitarianism in the service of an ego. *Kosmonav-tov* was a monument to totalitarianism in the service of tech-nology.

At regular intervals along the deep blue walls beyond the tracks were black oval bas-reliefs of space-walkers, space stations, satellites, cosmonauts and rocket-boosters falling to earth.

As trains swished in and out I sat on the steps that went down to the platforms from street level and remembered something Nastia the interpreter had said on an afternoon walk along the moraine beneath Peak Maxim Gorky in remotest Kirghizstan.

'I think all Soviet people in a way admired their country,' she had said with a catch in her voice after confessing to having been an evangelical member of the Communist Youth League as a teenager. 'Now they are all mad for America. The economy is in ruins and people hate the place.'

In *Kosmonavtov* I realized that if by some accident of sperm and egg I had been born into Soviet Uzbekistan I would have ignored any dark dissident rumours of gulags that came my way, and swallowed the darker official ones of western war-mongering and decadence. Like Nastia, I would have thrown myself with a passion into the whole Soviet shebang. It was, after all, an exhilarating experiment; the first time in human history that man had tried to reorganize the world in accordance with a set of ideas that aimed higher than the mere accommoda-tion of human nature on the one hand, and owed nothing to any sort of god on the other. The Soviet leadership, with the help of the Marxist-Leninist masterplan and the world's biggest cadre of bureaucrats and advisers, aimed at nothing less than doing everybody else's thinking for them. Every last significant decision, from how to spread the revolution down to the mixing of the alloy for a Ural's driveshaft, was to be taken by a single central brain motivated by a single big idea. Soviet Communism may have been doomed but down there in the cool efficient grandeur of the station of the Cosmonauts you had to applaud its *chutzpah*.

My critical faculties began to resurface on the way back to Sasha's, but *Kosmonavtov* still seemed at least a nobler cultural artefact than the Playboy Channel.

On my last evening in Tashkent, lingering over the inordinate luxury of a cup of coffee in the foyer of the Hotel Uzbekistan, I spied the Reuters correspondent who had lent her satellite telex to the BBC in Dushanbe. She was looking sharp. She had a lap-top slung from one shoulder and a delegation of Turkish businessmen in tow. They were off to the Istanbul for dinner. The Istanbul, across Pushkin Street from the hotel, was new and dollar-only, an underground haunt of daring expatriates and local mafiosi. I could not afford to go but when Mlle Reuter invited me I went all the same. We sat under an orange lampshade beside an aisle that was soon filled with thumping music and the shaking navels of belly dancers. Cold meats and vodka were brought. Mlle Reuter asked about my travels. I described my route since Dushanbe and then tried a little analysis on her.

'I have a theory that Soviet Communism was more popular in Central Asia than anywhere else in the Union.'

'And what is the theory?' she asked.

'That is. I just said it.'

'Aha,' she said crisply. 'What you say is not a theory. It's a fact.'

In the morning, I left Boris in Sasha's grotto, hoping vaguely that somehow, sometime he might find his way by train and boat to Shepherd's Bush. Then I took a bus to Kazakhstan.

The long-distance bus station was at the west end of the red metro line, out beyond the green reach of the oasis, far from the residual romance of the old town. It was a hub of easy routes across the deserts to Samarkand, Bukhara and Turkmenistan and north-east up the edge of the Tien Shan towards Alma-Ata, the capital of Kazakhstan. I squeezed on to the metro with a rucksack and shoulder bag. Their weight numbed my heels and pulled down the corners of my mouth. Queuing for a bus ticket put a knot in my stomach. Queuing again for a seat tightened it. The bus turned north once out of the city and crawled over the same smooth khaki hills in which the train journey to Bishkek had begun several weeks earlier. This time the windows were shut. Other passengers pulled down their blinds and slept.

I nursed a headache, forgave Boris all his breakdowns and missed him sorely.

Arriving in Chimkent I sulked. Traipsing down another Lenin Prospekt to another Karl Marx square in search of another shabby room seemed too much like hard work. I bought another ticket and got straight on to another bus, to Turkestan.

Turkestan was the empire-builders' name for Central Asia (land of Turkic-speakers, divided by the Tien Shan into its Russian and Chinese halves). But it was also a windy Soviet town, north-west of Chimkent, a hundred miles down the road to Moscow on the steppe. Tamerlane built a mausoleum-cum-*khanaga*-cum-seminary there in 1397; a religious multiplex to let the nomads know who was in charge on the northern reaches of his empire. Its domes made an incongruous silhouette as the bus rattled into town with endless Abba playing on the driver's radio. Facing the mausoleum from the west, with views across a waste of baked earth towards its turquoise tiles, there was a cold hotel.

It could only just be bothered.

'*Remont*,' said the less-than-loquacious *dyevuchka* at reception. Repairs. No heating.

I put on all the clothes I had and ate a plate of orange rice and a thin strip of reconstituted meat in the hotel dining room. The food was cold before it reached the table. There was no music. A sad silence hung over the tables with their cold steel legs and filthy brown tablecloths. Four Kazakh men were drinking vodka in the opposite corner. They kept their hats on – gangster hats with brims. One followed me to the urinal and stood behind me with his flies undone, waiting. The urinal was a scummy tin box. Its Lucozade-like contents were nearly overflowing.

'Bea-utiful,' I said in English as I tried to wash my hands. The man looked over his shoulder.

'You don't like Turkestan, Russki, is that it?'

'No.'

I left quickly with a distinct feeling that if he hadn't been peeing he would have socked me one.

Pilgrims were waiting on the guano-strewn forecourt of the mausoleum of Khodzha Ahmed Yasavi when it opened at ten the next morning. It was warm out there but cold again inside.

Under the largest intact medieval dome in Central Asia stood a replica of a two-tonne bronze vessel the height of a horse and the shape of a salad bowl inscribed with the words, 'This is a gift from Timur'. Photographers' lamps on tripods cast the vessel in a bright white light and believers, in neat family teams, took turns to climb three wooden steps and throw in money. They were Muslims, presumably. Yasavi was a Sufi holy man. But there was more than a whiff of paganism in this spotlit homage to the gift from Tamerlane, the warrior king who claimed descent from the Mongols and preferred to be worshipped than to worship.

In Turkestan's bus station a bored policeman ordered me into his office and fondled my passport for an hour. I used the time to ask about Baikonur.

'Closed,' he said. 'No foreigners allowed. No civilians.'

I showed him Hildebrand and asked whether Baikonur was marked in the right place. He surprised me by saying: 'There is not Leninsk on your map. Space City.'

He put a cross on it three hundred miles beyond Turkestan, further down the road to Moscow near a place called Tjuratam. I had seen Tjuratam described as a missile test range.

'And Baikonur?'

'Leninsk, Baikonur. Same place.'

Baikonur was shown on the map three hundred miles north of his cross, which was odd.

I had two hundred dollars left and didn't want to get stranded in the middle of the steppe. If Leninsk had been shown on my map I might have taken the policeman's word for it that Baikonur was the same place and tried to go straight there. But it didn't and I didn't and I ended up regretting it.

It seemed more important to complete Stephen Graham's route before the money ran out and winter came. I returned to Chimkent by bus. In the distance on the left were the Karatau hills, rising gradually towards their intersection with the Tien Shan. The view to the right, for the last sixty miles, was of one vast brown ploughed field. It looked too parched to grow anything but they had ploughed it anyway. Every kilometre a concrete post marked the distance from Moscow. 2145, 2146, 2147 . . . There was no shortage of kilometres out here. After all, we were on the far side of the land-ocean that had separated European Russia from her colonies.

Arriving colonists would probably have sighted port from further out than I did. Stephen Graham thought Chimkent 'a beautiful little town . . . with its mountain background, its white-stemmed magnificent poplars, its old ruins, its fortifications.'

The mountain background had since been obscured by smog from a big lead smelter, plus oil refineries and power stations and factories making tyres, textiles, drugs, asbestos and cement. But chiefly from the lead smelter. Chimkent made ammunition.

Some poplars survived on a hill on the edge of town where the tyre factory ran a hotel for its staff, to give them fresh air breaks on a rota. But the ruins and fortifications had been bull-dozed. A fighter plane pointed skywards from a plinth in the middle of a roundabout near the bazaar. Misha, a taxi-driver with a hare-lip who took me to photograph the lead smelter, didn't understand my question about whether they built fighters in Chimkent or merely flew them. 'Yes,' he said. 'Our town has many aeroplanes.'

We drove a short distance back towards Tashkent and turned away from the mountains along a raised tongue of land. The smelter was down to the right. It was actually a series of satanic furnaces letting off echoing bangs and noxious black belches every few minutes. A river ran through it, going in green and coming out black. From chutes under the furnaces an aerial tramway carried big black buckets of slag out of the smoke, over the river and up to the end of the tongue where a trip-wire emptied them over a slag heap, the latest in a line. It was steep, black and pointed. When it got near the tramway cables the trip-wire would be moved further out into the steppe to start another.

Misha sat in the car listening to the radio while I wandered round a half-burned rubbish tip under the cables with my camera, using it as foreground for the slag heaps and furnaces and feeling rather investigative.

Afterwards we went to Misha's girlfriend's flat: two dirty, cluttered rooms, one of them the kitchen, each with a bare bulb, four floors up in a peeling pale blue block plonked on a piece of scrubby flat earth dusted with cement and traced with random-looking lines of kerbstones. It was one of the more desperate dwellings I had seen in Central Asia.

Fariza lived there with a young daughter and memories of better times. She got out photo albums with conspicuous gaps in which dried glue seemed to be all that remained of an ex-husband. But still there were pictures of Tien Shan climbing holidays with Vietnamese and Russian friends, and of Fariza stripped to a bikini for a picnic on spring snow.

'Ten years ago,' she said smoking over my shoulder. 'We were students.'

Now she was manager of a sub-division of an oil refinery and work seemed to be what kept her going. At home she was on the edge of laughter one moment and tears the next, inviting us to join her in a shot or two of *divinosti shest*. She was lean of leg and wore tight jeans and a T-shirt. Underneath, she was actually Uzbek; a smoking, drinking, denim-wearing Uzbek woman. I guessed her husband had been Russian, though the fact of having been a citizen of Soviet Kazakhstan was probably another factor in her Russian-ness. Helped by massive Russian immigration in the 1930s and the lack of stubborn native cities on the steppe, Russification advanced further in Kazakhstan than in its neighbours. Mosques and *chaikhanas* were rare here. Soviet life had been Fariza's definition of stability even more than for the Kokand policeman. Now it had been pulled from under her.

That night the two top stories on the World Service were a victory for pro-Soviet forces in Tajikistan – they had marched into Dushanbe and ousted the caretaker prime minister – and the founding of a National Salvation Front composed of die-hard Communists and Russian nationalists in Moscow. They promised a return to law and order, an end to Yeltsin and in due course a new military state on the entire territory of the former Soviet Union. I suppose they would have had Fariza's vote.

The road over the high ground north of Chimkent passed low white farm buildings set in squares of poplars. Sheep and donkeys nibbled the greener folds of grassland. The best south-facing slopes were planted with the vines of a grape *kol-khoz*. Dzhambul came into view half an hour before we got there, far away on the plain beneath the west end of the Kirghiz Ala-Too. Graham's first impression was of 'a strange town hid behind the foliage of its long lines of trees'. Mine was of Lego. Instead of trees, electricity pylons cast their daddy-long-legs shadows on a phalanx of apartment buildings basking rather splendidly in the late afternoon sun. Factories with saw-blade roofs and tall chimneys pumped brown smoke into layers that hung over the town. Later on I learned that the f··mes were the result of mixing phosphorous and nitrogen for ...ilizer, and that cancer levels near the factories were forty-two times higher than the national average.

I spent that night in Dzhambul's Hotel Turizm, with the windows shut, and the next back in Bishkek as a guest of Vica and her mother. Valery Georgevich came round and so did Sasha – climbing champions old and new. We reminisced about the summer as if it had been years ago. Sasha was limping. He had survived Peaks Maxim Gorky and Pobieda, then axed his leg while chopping wood.

On a Wednesday in October I went down to Bishkek's bus station one last time and took the 9 a.m. Ikarus express to Alma-Ata four hours further east along the bottom of the mountains. I shared a taxi to the city centre and got out at the Intourist hotel. Tucked away behind reception was something called a service bureau. I went in and asked about rockets, just in case. The woman behind the desk looked startled.

'How did you know?'

'What?'

'About the rocket.'

'There's a rocket?'

'Yes.'

She paused. Her name was Galina. She was the service bureau's manager and she spoke English with hardly an accent. 'In two days there is a launch. A sputnik only, without cosmonauts. I am going to co-ordinate distinguished visitors.'

Shit. A launch. Incredible.

'Can I come too?'

'It is expensive.'

'How much?'

'Twelve hundred dollars, not including travel.'

Twelve hundred? I asked what it did include, if not travel. 'The excursion,' she said. 'Sleep in the Hotel Interkosmos, all meals including Kazakh national dish and sample of space food, special Intourist bus to the cosmodrome.'

The hotel was at Leninsk. The launch pad was at Baikonur, and as the policeman in Turkestan had explained they were practically adjacent on the lower Syr Darya. I asked if it would be OK to arrange my own accommodation and meet Galina at Baikonur. She said frostily that such a plan was out of the question and anyway physically impossible. Transport to Leninsk had to be specially arranged.

I cursed whoever had taken my money in Samarkand. Here by an amazing fluke was an opportunity to see a Russian space launch but whether I could take it was going to come down to pesky dollars. Mainly as a joke, I asked if Galina took credit cards.

'Visa card?'

'Yes.'

'Yes.'

YES! They took credit cards in Alma-Ata for space launches. I considered my credit limit and earning potential over the next few years.

'I'll pay by card, whatever it costs. I want to come.'

'I will ask.'

She had to ask the Foreign Ministry, and warned that normally they required at least a month's notice. Ignoring the warning, deeply thrilled at the prospect of a trip to the holy of holies of Soviet technology, I stepped out into a beautiful autumn afternoon in the city whose name means Father of Apples. There was a tall screen of oak trees opposite the hotel. Above them, from the middle of Panfilov Park, rose the wooden steeple of Zenkov Cathedral, once the tallest wooden building in the Russian Empire. The glaciers of the Kungey Ala-Too glinted next to the cross above the central dome. On the benches under the trees old men played chess.

Galina went without me.

She claimed afterwards to have asked the Foreign Ministry but I neither believed nor blamed her, much. She knew it would have been a futile quest. My own efforts started the morning before the day of the blast-off. The Foreign Ministry occupied a delightful single-storey building like a Louis-Quatorze hunting lodge on the upper edge of the city near the mountains, and knew nothing of space launches. They were sorry but they were quite unable to help.

At OVIR a dingy corridor was filled with ethnic Germans waiting patiently to emigrate. An ill-tempered woman named Aida told me I would need a letter from an official Kazakh sponsor for a Leninsk visa. I told her I had no sponsor and she said to try the Writers' Union.

As I was hailing a taxi to go to the Writers' Union a Korean cardiologist with the un-Korean name of Dr Vladimir Stepanovich Egai came running out of OVIR and across the street.

'Not the Writers' Union,' he said. 'Come with me to the *Alma-Ata Evening News*.'

He was a dapper chap, my *deus ex machina*, one of sixteen thousand ethnic Koreans in Alma-Ata descended from those transplanted to Kazakhstan from the Soviet Far East by Stalin, who was scared they might foment rebellion during World War Two.

On arrival at the *Alma-Ata Evening News*, Vladimir was granted an immediate audience with the editor. A letter was produced, which I took back to Aida. She said the editor must personally request permission from the KGB on my behalf. I asked why she hadn't mentioned this earlier and she ignored the question. Back at the paper the final edition had gone to bed and the editor was drunk, so I tried the KGB myself. Leninsk closed, they said. I returned to the Foreign Ministry. A chief assistant to some assistant chief said the consular department handled Leninsk protocol affairs. The consular department knew nothing about Leninsk protocol and helpfully suggested OVIR. At six in the evening I went to see Aida one last time. She called her commissar. The commissar stepped out of his office into the now empty corridor.

'Is this him?'

'Yes.'

I said hello.

'Come back in the morning. My colleague is off duty.'

'If I come back in the morning I will miss the rocket.'

'What do you want with this rocket anyway?'

'I love the cosmos, Gagarin . . .'

They both sighed.

'Wait here.'

The commissar came back a minute later with a Leninsk visa stamped on a square of low-grade brown typing paper.

It was a sweet moment. I went out into the tree-lined street and was about to salute the darkening cosmos when I remembered that Baikonur was still eight hundred miles away.

There was a flight to Kyzl-Orda, three-quarters of the way there, early next morning. At the downtown Aeroflot terminal they said it was full with no waiting list. At the airport they said the same thing, but lights were still on in the tiny international section, which handled China Airways services twice a week to Urumchi and a weekly flight to Frankfurt. I walked through several idle metal detectors and found a wonderful woman with a shot-putter's torso squeezed into a spotless dark blue uniform – a woman used to foreigners and authorized to take dollars. She made a call.

'I have one ticket,' she said, hanging up and smiling. It cost ninety-one dollars, more than half my remaining money. I bought it and slept in the Intourist hotel, paying by credit card.

Blast-off day dawned grey. The plane to Kyzl-Orda was a long thin Tupolev with three screaming engines bunched round the tail. It was going on to Ural'sk and Moscow and was very full. I sat next to Svetlana, a Russian woman with thick red hair and a beautiful pearly face, who worked for Kazakhstan's Ministry of Foreign Economic Relations helping companies like British Gas and Agip bid for drilling rights on the northern steppe.

For an hour and a half we flew over brown earth divided by dirt tracks into giant rectangles. It was not farm land so much as desert dotted with Soviet ghost-farms waiting for some miraculous climate change.

We came down over two yellow ribbons; reed beds along the banks of the Syr Darya. Everyone had to get out while the plane was refuelled. A bitter wind howled across the tarmac. I said goodbye to Svetlana and walked over to a gang of taxi-drivers who had driven out from the town centre to meet the plane. They were all wearing thick coats with upturned collars and none had ever been to Leninsk even though it was only two hundred miles away. They went into a huddle and produced a driver and a fare of five thousand rubles. I was relieved it was not more and anyway they did not seem interested in arguing.

We drove north-eastwards for three hours under a lowering sky, following the river, buffeted by the cross-wind along with choughs or crows or some other big black bird that would rise occasionally from the reeds and stagger sideways before getting into their stride, or their flap, or whatever birds get into. The driver did not seem keen on conversation.

The policeman in Turkestan had put his cross north of the river so when not nodding off to the drone of the engine I scanned the horizon to the right of the road. It was utterly bleak and empty. The rocket might go up at any moment if it hadn't already. I asked the driver to go faster. He said no, not for five thousand rubles. After about two hours he began to get nervous, suggesting that when we saw the town he would leave me to walk. I said no, not for five thousand rubles. The sky brightened a little. A low rise approached on the right. With a stab of excitement I thought I saw, further over in the distance, a giant structure like a square-cut silo. But it was the colour of the sky and might not have been anything. We drew level with the higher ground. Beyond it, a long way off but clearly visible, ending the uncertainty and delivering a slapshot of adrenalin, were three huge parabolic tracking telescopes with white towers and dark grey dishes tilted back in silent communion with outer space.

The driver slowed down. I promised him there would be no trouble, with no particular reason to know. Leninsk came into focus behind a grey wall ahead and to the left. From a distance it seemed to be little more than an army barracks. We reached a crossroads, turned right and came to a checkpoint where I showed the guards the scrap of paper from Aida's commissar. They nodded at it cheerfully from under their synthetic fur hats and said the launch was at eight. I realized I was actually going to see this thing happen. We drove back to the crossroads and another five miles beyond it, over a railway line, to Leninsk. I paid the driver and approached a gatehouse in the grey wall. Another amiable representative of the Red Army confirmed that a woman from Intourist had arrived at the Hotel Interkosmos. He drove me there.

All of Leninsk proper was walled. The railway station and a short street of kiosks and single-storey houses were outside the wall but access to Space City was by checkpoint only. The Interkosmos was a solid, clean concrete building on an open plot of tired-looking grass not far from the gate. Galina's special Intourist bus was parked outside it with Baikonur in big letters down the side. Inside, all was white marble, green upholstery and CCCR cosmo-bilia. Gagarin gazed down from every wall, dressed in space suits, lounge suits, tracksuits, and swimming trunks. Gleaming scale models of *sputniki* and rockets were arranged along the reception counter and the bar.

Galina was standing right there in the middle of the lobby, looking splendid in a fur coat and astrakhan hat. I went up as calmly as I could and said hello, and was sure I could see the blood draining from her face.

'How did you get here?' she said urgently.

'Taxi, aeroplane. I have permission.'

She began to splutter about reservations and VIPs. More ominously, dull-eyed men in raincoats were gravitating towards this little charge of awkwardness on the hallowed marble of the Interkosmos. Behind them Galina's distinguished visitors were draped over the green sofas; Hamburg ad-agency executives, as it turned out, filming a commercial for West cigarettes. West had put its name on the rocket and given the ad-men black leather jackets bearing their logo, a cigarette on a launch pad.

The dull-eyed men asked Galina what the hell was going on and I heard one of them mutter *'bolshoi skandal'*. I had hoped to join the official excursion to the blast-off but decided at this point to leave and make my own way. A hand gripped my shoulder at the door and a calm voice asked where I thought I was going. To find another hotel since this one was obviously full, I said. The man in charge of hotel security introduced himself and suggested a little sit-down on one of the sofas. More dull eyes. He asked some questions, wrote the answers in a notebook and went and chainsmoked into a telephone for half an hour. Shit, was what I was thinking.

When he hung up he came over and said, 'Wait', then joined Galina and the raincoats in muffled conversation by the bar.

The ad-men seemed to be avoiding my eye. After another quarter of an hour an army jeep arrived outside. A colonel in uniform got out and came and sat on the sofa and asked all the same questions and wrote down all the same answers in another notebook. He was a big man with a white face and white hair mostly hidden by his colonel's hat, which he did not remove. After questioning he wrote out a confession to be signed, which seemed to augur well. I signed it. He folded it and tucked it in his notebook.

'I am sorry but you must return to Alma-Ata,' he said politely. 'My driver will take you to the station.'

A minimum of twenty days' notice was required to visit the cosmodrome. The colonel gave the relevant paragraph and sentence of the Soviet constitution. I asked how Soviet laws could apply fourteen months after the end of the Soviet Union and he said they applied till new ones were written. I asked to speak to his commanding officer and he said his commanding officer was already at the cosmodrome. I asked to wait in the hotel until after the launch to find out from the ad-men what it had been like and he said no. Without possibility. They were flying straight back to Moscow. I reminded him I had a Leninsk visa. He said it was without validity.

The jeep went to the station via a full-size replica Soyuz rocket displayed horizontally on giant struts in the town centre. A photograph was permitted.

The station master was told to reserve the English guest a seat on the next train to Alma-Ata. He said it did not leave until two in the morning. The driver shrugged and drove back to Leninsk. Two in the morning. The station master unlocked a private waiting room and gave me the key. I went in, closed the door and sank miserably on to a couch in the corner.

It was getting dark outside. The horizon beyond a wide shunting yard was still bright, but the sky above it faded through bands of orange and violet to a blue-black in which the stars already flickered. Inside, the room was dank and cold but reasonably clean. There was a net curtain tucked into a clip to one side of the window and a neon light on the wall. I thought of the ad-men climbing into their bus with their cameras and tripods, the bastards.

Two in the morning. It was still only five to six. The launch was two hours away and there would be plenty of time to get back afterwards. Leaving the light on I drew the curtain, locked the door and set off on foot.

It seemed best to keep away from roads and headlights. There were some railway lines and ditches to cross but most of the walk was straightforward and adequately lit by the stars. Fortunately few others seemed to have chosen this particular night for a walk on the steppe. It took an hour and a half to come within sight of the first checkpoint we had tried that afternoon. A single arc light was positioned over the barrier and a dimmer light came from the window of the hut next to it. I joined the side road a safe distance from the checkpoint and was startled by a Kazakh soldier standing alone in the dark on the verge. I introduced myself a little awkwardly and was relieved to find he was a reluctant national service cadet hitching back to barracks inside the cosmodrome. He even pulled some spare fatigues out of a rucksack and offered to get me to the launch pad in disguise. It was tempting but too scary. Pulling on another army's uniform to trespass on its property seemed like asking to be accused of spying, so I continued in my own clothes to the checkpoint. A guard stepped out of the darkness between the hut and the barrier. I had my visa ready but we recognized each other from the afternoon. He tapped on the window with the end of his rifle and in a few seconds an officer appeared, turning up his collar. He looked at me briefly, his kepi silhouetted and his warm breath condensing in silver clouds in the arc light.

'Come on. Come on in.'

There was blissful warmth in the hut from a big electric bar fire. The officer gave his name – Sergei. I also shook hands with Valodya, his second-in-command, and with a cadet warming up before a stint in the cold. I told the truth about having been barred from the cosmodrome, which was a good thing because they knew already. The colonel had phoned. They laughed.

'So what are you doing? You want to cause a sensation?' Sergei asked. I said I just wanted to watch the rocket go up, and he told the cadet to put the kettle on. It was about ten to eight.

'May I stay to watch?'

'Of course. You are my guest.'

I asked how they could get away with this after their superiors had banished me to the station. Sergei said his superiors were idiots. Anyway, they would never know.

At 7.58 we went outside. At 7.59 there was a sudden orange glimmer away to the north-west. A moment later a blinding white tailflame cleared the horizon, lighting up the spreading explosion below it. The rocket rose vertically for a few seconds before tilting to the east. It cut an arc across the black sky for about a minute. Then in another orange burst it jettisoned stage one, the huge pod of solid fuel that had already been used up in its lunge away from gravity. The tailflame shrank to a bright pen-nib, racing backwards and upwards at eight kilometres a second.

'*Uzhe v kosmos*,' said Sergei. One hundred and twenty kilometres above the earth and already in space.

Three minutes after the launch we heard it; a long, angry roar that shook the hut and rattled the windows. Then silence. We went inside for tea.

The most outrageous show of strength ever conceived by man had been performed again. Hundreds of tonnes of chemicals and alloys had been sieved and sucked and hacked out of the earth's crust, and melted down and rolled out and purified and pressurized and riveted together, and thrown into space. The thing was there now. The satellite with 'West' on it had left this world in three minutes flat. I wouldn't have missed its departure for anything.

Semipalatinsk

~~~~~~~~

Back in the hut Valodya and Sergei talked proudly about the major pieces of Soviet space hardware as if they were sports cars. The rocket that had just gone up had been a Proton. The Soviet space shuttle was called Energia and its launch vehicle was Buran (pronounced 'boo-RAN', as Tarzan might).

Sergei laughed at my attempt to get to the launch pad. He said I had walked into the arms of the only people who still cared about security. Next time the thing to do was phone him in advance and everything would be arranged: padside seats, a visit to a secret space museum, and a safari to the drop zone where spent boosters fell to earth. All as Captain Sergei's Latvian friend. He had to be bragging.

After a while headlights appeared to the north and the cosmodrome commander's motorcade swept past on its way back to Leninsk. Galina and the Hamburgers were not far behind in their bus. Then came two more bus-loads: schoolchildren. Kids on a jolly.

'See what I mean?' said Sergei. I did see what he meant. Anyone who was halfway savvy could get into Baikonur nowadays, but I was too tired to mind very much.

He persuaded a passing jeep to give me a lift back to the station. I fell asleep in the waiting room, missed the first train back to Alma-Ata and caught one at breakfast time instead. No one seemed to mind. There was a bunk free in a compartment already being shared by a Russian from St Petersburg reading *Airport* in translation, and a Kazakh mother taking her daughter to a children's clinic in the capital. The daughter was a captivating seven-year-old called Lira who thought she could count to a hundred in English though in fact the tens got stuck at forty. When she tired of counting she would chant 'Willy, Willy, why you cry?' knowing I would laugh.

The hours and staging posts clanked by. Kyzl-Orda at lunchtime, Turkestan at dusk, Chimkent last thing before bed. I had spent the morning going over the episode in the Interkosmos, rewriting my lines with the benefit of hindsight and staring glumly out across the steppe. I should have stood my ground, demanded an interpreter, told them to arrest me. Yes! That would have been good. Would have.

Later on I passed the time imagining what eight kilometres a second looks like, eight kilometres a second being escape velocity for a rocket. The hazy view from the compartment window was always wide enough to pick out two points – camels, bushes, solitary posts – that might have been eight kilometres apart. Then you had to picture a Proton rocket blasting across the space between them in one second flat. Blam. It did my head in.

The overnight trek from Chimkent up the north side of the Tien Shan was my third and last. Daybreak found us already trundling through the rusting factories and wooden bungalows at Alma-Ata's suburbs. The sky was pristine and the mountain tops seemed to have had a fresh covering of snow. Outside, people were wrapped in thick clothes and breathing clouds of vapour. A banner across the front of the station building said in Russian, and what looked like Kazakh and Chinese as well, 'Peace and Friendship on the Great Silk Road'. Under it a digital thermometer gave the temperature: Zero degrees Celsius. Three days earlier the afternoon high had been twenty-five. Autumn hadn't lasted long.

I had fifty dollars left, plus ten pounds, ten Deutschmarks and some rubles. They had to stretch to the eastern tip of Kazakhstan and then to somewhere where a credit card could buy a plane ticket to Moscow. A carefully spent dollar did go embarrassingly far; ruble inflation had pushed it to nearly half the average Kazakh monthly wage. But Alma-Ata could also make you feel poor. Brand-name goodies had arrived at brand-name prices. The prestigious purchases at kiosks round the market were Snickers, Twixes, Marlboro and Johnny Walker. There was a Kodak photo lab behind the Intourist hotel. Hertz had an office opposite the twenty-storey Hotel Kazakhstan. An Arizona company had turned a former Party mansion into a

western business warlord's home-from-home with all the tools
and personnel needed for global conquest on call round the
clock: international phone and fax by private satellite connec-
tion, telex, fixers, drivers, limos, secretaries, conference rooms,
stenographers, interpreters and lawyers. There was a side of
Alma-Ata that was money town, a fashionable new stopover for
masters of the universe from Frankfurt and New York attracted
by Kazakhstan's Canadian-style bottom line: wide open spaces
(four times the size of Texas), not too many people (sixteen million in all) and abundant coal, oil, gas and ore. I avoided money
town and went to watch some ice-skating instead.

Alma-Ata sloped more steeply than Bishkek. The mountains
were closer and one of the ravines between them had been filled
in with the biggest, fastest speed skating arena in the world. It
had been put there to break records; something to do with the
dry air and the fast ice of the Tien Shan, and of course with the
Soviet need to break records.

The bus went from near Panfilov Park. It was a Sunday afternoon. Sunday afternoons were when the rink was open to the
public and everyone who got on had a breathless going-skating
look about them. We followed Prospekt Lenin past the Hotel
Kazakhstan, out of the city and straight into a world of pine
forests and picnic spots. We passed the entrance to the president's residence, snaked up between steep interlocking foothills
and stopped in a car park overlooked by a gigantic stadium with
arrays of floodlights on pylons at each corner, like insects' eyes
on stalks. There was *shashlyk* smoke and hard rock in the air
and western beer in cans for sale on tables lining the last grand
sweep of tarmac to the turnstiles. Still vaguely grumpy about
Baikonur and being poor, I didn't hire skates, but went and sat
high up on a sunny slope of seats to behold, from a distance,
post-Soviet Kazakhstan at play.

A great cosmopolitan crowd stumbled and glided round the
oval of fun. Most held on to each other for dear life in lines
abreast, while the élite of real skaters swooped among them.
One was a Russian woman in a tight red jersey. Young at heart
and firm at thigh, with short blonde hair and a face that could
have been a mask of Portland stone, she carved a sinuous swift
slalom through the dross as if it wasn't there. Her raised chin

and outstretched arms said, 'I was a champion once; watch me if you wish to learn.' People did, and you could almost see the pleasure welling up and being stored away inside her.

A cocksure male in an CCCP tracksuit skated nonchalantly round the inside of the herd, darting into space from time to time to leap spinning through the air and land beside a terrified admirer. A tall, brown, bearded Kazakh did endless laps of the perimeter wearing only skates and his baggy underpants, topping up on speed occasionally with a swing of a leg like the rare flap of an albatross's wing, but mostly cruising with both hands on his knees and a steady gaze that seemed to clear the way ahead. Young bloods in hockey skates nipped and tucked against the tide, usually backwards, never falling over, toppling lines of novices like dominoes.

Further up the ravine a terraced barrage three times the height of the stadium protected it from mudslides. I walked up the barrage. From the top a steep, narrow road, winding on up through the trees, led to a solitary ski lift. The ski season hadn't started but the lift was working; yellow chairs suspended from a cable, cranking slowly up towards the snowline. I paid one hundred rubles to go up and was greeted by six Kazakh businessmen coming down, one by one. They all wore suits and looked most uncomfortable without their desks.

The white peaks that separated Kazakhstan and Kirghizstan were above the lift to the south, turning pink as the afternoon wore on. Lake Issyk-Kul was a week's walk away when the passes were clear. To the north and far below lay the rink, the friendly face of Soviet gigantism, now spectacularly floodlit. Beyond that a brown duvet of smog hung over Alma-Ata, and beyond that, indistinct but definitely there, was the poor old beat-up steppe.

It would have been hard to miss the fact that large areas of the steppe had been pulverized by nuclear testing, even if I'd wanted to. The man who stopped the testing was a folk hero, and in the Central State Museum memorabilia from his campaigns had taken over half the space once devoted to the exploration of the cosmos.

I went to the museum first. Olzhas Suleimanov, the poet and former dissident, was shown in photographs with Shoshone Indian chieftains from Nevada, where most American nuclear tests took place, and the mayor of Hiroshima. It had been Suleimanov's brainwave to seek solidarity with other victims of actual nuclear bombing. They had been on peace marches together and he had given the museum some of his souvenirs: bandanas, banners, photos, beer mats and a tent. Also a T-shirt on which Doug of California had painted: 'Stay Warm, Eat Garlic, Sip Red Wine, Peace and Health'.

The Kazakh campaign dovetailed nicely with the end of the Cold War and gave a focus to the otherwise fuzzy surge in national consciousness that accompanied the Soviet collapse. After 465 nuclear explosions in forty-two years, testing at the site near Semipalatinsk was stopped in 1991.

Mr Suleimanov was not available for interview, but his son-in-law received me in the airy offices of Nevada-Semipalatinsk and talked very fast for an hour and a half. His name was Mirza Khan and he was a mathematician with a large head, thick glasses and a pants-on-fire racing commentator's way of speaking. I understood perhaps a quarter of his monologue. It opened with the early history of the movement – tense meetings chaired by Suleimanov at the Writers' Union, standing room only despite the possibility of a crackdown by the KGB; Suleimanov's central claim that Russia had no right to test its atom bombs on Kazakh land, least of all without permission. *Glasnost* had proved to be more than a slogan and Suleimanov's antics had been tolerated. His confidence and fame had snowballed. Mirza Khan described an anti-testing roadshow through the cities of the northern steppe in 1989, a rearguard action by the army in the face of mounting international pressure, a trip to Downing Street for Suleimanov, a partial military climbdown, and wild rejoicing when the Kremlin's edict was at last announced: 'Polygon at Semipalatinsk to close'. Polygon was the Soviet euphemism for nuclear test site.

For Mirza that was only the beginning. Testing continued on the Russian Arctic island of Novaya Zemlya and in the western Chinese desert at Lop Nor. Both names meant 'new lands', he said, spitting with contempt. There as in Kazakhstan the testing had to be stopped and local people compensated.

'The colonists invade and call these places New Lands and turn them into polygons. Then the people who always lived there are killed by invisible atoms and they don't even know what atoms are.'

Mirza said the people of the Semipalatinsk oblast had so far been paid three hundred rubles in compensation each, enough for a single piece of meat. He said their babies would be mutants for three hundred generations.

Using the Geiger counter I had borrowed in Moscow many months earlier I measured, for the sake of future comparisons, Alma-Ata's background radiation levels. They were too low to be a worry but this did not mean much. The test site was still six hundred miles away. Then I went to the station to catch a night train to Semipalatinsk.

The locomotive arrived with a bang at the far end of the platform and the bang travelled down the couplings like rolling thunder. People in huddled groups waiting to get on looked up, saw the wagons moving and shuffled with their bags to stay opposite their designated doors. Their breath rose into the glare of an arc light.

The train left at 1900 hours, Moscow time, 10 p.m. local. At quarter to ten the steward stepped down on to the platform. A loudspeaker announced boarding for the TurkSib express to Novosibirsk and the huddled groups scrambled in to find their bunks. Mine was in a compartment with two Kazakh women and two young Russian men. One of the women wished she was in third class, for the company. The other spent the journey sewing stoat skins together for a hat. The Russians had to share.

We left on time, heading north-east out of the glare. It was cold outside. Cold inside too. The compartment had no heating and the window was broken. During the night the cold bedded down with us. Dry snowflakes drifted in and gathered on the sill. The cold gave me a cold. Everyone slept badly in the thin blankets provided, except possibly the Russians who had each other for warmth. When the sun came up we couldn't see it because the sky was completely covered by cloud and it was snowing steadily. The steppe was white. To spare the compartment my sniffing I stood in the corridor in my blanket and watched the perfect freezing emptiness slide past.

Somewhere over to the east the northern end of the Tien Shan would at last be sinking under the plains, leaving the way clear from Xinjiang through the Dzungarian Gap. Genghis Khan led his cavalry through here in 1218. Nowadays it was where the international trains to and from Urumchi stopped to change their bogies. North of the gap sundry other ranges would break surface to keep the old empires apart and beyond them the Altai would begin, softer and greener than the mountains further south, but just as lonely. Hundreds of miles to the west were the Karaganda mines and the labour camps where the prisoners had lived who dug the coal to smelt the steel to build the tanks that beat the Germans, roughly speaking.

I felt feverish and exhilarated. Actually I felt like Omar Sharif in *Dr Zhivago*. The cold was miserable but epic. It seemed to have been conjured from the sheer bigness of the place. Meteorologists call Central Asia's climate extreme continental because the region is so far from moderating oceans. I thought back to the oven-train from Krasnovodsk to Ashkhabad and began to understand what they meant. I went back into the compartment.

The lady with the stoat skins was busy sewing. All the seams were on the inside of the hat and her final flourish would be to turn the whole thing outside in. The other woman was coaxing conversation from the Russians. I sniffed. She gave me another blanket and said the cold was only just beginning. She was right. The day never brightened beyond its original gloom. It just got colder, until moving became a bother because it emptied the pockets of warmth that had built up under the blankets. Every hour or so a village passed; a clutch of solid little homes with oil drums as water tanks. Imagine being born and raised out here, then going to university in Leningrad. I couldn't.

In the middle of the afternoon we stopped at Ayaguz where bundled women were waiting on the platform to sell us hot *chiburekki* and potatoes. Their pots were wrapped in swaddling clothes. A tractor passed with a thick black quilt strapped round its engine. I jumped down and had to laugh with everyone else as the cold bit my ears and stung my nose and pressed up from the icy platform on my toes. Laughing let in the freezing air and I choked on it.

Night fell. A Russian family from the next compartment came out to the corridor looking like royalty in fur hats and long fur coats. We rumbled over the River Irtysh, which meant we had almost arrived. The father peered down through the passing girders at the water. 'Hasn't frozen yet,' he told his wife and daughter snugly. 'Not cold enough.'

When the train stopped I ran for the nearest taxi, visions of a putrid Kazakh pneumonia ward dancing before my eyes. The driver wore furs too, and grew his own fur over most of his face. He looked at me as if I was naked and drove gingerly over the black ice to a cheap hotel. The Irtysh froze overnight.

Semipalatinsk wasn't supposed to be beautiful but when the spangles of frost melted off the outside of the double glazing in the morning they revealed a winter queen. The hotel was by the river, whose skin of ice the wind and snow had striped with shallow drifts. The far bank was forested and cloaked in white. It turned out to be an island but looked like the beginning of Siberia, which after all was only thirty miles away. Dark smoke from factory chimneys in the distance smudged the sky – the queen's mascara; perhaps she had been weeping.

To judge by the number of pedestrians and the gaggles at bus-stops down below, life went on in the nuclear city despite everything. I checked the background radiation levels. Gamma and beta counts were both lower than in Alma-Ata, which might have had something to do with it. More obviously, these people were dressed for the cold. They were huge. They had turned themselves into bear-people. I had to become one too, for as little money as possible.

The bazaar was a street of log cabins lined with stalls that were mostly glorified hanging rails. The stall-holders were their own models, fierce and friendly at the same time like their animal cousins, in black fur, brown fur, grey fur, golden fur and (less fierce and apparently more fashionable) long Chinese-made box-stitched winter coats. The weathered Kazakh men among them looked as if they might have trapped the furs themselves on snow-shoe expeditions to the *taiga*. I was tempted by a lion-coloured hat with useful-looking ear flaps but it was made in North Korea and too expensive.

There was no getting used to the cold and no standing around in it. I ran from stall to stall, pointing and asking prices and pining again for the dollars taken from my hotel room in Samarkand. In the end a charitable Kazakh couple came up with an affordable package consisting of a boxy hat in soft black rabbit skin (with flaps), a pair of loosely knitted gloves and a heavy grey wool greatcoat, double-breasted, with a magnificent collar of tightly curled Astrakhan lamb's wool in matching grey. I put them all on. The effect was of instant central heating. Never mind that I looked like an *apparatchik*. Semipalatinsk, against the odds, was suddenly my favourite city in the world.

Dostoevsky developed an affection for it too. He spent five years here as an army captain in the 1850s after being exiled to a prison camp near Omsk, a week or two's sleigh ride down the Irtysh, for unpaid gambling debts. His rank afforded him a sturdy log house near the river with glass windows, tasteful furniture and an upstairs study with a view. A museum had since been added, not to mention an entire Lenin Square of which local and regional secretariats formed the sides and Dostoevsky's house a corner. But the writer's rooms had been preserved and polished as a shrine. Presumably his portrait in *Crime and Punishment* of diseased pre-Communist St Petersburg made him a darling of Soviet censors and curators. He was certainly revered by the *babushka* who took me round. When we stepped into the study she could only whisper, 'Here he wrote.'

On a wall in the museum there was an engraving, enlarged to the size of a mural, of Semipalatinsk as a nineteenth-century garrison and trading post. It was a profoundly wholesome scene of wooden wagons, wooden storefronts, a wooden church and beyond them all the river and the steppe. *Crime and Punishment*, one of the grimmest novels ever to have an optimistic ending, had it here.

He sat down on a pile of timber by the shed and began looking at the wide, deserted expanse of the river. From the steep bank a wide stretch of the countryside opened up before him

. . . There was freedom, there other people were living, people who were not a bit like the people he knew; there time itself stood still as though the age of Abraham and his flocks had not passed. Raskolnikov sat there, looking without moving, and without taking his eyes off the vast landscape before him; his thoughts passed into daydreams, into contemplation . . .

This was the man who split open an old woman's head with an axe for her money, then drove himself mad trying to justify it to himself and deny it to everyone else. A man in a pickle. The denials failed to convince the police and he was exiled to Semipalatinsk, where, like his creator, two thousand miles from St Petersburg on the frontier between Asia's two great voids, he found solace.

Where Raskolnikov found solace I had found a morsel of romance where I least expected it, and a damn fine coat. Meanwhile the floor lady at the hotel had arranged a powerful cure for a streaming nose (grated onion up each nostril, followed by the inhalation of boiled potato vapours) and, halfway round the world, Bill Clinton had romped home against George Bush. Convinced that anything was possible I set about visiting the polygon. It might as well not have existed, for all I had heard or seen on the subject of nuclear testing since arriving. The kind *dyezhurnaya* who stuck the onion up my nose said sure, the earth had shaken every now and then and, sure, we knew it wasn't earthquakes. But she had never talked about it, even with her husband.

Urazaliv Marat was head of microbiology at the medical school and the local representative of Nevada-Semipalatinsk. The Med-Institut was a long pink building with a grand white portico across the square from Dostoevsky's house. Dr Marat's office was a calm retreat from white-coated students running everywhere and banging everything. He had tidy grey hair and half-moon spectacles. He sent his secretary outside. I asked him to show me where the polygon was and he drew a large circle on my map, south-west of the city. Inside it he marked a town, Kurchatov, which he linked with a line to a road shown on the map as a dead end. This had been public information for less than a year, he said.

'Before 1991 we were not permitted to discuss the polygon. It did not exist. The explosions did not happen. If we travelled in the Soviet Union or Eastern Europe we were not allowed to say we came from Semipalatinsk. Only from Kazakhstan. And no one from our city was ever granted a passport to travel to the West.'

He talked in clear, precise Russian with a slight smile.

'I saw a fireball once, before they stopped the air tests in 1963. But of course I didn't see it. No one did.'

He excused himself to go and give a lecture but said if I returned at four that afternoon he had something to show me. I returned at four. He put his white coat on a hanger in a cupboard, swapped it for a fur one, and led the way briskly out the back of the building and across the school's garden to the pathology library, which was housed upstairs in an old villa with closed shutters.

'It is unpleasant perhaps, but interesting,' he said on the way inside. I was expecting books, but was shown deformed babies in jars of formalin.

The library was a large room filled with specimens from all branches of the animal kingdom pickled in jars of various sizes and crammed on to overburdened wooden shelves. The human foetuses filled a pair of special cabinets. One had a single eye only, in the centre of its forehead. Its nose, mouth and ears were misplaced elsewhere on its skull. Another had two heads. Another had no skull and only a membrane attaching the brain to the body. Another had an open abdomen; there was no skin between the navel and the pelvis. The biggest jar contained twins joined at the neck, chest and abdomen. Both had hare-lips and tortured expressions.

All the foetuses came from the area of the polygon, Dr Marat said. All had been dead at birth. All were likely victims of genetic mutation as a result of nuclear radiation but the link was hard to prove without a detailed radiation map, which had not been authorized.

We didn't stay long. On the way back across the garden Dr Marat explained that monsters could be born anywhere at any time for no better reason than a freak genetic botch-up. The trouble was, statistically speaking, Semipalatinsk had enough for the entire Soviet Union.

I went to the bus station. Most buses drawn up outside were stubby old charabancs with protruding engines and hard seats. Those about to leave were having their bellies tickled by naked gas burners. It was dark again, snowing again, colder than ever. Spark plugs apparently didn't stand a chance on their own. Inside, the waiting area was full to bursting with muffled bodies giving off an animal fug.

There were no buses to Kurchatov, but there was one to Chagan, the place marked on Hildebrand as the end of the dead-end. Apparently that bus continued to Konyechnaya, which translated roughly as 'the end'. I queued up and asked for a ticket there.

'No seats left,' said the *dyevuchka*.

'Standing then.'

'No standing.' (This was tosh. People always stood.)

'How about tomorrow?'

'Do you have a *propusc*?'

So you needed a *propusc*. In a way this was a good sign.

'Yes.'

She looked at me as if she didn't believe me but sold me one anyway.

Dr Marat had apologized and said there was little he could do to help with getting access to the polygon. He had been there only once himself, as the guest of an official Japanese delegation. The army still ran Kurchatov and was not friendly with Nevada-Semipalatinsk. He suggested trying the offices of the regional Soviet. I did, the following day, with no expectation of anything but blank faces.

Oleg Vladirovich Popov worked on the fifth floor and smoked Chesterfields. He had sunken cheeks, an ill, grey pallor and five telephones that he was itching to use. He waved me in, sat me down, offered cigarettes and tea and dialled Kurchatov. I was already stunned.

'Yelnikov,' he barked down the phone, adding with a chuckle and a hand over the mouthpiece. 'The mayor. We get through to people here.'

Attaboy Oleg.

'OK. We'll meet him at the airport.'

Oleg hung up and hit the intercom. Edil the press attaché

walked in. Oleg warmed him up with a joke I didn't understand then explained for my benefit that Yelnikov was flying back from Alma-Ata after a meeting with the president. Edil would take me to meet him at the airport and ask permission to visit the polygon. Edil nodded meekly.

'You already have permission from the Ministry of Defence?' Oleg asked me, as if confirming a formality.

'No.'

'Then you have a problem. But go anyway.'

A Volga was summoned. We drove very fast to the airport then very fast back again, having been told by the first secretary of the oblast that there was nothing Yelnikov could do but that he himself would arrange it all on his Alma-Ata hotline in the morning. The first secretary, who had been at the airport to meet another dignitary, had oozed power and brooked no discussion. Edil, who had a face like a mouse and a generally put-upon air, had said we'd have to wait and see. I spent the next morning waiting in his office and trying not to irritate him. He passed the time cutting pieces of used typing paper into squares that fitted into a slot in his executive desk set. He seemed averse to all noise, including conversation, and would tip-toe even when approaching his own door from the inside.

The call came through at noon. Permission had been granted and Yelnikov telexed. A car was on its way.

I went down to meet it in a dizzy bubble of elation, not at the prospect of seeing a nuclear test site but at having seen the old machine at work, the bureaucracy that was supposed to have smothered the Soviet Union with its own corrupt obesity. On this occasion it seemed to have cut through red tape like a Ninja.

Then the car radio played a Russian version of 'I Did It My Way', and I decided to congratulate myself instead of the system. As we drove out on to the steppe I felt an absurd smug kinship with Frank Sinatra which I think, deep down, had a lot to do with knowing I would soon be going home.

'MIRU MIR,' proclaimed a banner across the road at the city limits. 'Peace on Earth.'

The transition from town to country was abrupt and eerie. Suddenly there was only the road, dead straight to the horizon, and limitless space on either side. We drove for an hour and a half with hardly a twitch of the steering wheel. At times the journey felt unreal, in the strict sense that it could have been happening in a simulator. The graphics would have been simple; a tapering grey line on a white screen. We did pass a pig factory, as Edil described it, and the turn-off to Chagan, which turned out to be a walled dormitory for Kurchatov. By this time there was a dark band of trees to the north; the Irtysh coming alongside.

We reached a fence and a checkpoint. Kurchatov was ahead and to the right beyond a few miles of easily strafed nothing. Edil had to get out and phone Yelnikov's office and hand the receiver to the guard before we were let through. I wouldn't have stood a chance on my own. Beside the road a simple four-sided post had been driven into the steppe with 'May Peace Prevail on Earth' on it in four languages, including English.

The road drew level with Kurchatov and turned sharply to the right, becoming Lenin Street. There were poplars down the middle and sides, then wide pavements and cosy-looking office buildings with sloping roofs and pastel pink façades with white shutters. Yelnikov was upstairs in one of them. Edil led the way through an ante-room and a boardroom into the mayor's office, where the mayor sat behind an empty desk – empty but for the usual bank of telephones and the glass top with lists of numbers underneath.

Nikolai Feodorovich Yelnikov was a big man in a beige suit who launched into his spiel without preamble. He said, fingers interlocking on the glass, that I would be interested in the tourist programmes planned by himself and the military commander of Kurchatov, General Yuri Borisovich Konovalenko, for the area of the polygon. *Tourist programmes for a nuclear test site?* I began to see how it had been possible to grant permission for this visit at short notice. Tourists would be able to visit Kurchatov's military museum and the site of the Soviet Union's historic first nuclear explosion in 1949. (Tourists, but not me. The 'facilities' were not ready yet.) There would also be the opportunity to catch and eat trout from Atomic Lake Shagan, created by a controlled nuclear explosion in the path of the River Shagan in 1963. I thought Comrade Yelnikov might join me in a little laugh at the idea of atomic lakes and eating their irradiated trout, but he did not. Then I pleaded to be allowed to see the test site and museum and he said that was up to General Konovalenko's second-in-command, who would see me next.

A colonel, all too reminiscent of the one at Baikonur, appeared in the doorway and led Edil and me back to the car. He sat next to the driver and gave directions to the military headquarters. They were not complicated directions because the military headquarters stared down Lenin Street from the far end like an invigilator.

The deputy commander was grouchy and inflexible but hard not to admire for sheer authenticity. He had a breastful of medals, an immaculate green uniform and a desk as empty as Yelnikov's but for a desk-top hammer and sickle.

'Welcome to Kurchatov. What do you want to see?'

The 1949 test site, I said, hoping he wouldn't ask why. There couldn't be much left at a nuclear test site after it had been used, especially if it had only been steppe in the first place. I suppose I wanted to see whatever devastated sort of nothing was left. It was a bit like the Aral Sea, but the gentleman behind the Soviet flag seemed unlikely to regard this as a constructive line of thinking.

'Impossible,' he said. 'You have permission for Kurchatov only.'

'And the museum?'

'Only the town. The museum is secret. We still work here you know; biological defence, radio-biological defence. It was better before but we are not useless yet.'

Better? What – more fun? More satisfying? Better for self-esteem and *esprit de corps* when the big bangs still went off once a month, shaking the earth for hundreds of miles around? My Russian wasn't up to asking, which was probably a good thing. General Konovalenko was away and his deputy seemed to see his role as stopping the rot; unblurring the line between test site and theme park. He left Edil and me with the colonel and our trip to the polygon turned out to be a walking tour of officers' dachas on the banks of the Irtysh. The colonel said the hunting was good here; ducks and boar. I took a picture of a monument to the plutonium atom in the dark square, and we ended up having a Pepsi in the officers' mess.

The colonel was actually a trooper. He spoke English and drew diagrams in my notebook of the two main ways of letting off a nuclear weapon underground: at the bottom of a vertical shaft in flat land or at the end of a horizontal one in mountains. He'd built the shafts for both kinds of test and filled them with concrete and lead. He was an engineer. The procedure was totally safe, he said. The explosion vaporized a sphere of the earth's crust, usually half a mile from the surface. The heat melted the skin of the sphere into a thick layer of glass which kept in most of the radiation. Aeroplanes flew over the site with sophisticated Geiger counters before anyone went near the shaft. No one he knew had suffered any harmful side-effects from working at Kurchatov, he said. The only people who complained were poorly educated Kazakhs from surrounding villages. And they did suffer, but not from radiation sickness.

'It is psychological,' he said, pronouncing the p. 'Radiophobia.'

I thought of the monsters in the pathology library and got out my Geiger counter.

'That's a toy,' he said, a touch too airily. I reckoned I had him in an awkward spot, but the measurements were the lowest yet.

Edil wasn't interested. Driving back towards Semipalatinsk and a blue-black eastern sky he said sadly that every foreign visitor to Semipalatinsk since independence had come to see the polygon. None had ever shown an interest in the Kazakh people. Did I know they were a minority in their own country? That two million of them died during collectivization? That before the Russians came the steppe had been a place of yurts and horses, like Kirghizstan? That his country's greatest writer came from a village on the edge of the polygon? He could take me there.

Next time, I said, partly ashamed and partly tempted to observe that, one way or another, nuclear testing had become a part of Kazakh history too.

The Road to Rakhmanovski

~~~~~~

The broad River Irtish flows placidly onward, five hundred miles to Omsk and thousands of miles to the Arctic Ocean . . . It flows from the silences of the Altai mountains, through the silences of Northern Asia, the noise of man hardly ever becoming more than a whisper upon it.

As Europe prepared for war, Stephen Graham left Semipalatinsk by river boat, sailing up the Irtysh at the end of the summer 'the wrong way, away from the interest of the world'.

I had to go by bus, what with the river being frozen over, but it was still a dreamlike journey. We left Semipalatinsk at dusk for the first stage to Ust-Kamenogorsk, rolling over new snow into wooded hills beside the river. Everything was muffled. I was wearing fifteen separate garments to keep warm and seemed to be surrounded by adorable young women wrapped in furs and talking softly, as if waiting for a play to start. (It was their hats that made them perfect, I decided, and my ear-flaps that made their conversation hard to hear.) Outside, trees slipped by like the crowd behind the cordon at a première, hiding bears and bobcats, surely.

Away from the interest of the world we rolled, reaching Ust-Kamenogorsk at midnight.

Here uranium was processed for the atom bombs they tested at Kurchatov, so Mirza Khan had said. Less secret but probably as dangerous were several other heavy metal smelters, sending up a noxious copper-coloured canopy to shield the city from the skies. The floor lady in Semipalatinsk had said that rain that had fallen through the air above Ust-Kamenogorsk could turn tomatoes brown. I was not able to confirm this. The bus to Katon-Karagai, three-quarters of the way to Rakhmanovski, left first thing in the morning.

In the bluish dawn Ust-Kamenogorsk was not obviously poisoned; simply bleak. The woods had shrunk back from the city, leaving it to wheeze in the bottom of a bare white basin.

The end of Soviet Central Asia was still two hundred miles away, not at an arbitrary map reference but at a natural node: the clustered summits of the High Altai. Here China ends, Mongolia begins, Kazakhstan narrows to a single valley at its eastern tip and Siberia slopes away northwards to infinity. It must be the least maritime place on earth and it was here that Stephen Graham found a village called Altaisky and holed up for a fortnight in such rustic bliss that he wrote it up as 'very paradise'. Times had changed. There was no Altaisky on my map. There was a road marked up that single Kazakh valley, though, and a dot at the very end called Rakhmanovski. I reckoned that at Rakhmanovski honour would be satisfied.

From Ust-Kamenogorsk the bus struggled up a long slope dotted with old mineheads. It was an ancient bulldog of a bus with a hammering engine under a hood by the driver's knee and a payload of long-suffering natives of the Altai (Kazakhs, technically, though their forbears were a shamanistic people called the Kalmyks). They had complexions like freshly risen wholewheat bread. Their overdressed bodies, and mine, and my unpopular rucksack, filled every cubic foot available. There was one bus a day to Katon-Karagai and this was it.

We left the mines behind and laboured all morning through hills that Hildebrand called the Kalbinsky Range. 'Here are sweeps of blue sage, mauve cranesbills poking everywhere, saffron poppies, grass of Parnassus, campanula, pink moss flowers and giant thistle-heads,' wrote Graham. Their seeds and bulbs were no doubt all around us, hibernating. The snowscape was decorated with coppices of larch and darker spreads of pine. Round every corner you could dream of summer picnics, but in mid-November the Kalbinskys had a desperately forgotten air, even from a laden bus.

In the middle of the afternoon we crossed the Irtysh on a ferry. The river had been dammed downstream and was as wide as Lake Geneva but without a soul as far as you could see on either bank. The ferry, with a red star above the bridge and space for twenty vehicles, was a welcome but surreal presence, condemned to chug forever between nowhere and precisely nowhere.

I was dozing when at last we rattled into Katon-Karagai. The bus stopped at a crossroads with a single streetlamp. The door flew open and the cold blast woke me.

'*Ashkhana*,' said the driver, turning wearily. Food. This was my stop.

It was dark and yet not dark. There was a full moon over the town and its enchanted valley. Mountains rose to the east and west, forested at first and then as naked snowcaps etched against the blackness. These were the Altai then. They had crept up very stealthily. The bus had gone. No one else had disembarked. Katon-Karagai consisted of a street or two of silent wooden houses, by the look of it, and the *ashkhana*, from which two windows' worth of filtered neon blended with the moonlight. I ate a plate of bloated oats and meatballs while the solitary kitchen hand on duty waited to close up. He pointed down a side street, over a cattle grid, to a place where visitors could stay. It was a low-grade Party guest-house beside a low-grade Party monument; a star on a concrete spike. Katon didn't seem to rate a Lenin.

On the subject of onward transport there were rumours only. Katon's bus station was a shed by a frozen stream and when I found it in the early-morning half-light hopeful passengers were already shuffling in and out like restless bears. Inside there was a faded *skhema* of the valley with symbols for the principal industry of each village: a cow, two deer, a sheep, a horse and what seemed to be a camel. Rakhmanovski had only fir trees. Was there a bus to Rakhmanovski? A woman behind a grille said *nieto*. To Berel maybe. Berel was the last village but one.

A chilly hour passed. An old man with a peg leg tapped up and down the shed. The sky brightened and the mountains seemed to shrink a little. Then there was a sudden growl of internal combustion outside and the bears stampeded.

It was slow going up the road to Rakhmanovski, sometimes following the frozen stream, sometimes hugging the left side of the valley, always twisting, stopping every few minutes to let people on or off. There was no chance of a seat. I stood wedged in the aisle with a view, which ever way I looked, of hat. In four hours we went fifty miles.

Berel consisted of a row of neat log houses, some with fenced front gardens, some with barns attached, some with paddocks out behind. It bore no trace of having been an outpost of the Soviet empire, nor of much else about the modern age. Beyond, the valley narrowed and the woods came down from either side to meet across the road. A sign said thirty-one kilometres to Rakhmanovski. The bus had emptied and gone back to Katon-Karagai, so I started walking.

The sky was clear and the snow crisp underfoot. After the wooded defile the valley opened out then curved to the east. As the light began to fade a tractor appeared, coming in the opposite direction. The driver stopped and said there was a steep climb ahead, and bears and wolves that were known to attack humans, especially after dark. I asked if he was joking and he said he wasn't, so I asked if there was anywhere closer than Rakhamnovski to spend the night. Berel, he said, and drove on.

He was right about the climb. The road zig-zagged up the side of the valley, alternately plunging into forest and emerging for brief views of the Altai, each one darker but more panoramic than the last. I became aware of not having eaten anything in two days except the oats and meatballs, but fear of man-eating bears and wolves seemed to compensate for the lack of fuel. I hoped the climb would end with a pass and a clear view of Rakhmanovski, but instead the zig-zags gave way to undulating forested upland. I found a good stick and rehearsed holding it up so the wolf would bite it instead of my throat. For bears I remembered reading that you act dead and hope they lose interest. To ward them off and for the edification of the trees I sang 'Liberame Domine' from Fauré's Requiem as a round, loudly and probably off-key.

As the moon rose again and the glaciers of the High Altai sank behind an approaching ridge of forest I asked the beasts of the wild, as a personal favour, to live and let live tonight of all nights. Like them I had a home and wanted to get back to it alive. At last the lights of Rakhmanovski appeared, perhaps a mile and a half away, scattered through the trees at the bottom of a moonlit cwm.

A few seconds later I heard the howling and jumped clean off the road. I listened again, trying to block out the banging in my chest. The sound came a second time, from between where I was and the village. It was a piercing wail, rising, falling and then rising even higher, too querulous to be a siren. It had to be a wolf. The next mile flashed by as if my rucksack was empty but the last half-mile was slower. By that time I knew the sound was not a wolf. It was an opera singer.

The music was too loud to be live, which could only mean one thing: a People's holiday resort, a *turbaza*. Loudspeakers in the trees were not quite Mr Graham's sort of paradise but there would be food here, and a bed. I knocked on the door of the director's cottage. He had been having supper and seemed surprised by what he saw. Not wishing to be turned away I explained in detail where I'd come from, and why, and how long it had taken.

'*Tak*,' he said, considering. He stood there in his porch for what seemed like a long time, then went to fetch his keys.

He led the way through the trees along duckboards laid out over the snow, to a cabin with a steep roof that came down almost to the ground. It was one of several that might have blended with the forest but for the moonlight. Inside there was a sitting room with big windows and four chairs tucked in under a card table. With the moon in the windows there was no need to fumble for switches. The manager handed me a key and pointed down a short passage to my bedroom. There was a *dyevuchka* staying upstairs, he said – not married, quiet, here for a cure. Supper would be ending soon.

It was a dour but perfect welcome. Resistance would have been too much but so would enthusiasm. Instead this monosyllabic backwoodsman from the lonely middle of the biggest continent on earth had seemed as unexcited by my ludicrous story as by his own remoteness, asking me only to register in the morning because his own supper was getting cold.

The bedroom was warm. I eased my rucksack off my shoulders and let it drop on to the narrow bed. It creaked. The adrenalin that had taken over at the sound of the wolf was gone. In its place was a sleeping consciousness of blisters and running on empty. I hobbled back along the duckboards to the dining room, which was in a chalet made of creosoted planks with small square windows and checked curtains drawn against the early winter. The longest table was taken by a group of Russian athletes in tracksuits and flip-flops – the kind with broad straps over the toes but none between, allowing socks. There were also four women sitting together, not so Russian-looking or athletic, and a singleton. There was subdued chatter and the tink of aluminium knives and forks on aluminium plates. I sat alone. A woman in a white coat brought a pot of tea and saucer of sugar. I drank the tea like a junkie, glass after sweet tepid glass. When the pot was finished I went up to the kitchen hatch for another and drank that too. When that was finished I ate a plate of bread and three bowls of noodles in tomato sauce. Then I returned to the cabin and took my boots and socks off. I put my feet up on the creaking bed and stared at them, reflecting that the middle of a continent was an odd place for a journey to end but that this one was ending nevertheless. Rakhmanovski was at a roadhead in a horse-shoe of mountains. The only way out was the way I had come. I had run out of money, and being unprepared for a Siberian winter had run out of time as well.

The air over the Altai warmed up a bit during the night. In the morning Radio Moscow sounded deadened – deadened by low white cloud and light snow falling the short distance to the forest floor. It was Radio Moscow that was piped to the loudspeakers in the trees. You could tell by the single bar of 'Moscow Nights' that introduced the news each hour on the hour.

The singleton from the dining room turned out to be the *dye-vuchka* staying above me. She was up and reading at the card table in a long skirt and calf-length boots with low heels. Her top half was enhosed in an un-sexy brown wool turtle-neck. She had a long nose and long chin. Except for her uncertain smile she might have been a model in a People's fashion show from the 1950s. She was here for a medically supervised balneo-logical programme, she said.

So there were baths?

Oh yes. Beneficial ones. Highly beneficial.

I asked if you had to be medically supervised to take a bath and she short-circuited our conversation by saying all you had to do was pop into the bath-house and the duty *medezin* would tell you what was wrong with you. Prompt, expert diagnosis. And the baths were quiet at this time of year.

Outside it felt like Christmas. The snow and the pine trees helped but the stillness settled it; the suspended animation that comes but once a year to the home counties when everyone stays in with the telly. I guessed it came more often than not to Rakhmanovski, but this was still a feast day as far as I was concerned, between half a year of coming and however long it took of going. I hummed so as not to let it pass unmarked.

The athletes had already breakfasted, leaving their plates and glasses stacked beside the hatch in the dining room. The four women who had supped together were now finishing their morning tea together. We exchanged greetings as they wrapped themselves in coats and scarves. It was eight o'clock and by *turbaza* standards I had overslept.

The white-coated woman who had refuelled me the night before put a plate of pancakes in the hatch and, after a moment's hesitation, asked who my doctor was. I wasn't sure how to answer.

'Which spring did they say?'

I went on looking blank. She heaved the athletes' plates through the hatch and started washing up. 'Try number ten,' she said. 'Tell them you're a sportsman.'

I ate the pancakes and then, following a sign to the baths, took the longest line of duckboards yet. They led further into the cwm, away from the cabins and over a clearing to a grey stone house in a steaming fenced enclosure. The steam rose off hot springs that looked like deep black puddles and were lined by more duckboards. Beyond them the ground sloped down to a new line of trees and beyond that, visible through a gap filled partly by a wooden jetty, was a lake. Its far shore was lost in cloud and its surface was frozen and white except where the warm stream from the springs ran into it beside the jetty, cutting a thin wedge into the ice, a monochrome Excalibur.

At the far end of the house there was a door marked fourteen. I went inside. A brisk Kazakh doctor gave me the sort of look gents get in Ladies and said this was a gynaecology clinic. Could she help? Three of the four women from breakfast were sitting there in bath robes, looking discomforted.

So the essentials hadn't changed. Maral deer did not seem to be bred here any longer for the baby-bringing power of their horns, but the Altai were still held to be a fount of life, endorsed by no less a god than science. I did not feel welcome enough to ask how balneology cured infertility, and backed out surmising that Rakhmanovski had become a sort of atheistic Osh, a place of pilgrimage for barren women driven by their secret struggles to Soviet quackery instead of Suleiman the prophet.

Spring number ten was at the other end of the house. I hadn't noticed it at first but returned there and, following instructions, introduced myself to the orderlies as a sportsman.

'Which sport?' they asked in unison.

(There were two orderlies; fleshy women in the inevitable white coats, nursing jam jars of tea and talking dirty about the men in *Los Ricos Tambien Lloran*, as far as I could make out.)

'Trekking.'

'Which team?'

'Independent. Solo.'

'Which doctor sent you here?'

They handed me a form on which I wrote in Cyrillic letters the name of the last doctor I could remember seeing. That had been somewhere off Fulham Palace Road. Then they shooed me down the hall with a warning not to wallow for more than fifteen minutes.

I got undressed in a clean, deserted changing room, took a towel from a neatly folded pile and went down into a blue tiled chamber three feet deep in hot mineral water. Daylight shone through a thin layer of snow on a roof window and bounced crazily off the water on to the walls. This was a limousine among hot tubs – exclusive compared with the teeming dungeons of Bukhara and salubrious compared with the sulphurous desolation of the spa at Dzilandi in the Pamirs.

The principal active ions were listed on a board: Mg, Cl, Ph, SO_4. I knelt down in the water, then sat, then lay half-floating with the back of my neck on a ledge, and let the periodic table go to work on my aches and rucksack weals. I had not expected to feel like Caesar Augustus in Rakhmanovski. Having got used to the absurdity and the pleasure of it I did some more humming.

A man appeared at the top of the steps. He walked down carefully and stopped halfway, grinning broadly.

'Not bad eh?'

'Not bad at all.'

He looked around for the right words and eventually settled for two, plus a kiss of his own fingertips.

'*Chiste voda*,' he said. Then he walked awkwardly back up the steps, leaning so as not to have to bend his right leg. When my fifteen minutes were up I found him perspiring but still grinning on a bench in the changing room.

'That water is one hundred per cent *naturalne*,' he said. '*Chiste voda*. Totally pure. For my pain it is the only answer.'

He introduced himself as Vyecheslav, head coach of the Russian national langlauf team. He had an arthritic hip for which he was taking a cure while supervising training for the coming World Cup season. The athletes from the dining room were his, some of them veterans of the Calgary and Albertville Olympics, some mere teenage prodigies.

He winced. I realized the sweat on his temples was from the pain of the hip. He would soothe it in the bath in a moment, but not before he'd said his piece on Rakhmanovski.

It was not only the water that brought him here. The air too was pure, so the snow fell clean and the skis ran faster over it than in the woods round Moscow. It was a good excuse to make the long, expensive journey to these training camps where he could keep the grinding in his hip at bay, but it was also true.

'Really true?'

'I don't know.' He laughed. 'I tell the Olympic Committee. They believe me, and myself, I do believe it. The lap times are faster. Even the fir cones here are the purest in Asia. In Soviet times we exported them for medicines.'

In Soviet times. *Kagda Soyuz byl*. The old chestnut. That old fir cone. I was practically nostalgic by now for a Soviet Union I had never even lived in. As Vyecheslav eased himself to his feet and limped down to the water I remembered setting out many months before with the easy notion that Central Asia had been somehow virginal until the Russian Revolution, an exotic idyll in a timewarp, while Soviet Communism had brought nothing but dirty and brutal contamination. It was true that the Aral Sea had all but disappeared, that the cotton belt was covered in a poisonous skin of salt and pesticides, that large areas of steppe were Emmentaled with nuclear potholes. It was also true that the little miracle I had envisaged while daydreaming in a London library had come to pass in Kirghizstan, the nearest place to paradise this side of the First World War. But where Rakhmanovski fitted in, with its pristine fir cones on the one hand and its gynaecology cures on the other, I wasn't sure. All I knew was that I liked it as it was, blue baths and all, and that it gave Vyecheslav relief from pain and the breakfast quartet hopes of motherhood. My tidy distinction between Soviet and pre-Soviet, spoilt and unspoilt, seemed to have come face to face with real life and been quietly chewed up.

The last few yards of this journey were done on skis, not for aptness's sake especially but because I wanted to push on a little further to see if there was a rock or tree stump I could touch and say I had truly, unquestionably, reached the end of Central Asia. The snow was deep. Snow shoes were not available but langlaufing equipment was. From a lean-to beside the dining chalet I was given a pair of slender wooden skis with curling tips like those of oriental slippers, and some blue lace-up boots attached by their toes to hinged steel bindings. Stabilizing poles were also provided. Without them I would have slid backwards at once into a tangle of torn tendons.

I set off along a marked *loipe*, grateful that no one was watching. The track skirted the north side of the cwm above the hot springs. It entered a patch of dense wood and came out on the edge of a white meadow where I paused for breath.

A sort of skiing dragonfly flashed past. It came from nowhere and vanished over a low rise made invisible by the shadowless light. Then another came, sucking a cold lungful out of the air in front of me and leaving a faint human vapour trail. Then a third. This time I followed it with my head and saw in a freeze-frame the stabilizers being used as silent rocket boosters.

Thus did the Russians langlauf, in streamlined goggles and wind-tunnel suits that flowed taut over their elliptical muscles, tirelessly lapping and relapping in the secret depths of their old empire. Two thousand miles away on the far bank of the Volga, Mother Russia would have been proud of them.

Fearful of snagging a ski and crashing in the path of an oncoming champion I pushed out cautiously over the meadow and was relieved to see my *loipe* disappearing into trees again on the far side. There was a single clean set of tracks to follow. Like rails, they did away with the problem of steering and I even got into a jerky sort of rhythm. I hardly noticed the trees closing in. When the tracks stopped abruptly the skis rode up on to the virgin snow and pitched me forward into it. As the fog cleared from my glasses I realized the *loipe* had petered out, not at a landmark but in the middle of a forest. There were ways forward – the twisting spore tracks that forests allow forest animals. They would go on forever, up and over to Mongolia, or China, bearing right, or the Arctic, bearing left. But instead of choosing one I turned my skis round in their tracks and stood there for a minute picking out snowflakes against the tree trunks, then headed back the way I'd come.

Out of the blue...

INDIGO

the best in modern writing

FICTION

Nick Hornby *High Fidelity*	£5.99	0 575 40018 8
Kurt Vonnegut *The Sirens of Titan*	£5.99	0 575 40023 4
Joe R. Lansdale *Mucho Mojo*	£5.99	0 575 40001 3
Joan Aiken *Mansfield Revisited*	£5.99	0 575 40024 2
Daniel Keyes *Flowers for Algernon*	£5.99	0 575 40020 x
Julian Rathbone *Intimacy*	£5.99	0 575 40019 6
Janet Burroway *Cutting Stone*	£6.99	0 575 40021 8

NON-FICTION

Gary Paulsen *Winterdance*	£5.99	0 575 40008 0
Robert K. Massie *Nicholas and Alexandra*	£7.99	0 575 40006 4
Hank Wangford *Lost Cowboys*	£6.99	0 575 40003 x
Biruté M. F. Galdikas *Reflections of Eden*	£7.99	0 575 40002 1
Stuart Nicholson *Billie Holiday*	£6.99	0 575 40016 1
Jessica Mitford *Hons and Rebels*	£6.99	0 575 40004 8

INDIGO books are available from all good bookshops or from:

Cassell C.S.

Book Service By Post

PO Box 29, Douglas I-O-M

IM99 1BQ

telephone: 01624 675137, fax: 01624 670923

While every effort is made to keep prices steady, it is sometimes necessary to increase prices at short notice. Cassell plc reserves the right to show on covers and charge new retail prices which may differ from those advertised in the text or elsewhere.